PHILOSOPHY

THE GREAT THINKERS

Capella

Author: Philip Stokes, with introduction by George Davidson
With contributions by George Davidson, David Downing, Cath Senker and Alex Woolf
Design: Zoe Mellors
Editor: Ella Fern

Picture credits: Cover image Art Archive, Mussini, Luigi, 'The Descendants of Plato from the Medici Court';
AKG Images 17, 48, 58, 65, 76, 79, 82, 87, 96, 107, 110, 121, 122, 129, 154, 163, 169, 191, 192, 207, 210, 212,
231, 236, 238, 243, 249, 254, 269, 270, 290, 291; Stuart Barrett 130; Etienne Boucher 181; Clinton Fowler 58;
Corbis Ltd 33, 34, 39, 47, 51, 55, 68, 70, 71, 85, 99, 105, 116, 119, 127, 135, 137, 143, 159, 165, 170, 173, 180,
198, 202, 234, 260, 263, 264, 275, 277, 285; Getty Images 9, 151, 175, 194, 223, 225, 240, 257, 276, 294; Mary
Evans Picture Library 138; 'Morally Superior One' (Flickr name) 145; Picture Desk 88; Piers Northam 10;
Anthony Lockhart 242; Shutterstock 22, 184, 205.

We have made every attempt to contact the copyright-holders of illustrations within this book.
Any oversights or omissions will be corrected in future editions.

This edition published in 2007 by Arcturus Publishing Limited
26/27 Bickels Yard, 151–153 Bermondsey Street,
London SE1 3HA

ISBN: 978-1-84193-702-1

Printed in China

CONTENTS

INTRODUCTION

Is there any meaning to life? Does the universe have a purpose? What really exists, and what does 'exist' mean? What is 'mind', and how does it relate to 'matter'? What do we know? Do we in fact know anything at all, or is everything we think we know just hypothesis? Do human beings have free will, or is everything we do determined by prior causes and circumstances? Are 'right and 'wrong' just matters of opinion? It is questions such as these that philosophy seeks to answer.

And if some of these questions seem somewhat removed from the realities of everyday life, then how about these? Is it ever right to go to war? Can abortion ever, or never, be justified? Should we care about people dying of hunger and disease in faraway countries? Do animals have rights, and if so, are they the same as or different from human rights? These questions – of immediate practical concern in the world we live in – are also the subject of philosophical inquiry.

So what, then, is philosophy? Is it a science? Is it an art? And how does it differ from religion?

Like science, philosophy seeks to find answers to questions by a process of investigation and argument, but it differs from science in that the questions it asks cannot be answered by means of practical experiment. Philosophical investigation is mental rather than experimental.

Like religion, philosophy considers the fundamental questions of life and death, of purpose and meaninglessness, of right and wrong. But unlike religion, philosophy addresses these questions by argument and demonstration, allowing no place to revelation and dogma.

Few people have regarded philosophy as an art-form, but the American philosopher Robert Nozick has suggested that, just as a composer works with musical themes, harmonic structures and metre, an artist with forms and colours, and a novelist with plots, characters and actions, so a philosopher works with ideas, concepts and questions which are moulded and shaped, developed and revised, ordered and reordered, and in so doing 'sculptures a view'.

Philosophy in an informal sense is probably as old as civilization itself, but as a mental discipline it does not become clearly separate from religion until the 6th century BC, among the Greeks living in southern Italy and around the Aegean Sea. However, under the influence of Christianity, philosophy and religion become entangled once again during the Middle Ages, and philosophy as a separate enterprise independent of religion and dogma begins once more with Descartes in the 17th century.

The main branches of modern philosophy are *metaphysics,* which inquires into the nature of reality and includes *ontology,* concerned specifically with the nature of being; *logic,* which establishes the principles of valid reasoning; *epistemology,* which investigates the nature of knowledge; and *ethics,* the study of moral values and principles. There are, in addition, philosophies of many specific branches of human study and activity: for example, art (*aesthetics*), law (*jurisprudence*), politics, science, the mind, religion and language.

Not only are there several branches of philosophy, there are also many schools of philosophy. Among these are the *Sceptics,* who question whether it is possible to truly know anything; the *Empiricists,* who claim that all knowledge is based on experience; the *Rationalists,* who base knowledge on thought and reason; the *Idealists,* for whom what is real does not exist independently of the human mind; the *Utilitarians,* who relate the notions of 'right' and 'wrong' to what makes people happy or unhappy; and the *Existentialists,* who begin their philosophical investigations with the concerns of human beings finding themselves in an apparently meaningless world and having to deal with such matters as personal freedom and responsibility. These and other schools of thought are represented by philosophers whose work is summarized in this book.

In the first half of the 20th century, one of the main focuses of philosophy in the English-speaking world was 'analytic philosophy', concerned with the careful analysis of language and the concepts it expresses, as in the work of Russell and Wittgenstein. Analytic philosophy remains dominant in the English-speaking philosophical world today, although its subject matter now ranges well beyond the confines of linguistic analysis, as for example in the work of Rawls and Nozick. Commonly contrasted with analytic philosophy is 'continental philosophy', European in origin though by no means limited to

European philosophers. Concerned with the human condition in all its complexities, it is more metaphysical and speculative than analytical philosophy, and is sometimes expressed in the form of works of literature, such as Sartre's philosophical novel *Nausea* and Nietzsche's *Thus Spake Zarathustra.*

Of course, as science and technology advance, they open up new areas in which philosophy can and should offer its particular insights. For example, the new sciences of artificial intelligence and robotics have led to renewed philosophical speculation on what exactly intelligence is, what consciousness is, what it is to be human, and so on. Among the philosophers associated with this field of inquiry are Alan Turing and John Searle.

Philosophy has been described as being 'brain-breakingly' difficult. Indeed, C.E.M. Joad, a former professor of philosophy, once wrote that 'most books on philosophy are unintelligible to most intelligent people' and that 'over half of what passes for philosophy is unreadable', something he attributed in part to the abysmal writing-style of many philosophers.

Whether you find such an opinion depressing or reassuring, it certainly underlines the need for a book such as *Philosophy: The Great Thinkers.* In these pages you will find clear and succinct outlines of the key thoughts of the leading philosophers from philosophy's earliest stages right down to the 21st century. All the main branches of philosophy are covered, and all the main schools. And if, having read the articles in this book, you want to explore the writings of the philosophers themselves, then the 'Essential reading' boxes will guide you towards what you should look at next. Even if half of philosophy is unreadable, the other half is well worth getting to grips with.

ANSELM, ST

1033–1109

Born at Aosta in Burgundy, Anselm was a pious child and sought admission to the monastic life at the early age of 15. The local Abbot, however, refused him on his father's insistence. After his mother's death, Anselm took to travelling. Eventually he arrived at the Abbey of Bec and began studying under the renowned Prior Lanfranc. He eventually took his monastic orders in 1060. Only three years later, when Lanfranc was appointed Abbot of Caen, the young Anselm succeeded him as Prior, much to the chagrin of older and more established candidates for the position. During the next thirty years he wrote his philosophical and theological works and was appointed Abbot of Bec.

Now remembered as the father of the Scholastic tradition and Archbishop of Canterbury from 1093 until his death, Anselm is of philosophical interest mainly for his logical arguments in two major works, the *Monologion* (meaning 'Soliloquy') and the *Proslogion* (Discourse), both of which gave various arguments intended to prove the existence of God. By the 12th century, the works of **Plato** and **Aristotle** had been rediscovered and reinterpreted by the scholastics who attempted to synthesize early Greek ideas with medieval theology. Following the Greek tradition, it is said that Anselm's students had been concerned to hear a rational justification for the existence of God that did not rely merely on the acceptance of scripture or doctrinal teaching. Anselm's most famous response to this challenge

God exists because the concept of God exists

was to become known as 'the ontological argument for the existence of God' which has been called by some one of the most hotly debated issues in the history of philosophy.

Consider, invites Anselm, that by the term 'God' we mean something than which nothing greater can be thought of. Given that even the non-believer or, as Anselm calls him, the Fool, accepts that this is what the concept of God entails, the existence of God would seem to follow necessarily from the definition. For it would be a contradiction to suppose that God is on the one hand something than which nothing greater can be thought of and on the other hand does not exist. For a God thought of that does not really exist is not so great as one thought of that does exist, and since one can clearly think of God and suppose he exists, then something than which nothing greater can be thought of must be something that exists.

St Anselm is shown here at work, surrounded by the accoutrements of his office, and entranced by a vision of the Virgin and Child.

could ever be. Since by definition the island is the most perfect it must exist, for by Anselm's reasoning it would be less than perfect if it did not. Thus, complained Gaunilo, Anselm's reasoning licences the existence of all sorts of imaginary objects and must therefore be faulty. In response, Anselm claimed that

The quality of perfection is an attribute that only applies to God

the quality of perfection is an attribute that only applies to God, and therefore his ontological argument cannot be used to prove the existence of imaginary islands or anything else.

Versions of Anselm's ontological argument were later used by both St Thomas **Aquinas** and René **Descartes** and were, much later still, heavily criticized by Immanuel **Kant**. Kant's principle complaint was that the concept of God as a perfect being does not necessarily entail that God exists since 'existence' is not a perfection. The concept of a perfect being that exists is no more or less great than the concept of a perfect being that does not exist. Philosophers agree that the problem with Anselm's argument revolves around the fact that we surely cannot ascertain whether something

Anselm's ontological argument is ingenious in its simplicity. While most people agree that there is something rather fishy about it, opinion has been divided as to exactly what is the matter with the argument. The earliest critic of Anselm was a contemporary Benedictine monk called Gaunilo of Marmoutiers. Gaunilo argued that if Anselm's reasoning were correct, then one could conceive of a lost island that was the most perfect island there exists or not merely by analysing the meaning of a word or concept. However, exactly what logical error is being committed by attempting to do so has remained a cause of much dispute amongst philosophers and logicians.

The argument was taken up again in more recent times, in the 1960s, when the philosopher Norman Malcolm revived a lesser known variant of Anselm's argument which sidesteps the objections made by Kant and others. According to Malcolm, Anselm argues in the *Proslogion* that if it is possible that a necessary being could exist, then it must exist, for it would be a contradiction to say a necessary being does not exist. God could only fail to exist if the concept of God was self-contradictory or nonsensical, and this, declares Malcolm, remains to be shown by opponents of the ontological argument.

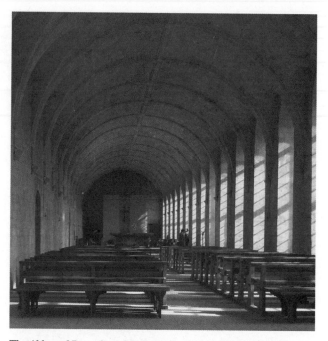

The Abbey of Bec, where St Anselm lived and worked, eventually rising to the post of Abbot.

▌ ESSENTIAL READING ▌

St Anselm wrote many religious books, including *Cur Deus Homo* (Why did God become Man?), but is best known today for his two philosophical works, *Monoglion* and *Proslogion*, in which he attempted to prove the existence of God.

Monologion (1076)

In this book, Anselm argues that the concept of 'goodness' would not be possible if there were not some absolute standard, some ideal of goodness, which all other 'goodnesses' were a reflection of. That ideal of goodness is God.

Proslogion (1077–78)

Not entirely satisfied with his efforts in *Monologion,* Anselm tried another proof of God, known as the ontological argument, in his next book: if we can conceive of perfection, but it exists only in our minds, then it is less than perfect. Yet, we *can* conceive of perfection – so therefore perfection, or God, must exist.

AQUINAS, ST THOMAS

1225–1274

The favoured philosopher of the Catholic Church, Aquinas is principally remembered for reconciling the philosophy of **Aristotle** with Christian doctrine. Born in northern Sicily, he was educated first at the University of Naples and later at Cologne, and lectured at Paris and Naples. Aquinas was canonized in 1323 by Pope John XII.

While much of Aquinas' work was Aristotelian in derivation, he also extended and clarified many of Aristotle's ideas and made many original contributions to Aristotelian thought. Chief amongst Aquinas' many achievements are the 'Five Ways', or proofs of the existence of God, from his *Summa Theologica*. The Five Ways are the clearest and most succinct attempt to prove the existence of God by means of logical argument.

In the first of the Five Ways, Aquinas says the existence of God can be proved by considering the concept of change. We can clearly see that some things in the world are in the process of change, and this change must be a result of something else, since a thing cannot change of itself. But the cause of the change itself, since in the process of change, must also be caused to change by something other than itself, and so on again, ad infinitum. Clearly, there must be something which is the cause of all change, but which itself does not undergo change.

For, as Aquinas says, 'if the hand does not move the stick, the stick will not move anything else'. The first mover, Aquinas concludes, is God.

'If the hand does not move the stick, the stick will not move anything else'

In the second Way, arguing in a similar manner to the first, Aquinas notes that causes always operate in series, but there must be a first cause of the series or there could not be a series at all. Interestingly, both the first and second Ways proceed on the assumption that a thing cannot cause itself. Yet this is precisely his conclusion, that there is a thing which does cause itself, namely, God. Philosophers have criticized this form of arguing as confused, since the proposition that appears to be proven in the conclusion is the very same proposition denied in the argument.

In the third Way, it is noted that we observe that things in the world come to be and pass away. But clearly not everything can be like this, for then there would have been a time when nothing existed. But if that were true then nothing could ever have come into being, since something cannot come from nothing. Therefore something must have always existed, and this is what people understand by God. The first, second and third Ways of Aquinas' arguments are often called variations of a more general argument, the Cosmological Argument.

In the fourth Way, Aquinas offers a version of the Ontological Argument (see **Anselm**). In Aquinas' version some things are noted to exhibit varying degrees of a quality. A thing may be more or less hot, more or less good, more or less noble. Such varying degrees of quality are caused by something that contains the most or perfect amount of that quality. For just as the sun is the hottest thing, and thus the cause of all other things being hot, so there must be some fully 'good' thing which makes all other things good. That which is most good is, of course, God.

A detail of Carlo Crivelli's 1476 *Demidoff Altarpiece* showing Aquinas, who was canonized in 1323.

Finally, in the fifth Way, Aquinas relies on Aristotle's notion of 'telos' or purpose. All things aim towards some ultimate goal or end. But to be guided by a purpose or a goal implies some mind that directs or intends that purpose. That director is, once again, God. Versions of Aquinas' cosmological and ontological arguments are still accepted by the Catholic Church today, though modern philosophers have almost unanimously rejected all five of Aquinas' Ways.

‖ **ESSENTIAL READING** ‖

Summa contra Gentiles *(1259–64)*

This is Aquinas' most important work. It aims to establish, mostly by philosophical argument, the truth of the Christian religion, proving the existence of God and then discussing the nature of God, creation and its purpose, the soul, ethics, sin, the Trinity, etc.

Summa Theologica *(1266–73)*

The *Summary of Theology* is a huge work, not what one might consider a summary. The first part discusses God, creation and human nature; the second part deals with morality; and the third part discusses Christ and the sacraments. Aquinas left the third part unfinished, having one day had a mystical vision, compared to which, he said, all he had written seemed like straw.

ARISTOTLE

384–322BC

Aristotle's achievements in the history and development of western thought are both stunning and unrivalled. More than just a philosopher, Aristotle was a scientist, astronomer, political theorist and the inventor of what is now called symbolic or formal logic. He wrote extensively on biology, psychology, ethics, physics, metaphysics and politics and set the terms of debate in all these areas right up to modern times. Indeed, his writings on justice are still required reading for undergraduates reading Law.

After his death his works were lost for some 200 years or so, but fortunately were rediscovered in Crete. Later translated into Latin by **Boethius** around AD500, Aristotle's influence spread throughout Syria and Islam whilst Christian Europe ignored him in favour of **Plato**. Not until Thomas **Aquinas** reconciled Aristotle's work with Christian doctrine in the 13th century did he become influential in western Europe.

Aristotle received his education from age seventeen in Plato's 'Academy', where he stayed for some 20 years until Plato's death. Later he founded his own institution, 'the Lyceum', where he

would expound a philosophy altogether different both in method and content from that of his former teacher.

More than any other philosopher before him, Aristotle made much of observation and strict classification of data in his studies. For this reason he is often considered as the father of empirical science and scientific method. Unlike his predecessor Plato, Aristotle always undertook his investigations by considering the regarded opinions of both experts and lay people, before detailing his own arguments, assuming that some grain of truth is likely to be found in commonly held ideas. Aristotle's method was nothing if not rigorous and lacked the proselytizing tone of many of his predecessors.

In contradistinction to both Plato and the Presocratics, Aristotle rejected the idea that the many diverse branches of human inquiry could, in principle, be subsumed under one discipline based on some universal philosophic principle. Different sciences require different axioms and admit of varying degrees of precision according to their

Aristotle studied under Plato, at the latter's famous Academy, for 20 years.

A 14th-century illuminated manuscript of Aristotle's *Ethics*, showing the allegorical figure of Dame Justice ruling over aspects of everyday life.

subject. Thus Aristotle denied there could be exact laws of human nature, whilst maintaining that certain metaphysical categories – such as quantity, quality, substance and relation – were applicable to the description of all phenomena.

If there is one common thread to much of Aristotle's work it lies in his conception of teleology, or purpose. Perhaps as a result of his preoccupation with biological studies, Aristotle was impressed by the idea that both animate and inanimate behaviour

Everything has a natural function and strives towards fulfilling or exhibiting that function, which is its best and most natural state

is directed toward some final purpose ('telos') or goal. It is common to explain the behaviour of people, institutions and nations in terms of purposes and goals (for example, John is sitting the bar exam to become a barrister; the school is holding a fête to raise funds for the roof; the country is going to war to protect its territory), and likewise modern evolutionary biology makes use of purposive explanation to account for the behaviour of, for instance, genes and genetic imperatives. However, Aristotle thought the concept of purpose could be invoked to explain the behaviour of everything in the universe. His reasoning lay in the idea that everything has a natural function and strives towards fulfilling or exhibiting that function, which is its best and most natural state. It is by means of the concept of function that Aristotle then ties his ethics to his physics, claiming that the natural function of man is to reason, and to reason well is to reason in accordance with virtue. Unlike the opposing ethical theories of **Kant** and **Mill**, both of which view actions as the subject of ethical judgements, Aristotle's ethics focuses on the character of the agent as that which is morally good or morally bad. This so-called 'virtue ethics' was revived with much critical success by Alistair Macintyre in late 20th-century moral philosophy.

‖ **ESSENTIAL READING** ‖

Aristotle's works cannot be precisely dated and it is likely that changes have been made to the texts down the ages. However, a substantial – and hugely influential – corpus has come down to us.

Nicomachean Ethics
One of the most important and influential works on ethics that has ever been written, the *Ethics* contains a discussion on virtue and its relationship to well-being and happiness. Aristotle's ethical views show a clear understanding of human nature and psychology.

Politics
In his *Politics*, Aristotle discusses the ideal city-state, and classifies and discusses the merits and demerits of various types of government. The book includes a defence of slavery.

Physics
In this book Aristotle discusses topics such as matter, form, causation, space, time and motion. The book is also interesting for its discussion of the nature of explanation.

ARNAULD, ANTOINE

1612–94

Last-born son of a lawyer who fathered twenty children, Arnauld became a theologian, logician and philosopher. He collaborated with both Nicole and **Pascal** on their famous *The Art of Thinking*, which later became known as 'the Port Royal Logic' or sometimes just 'The Logic'. He is also remembered as the author of several of the replies to **Descartes**' *Meditations on First Philosophy*, gaining in the process a reputation as an intellectually rigourous and perceptive critic, and bringing attention to the problem now known as 'the Cartesian circle'.

Like Descartes, Arnauld is a firm rationalist. In *The Art of Thinking*, he proclaims that the main aim of logic is to inculcate clear thinking. Thus he writes, 'nothing is more to be esteemed than aptness in discerning the true from the false. Other qualities of mind are of limited use, but precision of thought is essential to every aspect and walk of life. To distinguish truth from error is difficult not only in the sciences but also in the everyday affairs men engage in and discuss. Men are everywhere confronted with alternative routes – some true and others false – and reason must choose between them. Who chooses well has a sound mind, who chooses ill a defective one. Capacity for discerning the truth is the most important measure of minds.'

The Art of Thinking consists of four parts corresponding to the principal operations of the mind: conceiving, judging, reasoning and ordering. Conceiving and judging imply a knowledge of

'Capacity for discerning the truth is the most important measure of minds.'

language, since it is concepts and propositions, essentially linguistic items, that are conceived and judged. Reasoning is a higher-level function of conceiving and judging, required when the concepts that form a proposition are not sufficiently clear for a judgement to be made. Finally, ordering is a mental activity which reflects the method of the new inductive sciences.

Arnauld accepts the general tenets of Cartesian thought. In line with Descartes' ontological dualism, Arnauld commits himself to the idea that speech is part of the material world and bound by its laws, but thought, belonging to the essence of the mind, is not so constricted. This leads to a distinction in Arnauld's work between grammar on the one hand, which belongs to speech; and logic, which belongs to the realm of thought. In the four-fold classification of *The Logic*, Arnauld places logic itself firmly within the faculty of reason, but insists that reasoning is merely an extension of judging.

This idea is important for it reflects one side of a foundational debate concerning the status of logic. Is logic, as Arnauld would have it, merely a tool of clear thinking in order to aid rhetoric, or does it reflect universal laws of thought that correspond to reality? This latter view, to which Arnauld and the Port Royal logicians were hostile, holds that there are three laws of thought that are necessary principles for any rational creature, even God. These are the law of non-contradiction, the law of identity, and the law of the excluded middle. These state respectively that a proposition cannot be simultaneously asserted and denied; that if A is identical to B, then anything that is true of A is also true of B; and that every proposition is determinately either true or false. Modern developments in both logic and physics (quantum physics) have cast doubt on the universality of at least two of these so-called laws, giving support to the Port Royals' contention that logic is merely the refinement of clear thinking in aid of argumentation, or rhetoric.

One of twenty children, Arnauld grew up to be an eminent rationalist and logician, sometimes referred to as *Le Grand Arnauld*.

▌ ESSENTIAL READING ▌

The two most important philosophical works by Arnauld are *Port Royal Grammar*, co-authored with Claude Launcelot, and *The Art of Thinking* (or *Port Royal Logic*), on which he collaborated with Pierre Nicole and Blaise Pascal.

Port Royal Grammar (1660)

In this book, he argues that our mental processes and grammar are deeply connected. Since mental processes are carried out by all human beings, we need a universal grammar.

The Art of Thinking (1683)

In his most famous work, Arnauld argues that the main aim of logic is to develop clear thinking and to enable a person to distinguish truth from falsehood, both in the sciences and in everyday life.

AUGUSTINE, ST

354–430

Religious scholar and philosopher, Augustine produced works, principally his *Confessions* and his *City of God,* that are classics in both the philosophy of religion and Christian doctrine. Born in Algeria, he studied in Carthage, Rome and Milan before returning to North Africa to found a monastery. He was made Bishop of Hippo Regius in 395.

Rational thought is the servant of faith:
'unless thou believe thou shalt not understand' Isiah

At the heart of Augustine's philosophy is the belief that only through faith can wisdom be attained. He saw both philosophy and religion as quests for the same thing, namely truth, but with the former inferior to the latter in this pursuit. The philosopher without faith could never attain to the ultimate truth, which for Augustine was beatitude, or 'the enjoying of truth'. Although reason alone could attain to some truths, Augustine maintained that rational thought was the servant of faith.

One of Augustine's favourite texts, quoted from Isaiah, held that 'unless thou believe thou shalt not understand'. One must believe in order to acquire understanding. This idea of Augustine's was not mere slavish following of Christian doctrine. Indeed, in his youth he had renounced religion, finding the scriptures intellectually unsatisfying. After converting to Christianity in his early thirties, it became his aim to show how reason could prove the tenets of faith. This was the idea that informed his philosophy.

Augustine's use of reason to justify the doctrines of faith is best known, famously or infamously depending on one's point of view, for putting down the so-called 'Pelagian heresy'. Pelagius had questioned the notion of original sin, and further held, in accordance with the notion of free will, that when a person does good they do so from the virtue of their own moral character. As a result they are rewarded in heaven. Augustine found this doctrine subversive and distasteful. He argued, following the Epistle of St Paul, that all men are born in sin. Redemption is only possible by the grace of God regardless of our actions on earth. Adam, in taking the apple had condemned himself and all of mankind to damnation. Our only salvation lies in repentance, but this does not guarantee that we will be chosen to go to heaven and not to hell.

Augustine's arguments, later revived by Calvin and eventually abandoned by the Catholic Church,

This 15th-century panel shows the Devil presenting St Augustine with the book of vices.

are skilled rationalizations of St Paul's *Epistle to the Romans*. But nowhere does he question the assumptions of the Epistle, concentrating instead on drawing out the logical conclusions of the Scripture.

In more recent times, Augustine's *Confessions* received attention from **Wittgenstein**, not for its religious or even philosophical pronouncements, but for the way in which Augustine describes the learning of language:

'When they (my elders) named some object, and accordingly moved towards something, I saw this and I grasped that the thing was called by the sound they uttered when they meant to point it out. Their intention was shown by their bodily movements, as it were the natural language of all peoples: the expression of the face, the play of the eyes…Thus as I heard words repeatedly used in their proper places in various sentences, I gradually learnt to understand what objects they signified; and…I used them to express my own desires' (*Confessions*, I. 8).

At the beginning of his posthumously published *Philosophical Investigations*, Wittgenstein famously called this common-place conception 'the Augustinian picture of language'. Much of the rest of the *Investigations* is a successful repudiation of the Augustinian conception of language.

St Augustine is shown here wearing a monk's habit under his bishop's robes. He was appointed to the bishopric of Hippo in 395.

‖ ESSENTIAL READING ‖

Confessions (397–398)

This is an autobiography in 13 volumes, charting the evolution of Augustine's philosophy of religion. He records his regret at leading a sinful life, his growing awareness of the evils of astrology and Manichaeism, his conversion to Christianity, and understanding of the importance of sexual morality.

City of God (413–427)

Divided into 22 books. The first 10 argue against belief in religions and philosophies other than Christianity. The last 12 retell the biblical story of human history from Genesis to Revelation in terms of a conflict between what he calls the City of God (those who live according to Christian values) and the City of Man (those who have strayed from the City of God).

AURELIUS, MARCUS

AD121–80

Adopted son of the Emperor Pius, Marcus Aurelius himself became Roman emperor for almost 20 years until his death in AD180. He is known for his only work the *Meditations or Writings to Himself,* written, according to critics, in the midst of the Parthian war when he might have better used his time directing the army. Still, as a 'converted' Stoic, he had great concern for the social problems of the poor, slaves, and the imprisoned. Despite this, he continued, as emperor, with the persecution of the growing Christian population, undoubtedly because he saw them as a threat to the Roman religion and way of life, based as this was on conquest, polytheism, and the deification of dead emperors. His own life ended as a result of the plague, whilst he was planning a campaign to increase the domain of the Empire to the north.

The importance of his *Meditations* lies in their practical and aphoristic Stoic message. A loosely organized set of thoughts relating to Stoic philosophy, they nevertheless represent an example of a living ethic, of a teaching closer to religion than to philosophic speculation. For example, the following is typical of Marcus Aurelius: 'The happiness of your life depends on the quality of your thoughts: therefore, guard accordingly, and take care that you entertain no notions unsuitable to virtue and reasonable nature'.

Like **Seneca** before him, Marcus Aurelius believed that a divine providence had placed reason in man, and it was in the power of man to be one with the rational purpose of the universe. The Stoic

> *'The happiness of your life depends on the quality of your thoughts: therefore, guard accordingly, and take care that you entertain no notions unsuitable to virtue and reasonable nature.'*

philosophy was primarily concerned with living in accordance with both one's own nature and universal Nature, perhaps best understood in the sense meant by Taoist philosophers of the East. Simple living and contentment with one's lot go hand in hand with Stoicism, but run the risk of leading to quietism. As a means of social control Stoicism is the ideal 'religion', since the more that people are willing to accept that things are just as they are, the less trouble they are likely to give the Emperor. Though it is unlikely that Marcus Aurelius professed Stoicism for political purposes – the

Meditations seem sincere enough – it is a factor of his philosophy that should not be ignored.

The rationale behind the Stoic insistence on living 'in accordance with nature' stems from a certain biological outlook. According to the Stoics, all 'ensouled beings' (by which they mean what we would now call 'sentient life') strive towards self-preservation. Self-preservation leads a being to look for that which is in tune with its nature and appropriate to its own being. Man, being endowed with reason, seeks not just food, warmth and shelter, but also that which is good for the intellect. Ultimately, reason allows us to choose that which is in tune with our true nature with greater accuracy than if we merely follow our animal instinct.

Central to this Stoic outlook is an understanding of what constitutes the good or most appropriate life for human beings. Whilst many thinkers might suppose health or wealth, the Stoics insist that the ultimate good must be good at all times. It is conceivable that wealth might sometimes be detrimental to a person, and so too even health, if for example, my strength were put to ill-doing. Accordingly, the Stoics conclude that the only infallible good is virtue. Virtue includes the usual list of Greco-Roman excellences: wisdom, justice, courage, and moderation.

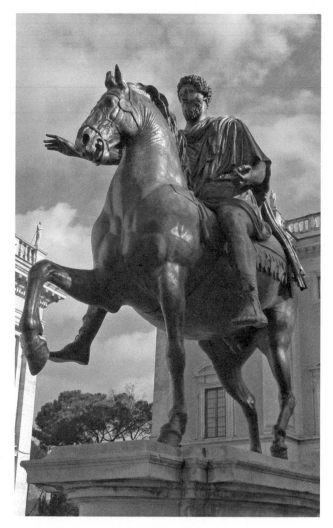

Roman emperor, military campaigner and Stoic philsopher, Marcus Aurelius cuts a larger-than-life figure in the Western tradition.

‖ ESSENTIAL READING ‖

Meditations

The practical application of Stoic philosophy set out in the *Meditations* has been adequately described in the above essay on Marcus Aurelius. Although written almost 2,000 years ago, the wisdom they encapsulate is no less applicable in the modern world than in the Roman world.

AUSTIN, JOHN LANGSHAW

1911–60

Professor of Moral Philosophy at Oxford and a prominent figure in the 'ordinary language' school of philosophy, Austin produced two major works in his career, *Sense and Sensibilia* and *How to Do Things With Words*.

Austin's approach begins with an analysis of the different kinds of thing we do with words. Philosophers have long been impressed with the fact that language is used to represent how the world is, to say what is or is not the case, and thus

> *Austin points out the many things we do with words: we ask questions, give commands, tell jokes, make promises, make suggestions, give advice, insult, persuade and intimidate, all through the use of words*

the notion of truth has been central to the philosophy of language. But Austin, like the later **Wittgenstein**, is keen to point out the many other things we do with words. We do not just represent how things are, we ask questions, give commands, tell jokes, make promises, make suggestions, give advice, insult, persuade and intimidate, all through the use of words.

This led Austin to draw a three-fold distinction between different kinds of 'speech-act'. First, words have a distinct, conventional, meaning. The expression 'the cat sat on the mat' refers to a cat, a mat and a relation between them, of one sitting upon the other. This ordinary sense of meaning constitutes the 'what is said' of any particular speech act, and Austin gives it the technical name of 'a locutionary act'. Secondly, Austin notes, in saying certain words one actually commits an act e.g. in saying 'I do' at a wedding, one makes a promise, in saying 'will you?' one asks a question, and saying 'you will!' one gives an order. Austin calls such acts 'illocutionary'. Finally, he points out that by saying something, one often performs an action, by saying 'I do' one weds, by saying something like 'I will give you a better deal than the shop along the street', I may cause a buyer to be persuaded, and so on. Such an act Austin calls a 'perlocutionary act'.

These different functions of words are not necessarily exclusive. Austin is aware that many utterances can involve all three kinds of acts. Consider someone saying 'It's cold', a locutionary act describing how one feels. It might also be taken, in the context of a room with an open window, as an illocutionary act – a request to close the window. Finally, insofar as the hearer responds by closing the window, the single utterance has also performed a perlocutionary act.

These distinctions significantly increase and deepen our understanding of the way in which language functions and have profound effects on what is required of a theory of meaning. In particular it is interesting to note that what locutionary and illocutionary acts are performed depend on convention, the rules by which we understand the meaning of the words. Perlocutionary acts, however, are causal: if successful they cause the occurrence of an event.

In his other main work, *Sense and Sensibilia*, a play on the title of a work by another famous Austen,

Austin worked for the British intelligence services during the Second World War, before taking up his post at Oxford.

Austin attacks the sense-data theory championed by **Ayer**. Austin's method is similar to that of Gilbert **Ryle**, though he does not formally introduce the notion of 'category-mistake', but he does use an analysis of the ordinary use of words to show how they are presupposed and relied upon, often illegitimately, in philosophical contexts.

The 'ordinary language' school of philosophy thus ushered in by the work of Austin can be celebrated for two primary achievements. First, it forced philosophy and philosophers to pay greater heed to the way in which they described and explained their theories, on what notions they were borrowing from other contexts and whether those borrowings were consistent or not. Second, it helped to inform pragmatics or speech-act theory, which itself is a major school of thought in both linguistics and philosophy.

‖ ESSENTIAL READING ‖

How to do Things with Words (1962)

In this book, Austin attacks the view that the main purpose of uttering sentences is to state facts, which can either be true or false. He argues that uttering some sentences is neither to state a truth or a falsehood, but to perform a kind of action, known as an illocutionary act; other sentences can cause an action to take place, known as a perlocutionary act.

Sense and Sensibilia (1962)

This is a critique of sense-data theory – the idea that within our minds there are internal objects of perception that represent physical, external objects, and that this can sometimes cause misperceptions. Austin argues that this is not a helpful way of explaining misperception, as it implies that all misperceptions are of the same nature.

AVICENNA

980–1037

The Persian Islamic philosopher Avicenna was responsible for bringing **Aristotle**'s works into the wider consciousness in the post-Classical era. He originated a version of the Argument from First Cause for the existence of God. Avicenna was also widely respected in his day for his medical writings, and his textbook, *The Canon of Medicine*, remained a standard work until the 17th century.

Born near Bukhara in modern-day Uzbekistan in 980, Avicenna had memorized the Koran by the age of 10 and by 21 was a well-rounded intellectual, accomplished in all areas of learning including medicine, mathematics, music, astronomy and logic. Avicenna lived in turbulent times, when Turkish forces were fighting for dominance in Central Asia. At the same time, local Iranian dynasties were struggling to gain independence from the central Muslim dynasty, the Abbasid caliphate, which was based in modern-day Baghdad, Iraq. Despite having to move from town to town in Khorasan (north-eastern Iran and modern western Afghanistan) to work for a living as a physician and an administrator, Avicenna managed to further his intellectual pursuits and wrote around 200 treatises as well as several major works, of which the most famous are the *Kitab ash-shifa (Book of Healing)* and *al-Qanun fi at-tibb (The Canon of Medicine)*.

Avicenna's major contributions were in medicine and philosophy. Reason and reality were central to his philosophy. He stressed the importance of gaining knowledge. He believed that through

Avicenna held that God, the originator of existence, is pure intellect

reason it was possible for an individual to progress through various levels of understanding and eventually reach the truth about God, the ultimate object of knowledge. Avicenna held that God, the originator of existence, is pure intellect.

As a Muslim, Avicenna attempted to integrate elements of Aristotle's and **Plato**'s philosophy with his belief in God as the Creator. In this area, he departed from Classical thinking. Avicenna took on the central subject of metaphysics: the existence of God. Drawing on Plato's ideas, he made a distinction between essence and existence. Essence is the nature of things, while their physical manifestation is separate. For example, the essence of a 'horse' or a 'stone' does not imply that a particular horse or stone exists. Existence has to have been created by a necessary essence that is itself not caused. Put another way, for the material world to have come into being, another factor must have caused it; in turn another factor must have brought this factor into being. Avicenna proposed that an essential cause and its effect cannot be part of an infinite chain. There has to be a First Cause, and this is God.

There has to be a First Cause, and this is God

God is the necessary existent, and the world emanated from him. In this way, Avicenna believed he had proved God's existence.

Avicenna went on to show that God, reflecting on his own existence, emanated a First Intellect (an intelligence or consciousness); the self-awareness of this intellect in turn gave rise to a Second Intellect. Successive levels of intelligences emanated from them, creating the universe and the matter that fills it; the tenth and final intellect produced the material world. For Avicenna, the nature of God means that the universe has to exist as it does. Every stage from the First Intellect through all the emanations to the creation of the material world was entirely necessary, not the work of a deity that decided the form of creation. Thus the creation of God and the universe were all part of the same process. This contradicted the biblical and Koranic theory of Creation as an act of free will on the part of God.

For individuals to gain knowledge and grow closer to the truth about the Creator, they had to attempt to grasp the intelligible, using reason and logic. Avicenna followed Aristotle's thought in *Prior Analytics,* in which he identified the capacity for a person to hit upon the middle term of a syllogism to develop arguments. (A traditional syllogism has

Avicenna was both a physician and a philosopher. In this 15th-century woodcut, he is shown examining a urine specimen to make a diagnosis.

two premises and a conclusion, such as 'All mortal things die. All men are mortal things. All men die.' The middle term is the term that the two premises have in common – in this case, mortal things.) For Avicenna, when a person understood such intelligibles, he or she came in touch with the Active Intellect, the final level of being that emanated from God. The capacity for gaining knowledge varied enormously between people; a prophet, who knew virtually all of the intelligibles, had the greatest capacity.

For Avicenna, it was the human soul that engaged with the task of gaining knowledge of reality. The human soul was incorporeal – separate from the material world. This was because an intellectual thought, in order to remain a coherent concept, could not belong to different intellects, but instead was held by one single intellect. The soul was therefore also immortal; the disintegration of the body after death did not affect it.

In Avicenna's final major philosophical work, *Kitab al-isharat wa at-tanbihat (Book of Directives and Remarks)*, he wrote of the path of knowledge from the beginning to the final vision of God. It was written during the last 14 years of his life in which he lived relatively peacefully in the employ of Ala ad-Dawlah, the ruler of Esfahan, Iran. Avicenna died in 1037 in Hamadan.

In the century after his death, *The Canon of Medicine* and part of the *Book of Healing* were translated into Latin. The translation brought Avicenna's ideas to a European audience and was at first perceived as a mere commentary; a century later, his efforts to integrate philosophy with faith were greatly appreciated by Christian scholars. The foremost Scholastic Christian theologian Thomas **Aquinas** (1274–1323) included some of his proofs, for example, the distinction between essence and existence, in Catholic theology. Avicenna's works in philosophy, theology and medicine had a dominant influence in the Islamic world after his death and remain of significance today.

|| **ESSENTIAL READING** ||

Avicenna made notable contributions to the fields of philosophy and medicine. His most significant works are the *Kitab ash-shifa (Book of Healing) and al-Qanun fi at-tibb (The Canon of Medicine),* both written in the early 11th century.

Book of Healing

In this work, Avicenna covered logic, mathematics, the natural sciences, music and metaphysics. Drawing on Aristotle and other Greek philosophers, he developed an argument for God as a necessary existent from which the entire universe was created.

The Canon of Medicine

This encyclopaedia drew on the medical knowledge of the Greek physicians of the Roman imperial age and of Arab physicians, as well as his own experience as a physician. A summary of over one thousand years of the history and traditions of medical practice, it remained a standard textbook of medical knowledge in Europe until the 17th century.

AYER, ALFRED JULES

1910–89

Oxford philosopher famous as a broadcaster, Ayer was, in some eyes, a political radical: the Times Literary Supplement warned its readers that his work had 'successfully carried the red flag into the citadel of Oxford University'. He is best known, however, for his 'logical positivism' and his commitment to a robust empiricism grounded in 'sense-data', a position known as 'phenomenalism'. His best works are *Language, Truth and Logic* and *The Problems of Knowledge,* though he also wrote on pragmatism, freedom and morality, **Russell**, **Hume** and **Voltaire**.

Ayer's brand of 'linguistic phenomenalism' pervades his early work. It informs his view on scepticism, perception, memory and personal identity. In the phenomenalist view, talk of material objects is legitimate, but misconceived if such objects are taken to be 'behind' or 'beyond' what appears to our senses. On the standard version of this view, material objects turn out to be 'logical constructions out of sense-data'. Ayer's 'linguistic' brand of phenomenalism does not quite endorse this view. Rather, statements about material objects can be reduced to statements about 'sense-data' – the perceptual input from environment to subject. What this means, according to Ayer, is that although 'the manner in which sense-data occur can be explained in terms of entities which are not themselves observable; [the phenomenalist] will, however, add that to talk about such unobservable entities is, in the end, to talk about sense-data'.

Statements about material objects can be reduced to statements about 'sense-data'

How this works, Ayer tells us, is that any statement S is reducible to a class of statements K just so long as K is 'on a lower epistemological level than S, that is, that they [K statements] refer to 'harder' data'. By 'harder data' here Ayer means the primary evidence of sensual input.

Problematic for Ayer, here, of course, is that in rejecting the tougher phenomenalist line in favour of the linguistic line, he cuts away the ground of explanatory force from his own theory. If the postulation of unobservables is supposed to explain the occurrence of patterns or regularities in sense-data, and yet such explanations are themselves reducible to just those occurrences of sense-data, then it would look as though the sense-data are being invoked to explain themselves. Ayer is aware of this problem, and passes the explanatory power to the subjunctive conditional. In other words, regularities in sense-data are explained by hypothetical statements about what sense-data one would receive in certain conditions. So, for example, the fact that a tree exists in a garden is explained by reference to the hypothetical claim that anyone who goes into that garden will receive sense-impressions of a tree-type nature. The tree, we can suppose, exists as a cause of those sense-impressions, but the meaning of this statement cannot amount to anything more than the claim that being in a certain space-time region (i.e., the garden) will occasion impressions of a tree-type sort.

Clearly, there are worries about such a view. In particular, the worry is that this 'hard empirical' theory seems to explain less and bring into doubt more than our original common-sense conceptions that it was designed to replace. Indeed, Ayer was aware of the problems faced by phenomenalism, and his later work is a continual refinement of the position in light of criticism. In the end, it is probably fair to say that Ayer had to weaken his position to such an extent that it lost all semblance of plausibility. However, in the progress and defence of his work, Ayer made very many important contributions to the development of issues central to 20th-century philosophical thought.

Born into a wealthy European family, Ayer published his most famous work, *Language, Truth and Logic*, when he was 26 years old.

▌ ESSENTIAL READING ▌

Language, Truth and Logic (1936)

This is the classic description of logical positivism. Ayer limits meaningful statements to those which are empirically verifiable and those which are self-evidently true or false. Religious and metaphysical statements belong to neither group and are therefore meaningless. There is also a discussion of the purpose of philosophy.

The Foundations of Empirical Knowledge (1940)

In a refinement of those views expressed in *Language, Truth and Logic*, Ayer argues that statements about physical objects can be translated into statements about sense-data, a view that was criticized by **Austin**.

The Problem of Knowledge (1956)

Ayer considers what is meant by 'knowledge', and goes on to discuss scepticism and certainty, perception, memory, personal identity, and one's knowledge of other minds.

The Central Questions of Philosophy (1973)

An accessible book based on a series of lectures Ayer gave in 1972–73, it provides a useful introduction to Ayer's mature views on philosophy.

BACON, FRANCIS

1561–1626

English philosopher of science, Francis Bacon was the forerunner of the famed British school of philosophers that include **Locke**, **Berkeley**, **Hume**, J.S. **Mill** and Bertrand **Russell**. Bacon's important works include *The Advancement of Learning, New Atlantis* and the *Novum Organum*. Bacon was also an essayist and enjoyed a successful legal and political career, in particular after James I's succession of Elizabeth, whereupon he was made Lord Chancellor until being found guilty of corruption.

Attributed as the originator of the saying 'knowledge is power', his importance as a philosopher is most notable with regard to his concern for scientific method. Bacon was troubled by the two schools of thought that had come out of

Moving away from the ideas of Plato and Aristotle, Bacon championed a science based on observation and inductive hypotheses.

Platonism and Aristotelianism respectively. Firstly, the rationalist view that knowledge could be gained by examining the content and meanings of words – a view Bacon dismissed as like spinning a web from the inside of one's own head. Secondly, the Aristotelians, intent on collecting masses of empirical data, where equally useless at helping a man arrive at any scientific hypotheses. What was needed, insisted Bacon, was a new way of collating and organizing data that would help generate inductive hypotheses.

Bacon, like many of his contemporaries and predecessors, had been concerned with the problem of induction, a problem that would later receive an astonishingly sceptical response from Hume. The problem of induction, as Bacon's contemporaries saw it, was that the mere repetitive occurrence of an incident does not guarantee that the same thing will happen again. To give a simple example, suppose a man draws nine blue marbles out of a bag of ten. It is no more likely that the tenth marble will be blue than it is that it will be red. The previous instances do not guarantee anything about the following instance.

Bacon saw that the answer to this problem lay in placing the emphasis of investigation on looking for negative instances to disconfirm hypotheses, rather than finding ways of confirming them. This is a striking precursor to Karl **Popper**'s 20th-century falsificationist scientific methodology and his much vaunted claim of 'solving the problem of induction'. As Popper readily admits, he owes much to Francis Bacon.

However, unlike others of his time, and later, Hume, Bacon was less interested in the problem of justifying inductive generalizations, than in how to generate good inductive hypotheses out of the

This title page to a volume of Bacon's *Magna Instauratio* shows a ship passing through the pillars of Hercules, a symbol of man's exploration and advancement in learning.

masses of data collected by observation. Bacon devised a new method. To illustrate it, Bacon shows how one might generate an hypothesis on the nature of heat. One should, Bacon tells us, list all those things in which the property under investigation, in this case heat, is present, then all those things in which the property is absent and finally all those cases which admit of varying degrees of the property in question. From such a list, Bacon believes the natural hypothesis will present itself, which in this case, as he well knew at the time, is that heat is produced according to the movement or excitation of molecules within a body.

Although Bacon's method is undoubtedly one way of applying order to a body of data, and even perhaps a useful way in some cases, it nevertheless seems unlikely to fulfil his ambition, which was to find a systematic way of deriving scientific hypotheses from the arrangement of data. It is unlikely that there ever could be such a system. Bacon failed to take into account the creativity and imaginative aspect of scientific theory building. No matter how systematically one organizes data, inductive hypotheses cannot be guaranteed to appear out of them. One may find that some facts deductively follow from a certain ordering of data, but that is not what Bacon was after.

What was needed, insisted Bacon, was a new way of collating and organizing data that would help generate inductive hypotheses

Despite his failure in this regard, Bacon nevertheless made some important contributions to the philosophy of science and to the problem of induction, not least, as we have seen, in being the first to stress the importance of negative instances.

▌ ESSENTIAL READING ▌

Novum Organum or *Novum Organon* *(1620)*
Intended as the second part of a much larger work on human knowledge (the *Magna Instauratio*, which was left unfinished), this 'New Tool' contains Bacon's views in the correct methods for investigating nature, which is by experiment. In it Bacon also describes various 'idols' – illusions, prejudices, linguistic confusions and philosophical dogmas – which prevent us from truly understanding the world.

On the Dignity and Advancement of Learning *(1623)*
This was intended as the first part of the *Magna Instauratio*. In it, Bacon divides knowledge into three categories: history, 'poesy' (that is, poetry or literature) and philosophy, based on the three human faculties of memory, imagination and reason. He also considers some of the main obstacles to learning.

The New Atlantis *(1627)*
Written in the form of a novel, this book describes the then revolutionary idea of a scientific research centre where researchers collect data, carry out experiments, and apply their knowledge to the production of useful things which are then shared with the whole population.

BEAUVOIR, SIMONE DE

1908–1986

French novelist and philosopher, de Beauvoir is largely responsible for inaugurating the modern feminist movement as well as significantly influencing the later views of **Sartre**. De Beauvoir has become, wittingly or otherwise, the heroine of feminists across the world. Her most significant philosophical works are *The Ethics of Ambiguity* and, the bible of feminism, *The Second Sex*. Both are superior works whose philosophical import has often been overlooked because of the determination to marginalize de Beauvoir within the feminist movement. In the words of Brendan Gill's 1953 review in *The New Yorker, The Second Sex* 'is a work of art, with the salt of recklessness that makes art sting.'

De Beauvoir's thought is a development of existentialist themes found in Sartre. In particular, her most famous expression, 'One is not born, but rather becomes, a woman', can only be understood against the background of Sartrean 'bad faith'.

According to Sartre, freedom of choice is an ever-present condition of human life. However, because of the enormous weight of responsibility that this entails, we are apt to make excuses, to deny our freedom to choose. Such excuses can typically involve blaming the kind of person that we are on our human nature. But Sartre says cowards and heroes are not born, they are defined in action. What we are is what we do. Thus anyone who acts heroically is a hero, anyone who acts cowardly is a coward. But one always has the choice to act differently next time. There is no such thing as 'nature' which determines how we must act. Denial of this radical freedom is a kind of self-deception, or 'bad faith' as Sartre calls it.

De Beauvoir met Sartre at the Sorbonne in Paris and the two became lifelong companions.

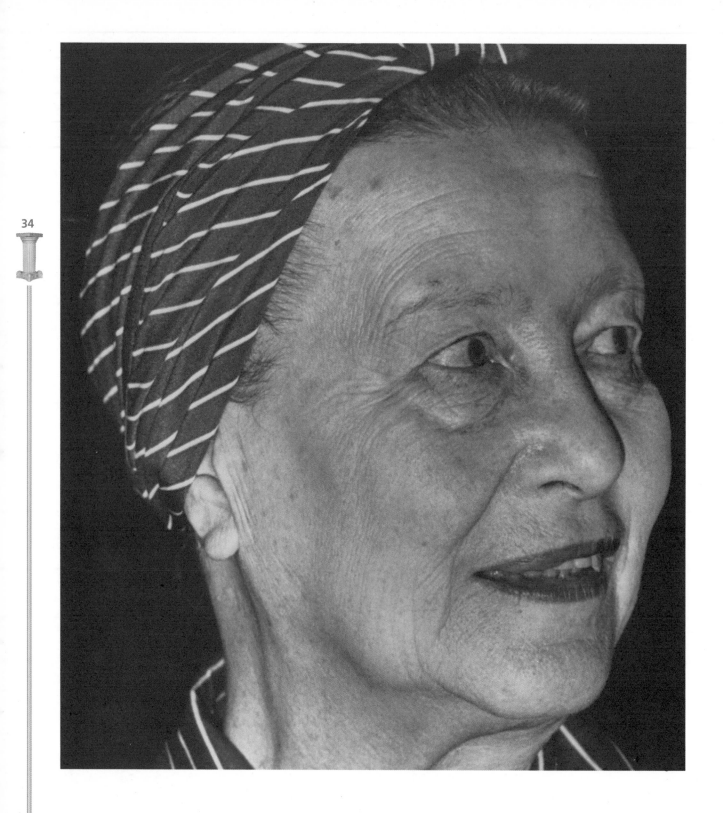

BEAUVOIR, SIMONE DE

Influenced by early feminists like Mary Wollstonecraft, de Beauvoir was herself a key figure for the 20th-century feminist movement.

Working within Sartre's framework, de Beauvoir accepts that an individual is born free, without essence. But the identification of ones biological gender serves, in the case of the female, to define her personhood. The female becomes 'a woman', the meaning of which is defined by culture and society, be it the 'domestic goddess' mother and wife of the 1950s or more recently, the 'Supermom' of the 1990s. Even biological facts such as menstruation are always culturally interpreted, says de Beauvoir, such that the fact of it could be lived either as 'a shameful curse, or a sexy reaffirmation of the healthy functioning of one's body', according to societies' conceptions. Consequently, one is not born a woman. The female becomes one by accepting and living the role society defines as appropriate. This acceptance, however, is not automatically 'bad faith' as Sartre would have it, and it is crucial to see how de Beauvoir extends and develops this concept.

De Beauvoir insists that acting in bad faith presupposes that one is aware of the potential for freedom in one's situation, which one then chooses to ignore. But the presence of this awareness is not a given. Children, for instance, cannot act in bad faith, because others define their being, since the child lives in the world of its parents or guardian. Only when they reach an 'awakening' in adolescence does existentialist angst take hold. Similarly, de Beauvoir argues, women have historically had their being defined for them through socio-economic circumstances. Consequently they have been ignorant of the potential for freedom in their situation, and hence could not be acting in bad faith.

It is easy to see how many of de Beauvoir's feminist ideas – that women must recognize their own freedom, define their own being, and free themselves from the 'enslavement' of a society whose rules and values are defined only by men – could be taken up as a war-cry by the women's liberation movement.

'One is not born, but rather becomes, a woman'

║ ESSENTIAL READING ║

The Ethics of Ambiguity (1947)

This is de Beauvoir's attempt to formulate a set of existential ethics. She argues that free will can overcome human nature and so we must accept responsibility for our own behaviour, but that a person must first be aware of the potential for freedom in their situation before they can choose to be different. Finally, she describes human existence as 'becoming' – a striving towards a fixed essence or identity.

The Second Sex (1949)

De Beauvoir's most famous work and a milestone of feminist literature. The book sets out to define what a woman is. It looks at the treatment of women throughout history, claiming that historically women have been defined as an aberration from the 'normal' male sex. De Beauvoir argues for women's equality while insisting on the reality of sexual difference.

BENTHAM, JEREMY

1748–1832

Born in London, Bentham was trained to become a lawyer but became dissatisfied with its over-complex language and conflicting principles. He undertook instead an inquiry into the very nature and basis of law, morals and politics, which he found could be united by a single principle. This principle, which insists that the good for man is the attainment of

> **'Nature has placed mankind under the governance of two sovereign masters, pain and pleasure...'**

pleasure and the absence of pain, is a reflection of the simple hedonistic psychology known and promoted since the time of **Epicurus**. However, Bentham wove the principle – which he called the principle of utility – into the very fabric of philosophy, society and culture, popularizing a system of ethics, known as 'utilitarianism', that is still of major importance today.

Bentham's genius was to show how the covenants of law, politics and ethics could all be recast in the more simple language of utility, which is concerned only with maximizing that which we desire and minimizing that which we fear. Utilitarianism is based on a very simple view of human nature. Bentham says:

'Nature has placed mankind under the governance of two sovereign masters, pain and pleasure… They govern us in all we do, in all we say, in all we think: every effort we can make to throw off our subjection will serve but to demonstrate and confirm it. In words a man may pretend to abjure their empire, but in reality he will remain subject to it all the while.'

From this follows one simple moral rule, that what one ought to do is to maximize pleasure and minimize pain. As a keen reformer of political, legal and social institutions, Bentham argued that such institutions should be set up in accordance with this rule. He famously designed a prison, the 'panopticon', in which prisoners would be visible to the authorities at all times, and thus encouraged to naturally do what they ought to do, in other words, to promote the greatest good for the greatest number, in order to avoid pain. Punishment was thus always intended as a means of reform and carefully calculated so that its long-term consequences, though painful for the punished in the short term, would lead to an increase in pleasure. Bentham even constructed a 'felicific calculus', to aid the calculation of the exact quantity of pain and pleasure that would result from a given action.

It is interesting that Bentham makes no distinction between happiness and pleasure. To experience pleasure is to be happy as far as Bentham is concerned, a view that would be criticized by his utilitarian successor, John Stuart **Mill**. Moreover, Bentham's idea that pleasure and pain can be calculated quantitatively, in units of equal value, counted like buttons in a jar, makes no allowance for the different quality of various experiences; again a problem Mill would later wrestle with in his developments of the utilitarian ethic.

Perhaps the greatest problem faced by Bentham's system, and to a certain extent one even modern day utilitarian theories have not fully resolved, is that created by the subjugation of individuals for the good of the majority. If all that matters in an ethical dilemma is 'the greatest happiness of all those whose interest is in question' as an aggregate total, there seems no obvious reason why one person's entire pleasure should not be sacrificed for the aggregate good of the whole. What Bentham's utilitarianism lacks, in similar fashion to the 'social contract' of **Rousseau**, is any notion of an individual's rights. Despite this, the ethical system popularized by

Bentham rejected the legal profession and turned to philosophy, becoming a leading advocate of utilitarianism.

Bentham and developed by Mill and many others has held, and continues to hold, a strong intuitive appeal to many thinkers.

▌ ESSENTIAL READING ▌

A Fragment on Government (1776)

Marking the beginnings of philosophical radicalism, Bentham here advocates basing laws on rational principles rather than on tradition and case law. He is also critical of conceptions of political obligation.

Introduction to the Principles of Morals and Legislation (1789)

The first document to outline utilitarianism, this provides a detailed account of Bentham's 'greatest happiness' principle of morality, and its application to law: legislation should promote the greatest happiness of the greatest number of people and produce harmony between the interests of society as a whole and those of the private individual pursuing his own happiness.

BERGSON, HENRI LOUIS

1859–1941

38

French philosopher whose work influenced Alfred North **Whitehead**, Bergson was once described as not appearing to be in vogue 'because everybody believes his philosophy more or less'.

Bergson's philosophy proceeds from a fundamental distinction between life force, the 'élan vital', and matter. These are really two conflicting impulses of the universe. The one, the urge to continually create and diversify, the other an entropic compulsion to make everything uniform, to dissipate energy and resist the flow of life.

The 'élan vital' is the driving force of novelty

These two conflicting forces are reflected in Bergson's theory of knowledge. According to him, the intellect which interprets the 'flux of experience' in terms of discrete, repeatable items of observation represents the way of matter. Its greatest achievement is geometry. It denies the continuous flow of experience and attempts to know reality by means of identifying and classifying experience into repeatable and discrete units. Contrasted with this is 'instinct'. Instinct is the creative force, less concerned with space than with time. Since succession is the characteristic of

experience, the creative force has always the quality of 'duration', of perpetually 'coming-into-being' without ever being made.

This complex idea rests on Bergson's notion of 'duration'. The intellect attempts to deal with the continuous flow of experience by breaking time up into discrete 'moments'. But Bergson claims the discretion is artificial. In experience there is a constant interpenetrability of past and present. Change is continuous and dynamic, not discrete and static.

Bergson is careful, however, not to fall into a trap of claiming that the 'élan vital' is progressive or moving towards some purposed fulfilment. It is, in his view, an aimless meandering, struggling and adapting itself as it meets its antithesis, matter, which is always trying to limit and constrain it. Bergson rejects any kind of 'teleological' explanation of evolution, such as that found in **Aristotle**'s idea that everything is striving to fulfil a pre-ordained purpose. This sort of conception Bergson calls 'inverse mechanism' – the idea that everything is determined not by prior cause but by some future potentiality. Bergson rejects both as deterministic. The 'élan vital' is the proof of free will. It is an unpredictable force of change that settles for a time into organized forms, because of

Starting out as a teacher, Bergson became a philopsher of international stature
and was eventually promoted to a professorship at the Collège de France.

Change is continuous and dynamic, not discrete and static

the downward pressure of matter, before moving and diversifying once more. Thus Bergson gives an account of how matter was forced to diversify into animate and inanimate forms, how the animate diversified into plants and animals, and how animals, through the diversification that is man, produce the further diversification between intellect and intuition. The 'élan vital' is the driving force of novelty, as seen in works of art and literature. Such works, Bergson maintains, are always a product of prior influence, and yet they are much more than just the sum of their parts. They embody a unified idea which can only arise from the intuition of the artist.

In his later work Bergson connects the 'élan vital' with the notions of love and God. Although Bergson says the opposing realities of life and matter, 'a reality making itself in a reality unmaking itself', are inextricably linked, it is clear he thinks the 'élan vital', the way of intuition and instinct, superior and more worthy of veneration than the way of matter, of intellect and ultimately of reason. His work thus continues a trend of anti-intellectualism in French philosophy that began with **Rousseau** and continues to this day in **Derrida**.

▌ ESSENTIAL READING ▌

Matter and Memory (1896)
In this early work, Bergson used recent studies of the brain to try to prove that the mind is independent of the body.

Creative Evolution (1907)
In this his most famous work, Bergson introduced the concept of *élan vital*, the creative impulse that shapes all life, claiming that this, not Darwinian natural selection, lay at the heart of evolution.

An Introduction to Metaphysics (1903)
Here Bergson argued that intuition, not intellectual analysis, reveals the truth about the world.

The Two Sources of Morality and Religion (1932)
In his final major work, Bergson explores two antagonistic moralities: the static, conformist and mechanistic morality, expressed in the laws of society and science, and the dynamic, aspirational morality that reaches out, breaks barriers and changes the world, expressed in the creativity of art and the mystical experiences of saints.

BERKELEY, GEORGE

1685–1783

Irish philosopher and Bishop of Cloyne, Berkeley is renowned as the father of philosophical idealism, who endeavoured to show how, using their own assumptions, the materialism of **Locke** and **Newton** was untenable. His most famous adage is 'esse est percipi' ('to be is to be perceived').

Following Locke's own causal theory of perception, Berkeley, like others, noted that it implies a logical gap between the subject and reality. This logical gap, often called by philosophers 'the veil of perception', is generated in the following way. The causal theory of perception holds that objects in the external world have a causal effect on our senses and in so doing produce ideas in the mind of the observer. Thus an ordinary vase begins a chain of causal events first in the retina of the observer, and subsequently in the neural pathways of the observer that lead him to see 'a vase'. The seeing of the vase, however, is a construct inside one's mind, a fact seemingly supported by the existence of hallucinations, and visual images in dreams.

If the perception of the vase is a construct – or 'idea' to use Berkeley's term – in the mind, then it follows that what we actually see is not the real cause of the idea, the actual vase, but only the idea itself. Accordingly, it is a matter of conjecture to suppose that the cause of the construct actually resembles what we perceive. It could be, for all we know, that ideas of vases are caused by something wholly un-vase like. But since all our perceptions of the world are generated inside the mind, we have no way of telling whether reality really does resemble our ideas or not.

'esse est percipi' ('to be is to be perceived')

Using a series of arguments employing this 'veil of perception', Berkeley concludes that since we never perceive anything called 'matter', but only ideas, it is an untenable conjecture to presume that there is a material substance lying behind and supporting our perceptions. Locke and others had resisted this suggestion by making the distinction between primary qualites, such as solidity, extension and figure, and secondary qualities, such as colour, taste and smell, claiming only secondary qualities are mind-dependent. But Berkeley's arguments appear to show that there is no valid distinction between primary and secondary qualities in perception. As a result, everything turns out to be mind-dependent. If something fails to be an idea in someone's mind, it fails to exist, hence Berkeley's famous saying 'to be is to be perceived'. Of course, such a view leads to an immediate criticism, which is that if there were no

George Berkeley (right) with his family. In 1734, Berkeley was consecrated Bishop of Cloyne in his native Ireland.

closed room still exists since it is perceived in the mind of God.

The following limerick by Ronald Knox sets out the objection to Berkeley and his reply:

There was a young man who said, 'God
Must think it exceedingly odd
If he finds that this tree
Continues to be
When there's no one about in the Quad.'

Reply:

Dear Sir:
Your astonishment's odd:
I am always about in the Quad.
And that's why the tree
Will continue to be,
Since observed by
Yours faithfully,
GOD.

material substrate behind our ideas, how is it that things persist when no one perceives them? When I close the door on the bedroom, it would seem to fail to exist according to Berkeley, if there is no one inside to continue perceiving it. Berkeley's reply is that our perceptions are ideas produced for us by God. God perceives everything at all times, so the

❘❘❘ ESSENTIAL READING ❘❘❘

A New Theory of Vision (1709)
Berkeley's aim in this book was to show 'the manner wherein we perceive by sight the distance, magnitude, and situation of objects'.

Principles of Human Knowledge (1710)
This is Berkeley's greatest work, in which he sets out a clear and well-argued description and defence of philosophical idealism. It includes a proof of the existence of God based on his idealistic principles.

Three Dialogues Between Hylas and Philonous (1713)
In these dialogues, Hylas personifies educated common sense and Philonous is Berkeley. Philonous explains and defends idealism.

De Motu or On Motion (1720)
In this book, Berkeley discusses Newtonian physics in terms of idealism, and rejects Newton's views on space, time and motion.

BOETHIUS

480–524

Boethius' life was cut short when he was executed by the Gothic King, Theodoric. This singular misfortune was to prove of enormous consequence upon, not to mention benefit to, the development of Western thought. For it was while imprisoned and awaiting execution that the Roman senator Boethius wrote his *De Consolatione Philosophiae (The Consolation of Philosophy)*, the most widely read and influential book, after the Bible, up to and throughout the Middle Ages.

An illuminated manuscript of *The Consolation of Philosophy*. The left hand panel shows Boethius teaching (top) and imprisoned (below).

The Consolation takes the form of a dialogue, between Boethius and Philosophy. The style is

Boethius' status as Roman senator is commemorated in this bas-relief, where he is shown wearing consular robes.

unusual, being alternately written in prose and verse. Boethius' thoughts and reflections are written in prose, whilst the wisdom of his interlocutor, Philosophy, appears in verse.

'The substance of God consisteth in nothing else but goodness'

Boethius, faced with execution, seeks to find solace for his misfortunes. Despite being a Christian and a hero of the Catholic Church, unlike **Augustine**, Boethius appeals to reason rather than faith for his consolation. In the book he sets out and defines some of the perennial problems of philosophy, including the problem of evil, free will and determinism, the nature of justice and of virtue. Boethius, primarily motivated by **Plato** in his philosophical views, finds that, 'The substance of God consisteth in nothing else but goodness'. In other words, for Boethius, God and 'Goodness' are synonymous.

This entails an interesting theological development, given that Boethius is revered as a Christian scholar. For Philosophy goes on to reveal to Boethius that in so far as any man is truly good he is a god. 'They who obtain divinity become gods. Wherefore every one that is happy is a god, but by nature there is only one God, but there may be many by participation'.

The discovery that God is synonymous with Good leads Boethius into considering the so-called problem of evil (see **Epicurus**). Boethius' solution is Aristotelian in essence, conceiving the divine providence as rather like a spectator of the Universe rather than an intervening agent. In effect, this amounts to a denial of God as an omnipotent being. Nevertheless, there are elements of karmic retribution in Boethius' philosophy. For he maintains that those who do ill shall suffer more if they are not caught than those that are. Boethius' logic, however, is straightforward rather than mystical. Those who avoid punishment continue to be bad, rather than good, and therefore move themselves yet further from blessedness and ultimate happiness. 'Virtuous men are always powerful, and bad men always weak,' claims Boethius, 'for both desire the good but only the virtuous get it'.

This 6th-century woodcut shows Boethius (left) competing against Pythagoras at calculations, presided over by the allegorical figure of Arithmetic.

Boethius goes on to discuss the perennial problem of free will and determinism. The problem arises for him because of the paradox between man being free to choose whether to be good or bad, and God's foreknowledge of everything that will happen. If God knows that you intend to do something before you even do it, you could hardly do otherwise. But if you could not do otherwise then it appears you do not have free will. Boethius' solution is a rather unsatisfactory compromise that allows free human agency in regard to moral choices. Nevertheless, there can be no denying that Boethius' work, written while under the threat of execution, is a masterpiece of philosophical sincerity equal to *The Last Days of Socrates*.

▌ ESSENTIAL READING ▌

Boethius wrote a number of theological works and philosophical commentaries, but his most famous work is *Consolation of Philosophy,* written while in prison awaiting his execution.

Consolation of Philosophy (c. 524)

This book has been described as the most influential work of medieval and early Renaissance Christianity and the last great work of Classical literature. In it, Boethius debates such questions as God's role in human affairs, why evil men sometimes prosper and good men suffer, and whether human nature is essentially good or bad. Boethius believed in harmony between faith and reason, so he answers these religious questions without reference to Christianity, using the techniques of classical philosophy instead.

CAMUS, ALBERT

1913–1960

Celebrated French-Algerian author, playwright and philosopher. Camus became great friends with Jean-Paul **Sartre** in Paris, where they worked together on the radical left-wing newspaper, *Combat*. However, they fell out in 1951 and never spoke again. Camus' best known works are *The Stranger, The Outsider* and *The Plague*. Undoubtedly his most important contribution to existentialist philosophy, however, is *The Myth of Sisyphus*.

'The absurd is born of the confrontation between human need and the unreasonable silence of the world'

In *The Myth of Sisyphus*, Camus develops the central existentialist theme of 'absurdity'. Human existence, Camus claims, is absurd. This absurdity arises out of our attempts to make sense of a senseless world. Camus tells us 'the absurd is born of the confrontation between [this] human need and the unreasonable silence of the world'. For Camus, 'absurd' is meant to be taken in its original comic sense, which arises out of a comparison of the ridiculous with the sublime, such as a man attacking a machine-gun nest armed only with a sword, or the fate of Sisyphus, condemned by the Gods to eternally push a boulder up a hill only to have it roll back down again as he reaches the summit.

Sisyphus' fate, Camus insists, illustrates the futility and hopelessness of labour. We, like Sisyphus, live our lives accomplishing nothing. For, as in **Russell**'s poetic words, 'all the labour of the ages, all the devotion, all the inspiration, all the noonday brightness of human genius, are destined to extinction in the vast death of the solar system, and the whole temple of man's achievement must inevitably be buried beneath the debris of a universe in ruins'.

Given such a pointless existence, in an uncompromisingly irrational universe, Camus must ask 'why should I not commit suicide?' It is the inevitable conclusion of existentialism, which he considers other writers – **Husserl, Kierkegaard**, Karl Jaspers and Sartre – all shied away from. For one by one they failed to stay faithful to the original premise of their existentialist philosophy, which is that the absurd is a consequence of the encounter between a rational human being and an irrational world. One must not, Camus insists, as they have done in their philosophies, make any attempt to resolve the conflict. It is irresolvable, because it is a

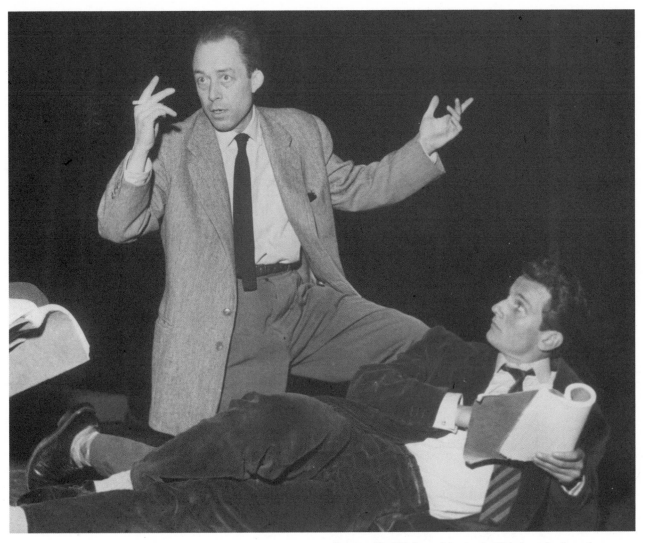

Camus said of his love of theatre that 'it is the only place where one can find innocent happiness'.

given of human existence. To resolve it is to deny the very phenomenon one began with. Suicide is just another attempt at resolution.

Undoubtedly Camus backs himself, and his reader, into an inescapable corner. To accept absurdity is to accept death. To refuse it is to accept a life on the precipice, where one cannot leap to comfort, but only live 'on the dizzying crest – that is integrity, the rest subterfuge'. The dizzying crest he describes is the fully conscious experience of being alive, like Sisyphus, in the face of death and the pointlessness of one's toils in life.

In the face of the absurd we must, he says somewhat metaphorically, 'revolt'. 'Revolt' is the awareness of a crushing fate, but without the resignation that ought to accompany it. Thus Sisyphus, who is condemned to eternal repetition and fully aware of it, finds that 'the lucidity that was to constitute his torture at the same time crowns his victory'. We must, Camus famously says, imagine Sisyphus happy, for 'being aware of one's life, and to the maximum, is living, and to the maximum'.

Camus thus rejects suicide as an option. We cannot solve the problem of the absurd by negating its existence. It is a necessary condition of the confrontation between man and world. Suicide, as a resolution and termination of the absurd, would be a defeat, a denial of the very condition of man's existence.

In 1957, Camus was awarded the Nobel Prize for Literature, just three years before his death in a car crash.

‖ ESSENTIAL READING ‖

The Myth of Sisyphus (1942)
In his most important philosophical work, Camus introduces his concept of the absurd: our futile search for meaning in a meaningless world. He suggests several ways of coping with absurdity. In the final chapter he compares human existence with the situation of Sisyphus. The book concludes: 'The struggle itself is enough to fill a man's heart. One must imagine Sisyphus happy.'

The Stranger (1942)
Camus weaves his absurdist philosophy into this famous novel about an alienated man, Meursault, whose unreflecting, unapologetic approach to life is his response to its essential meaninglessness. Only his imminent execution for murder forces Meursault to acknowledge responsibility for his actions.

The Plague (1947)
In this novel about a plague sweeping an Algerian city, Camus conveys his philosophical belief that ultimately we have no control over our lives in a meaningless world. Through the various characters in the novel, he demonstrates different human reactions to the absurd.

CARNAP, RUDOLPH

1891–1970

German positivist philosopher and leading member of the 'Vienna Circle', Carnap was a dominant figure in the development of post-War philosophy in the USA. A student of **Frege** at Jena, he went on to Vienna and became heavily influenced by the work of both **Russell** and **Wittgenstein**. However, with the rise of National Socialism he left Europe for America, where he remained for the rest of his life. The corpus of his work consists of over 20 books and some 80 articles which together have made major contributions to logic, semantics and the philosophy of science. The most important of these are *The Logical Structure of the World* and *The Logical Syntax of Language*.

Along with **Schlick** and Carl Hempel, Carnap was a strong proponent of the verification principle. For Carnap, this principle meant that anything that might count as a contribution to human knowledge can either be justified by observation and experience or is merely formal and expressed in tautological propositions. Carnap's best contribution to this idea was his meticulous working out of the nature of these formal, tautological propositions, which he described as the 'logical syntax of the language of science'.

This logical syntax, Carnap held, provides the conventional rules that set out the possible forms of any meaningful proposition. In the past, philosophers have mistaken such rules for substantive philosophical claims, but a proper understanding of their nature shows them to be what Wittgenstein would later call 'norms of representation'. For instance, the claim 'time extends infinitely in both directions' can be shown to be nothing more than the 'syntactic' proposition that any positive or negative real number can be used to represent a time-coordinate. Such a proposition possesses no empirical or cognitive content, but rather expresses a rule for the use of signs.

Logical syntax and empirical content are two distinct and unrelated studies

Carnap believed that the logical syntax of science could be laid bare by a thorough investigation into all the possible forms of a proposition, in other words into the structural relationships between all the signs in a language. This, Carnap held, should be the task of philosophy, making philosophy purely the business of linguistic analysis. At this point in his work Carnap was convinced that the syntactic investigation into the possible combination of signs, logical syntax, could not have

A prominent member of the Vienna School, Carnap left Hitler's Germany in 1935 and settled permanently in the USA.

any connection with what those signs were actually used to represent. In other words, logical syntax and empirical content were two distinct and unrelated studies. The first belongs to philosophy, the second to the various branches of science.

Under the influence of **Gödel** and **Tarski**, however, Carnap was forced to revise this position. It became clear that some philosophically important properties of language could not be reduced to syntactic structures, in particular the property of truth, which required a semantic analysis. Since Tarski had shown that it was possible to develop a formal theory of semantics using a meta-language referring to an object language, Carnap now set about defining semantic rules, or definitions, for a theory of truth. To this branch of logical analysis he made significant contributions which would heavily influence his student and disciple, W.V.O. **Quine**.

ESSENTIAL READING

Carnap believed that many philosophical problems are the outcome of a misuse of language and that therefore the logical analysis of language becomes the principal instrument in resolving many philosophical problems. He explores this in three major works:

The Logical Structure of the World (1928)
In this book Carnap put forward his idea that statements are only meaningful if every non-logical (e.g. psychological or cultural) term is defined using a very restricted type of objective language containing terms for things only.

Pseudoproblems in Philosophy (1928)
Carnap asserts that many philosophical questions were meaningless and a product of a misuse of language.

The Logical Syntax of Language (1934)
Carnap took his theory a stage further with this book, in which he looks at how an artificial language that can express mathematical and scientific theories can be constructed.

CHOMSKY, NOAM

1928–

Born in Philadelphia, Pennsylvania, the son of a well-known Hebrew scholar, Chomsky is perhaps one of the most widely known thinkers of our time. His work has been pivotal in the development of linguistics in the 20th century. However, it is important to realize, as shall be outlined below, that Chomsky's work in this field proceeds from a very distinct, and by no means uncontroversial, philosophical viewpoint with a long heritage. He is also known for his social and political commentaries, which to a certain extent are also informed by the same philosophical assumptions. After being dissuaded from dropping out of his University studies by the renowned professor of Linguistics, Zellig Harris, Chomsky went on to write his seminal work *Syntactic Structures*, published in 1957, which defined the field for the rest of the century. Since that time, Chomsky has developed and modified his views in a number of important works, particularly in his *Aspects of the Theory of Syntax, Language and Mind,* and more recently *The Minimalist Program*. Of his many political writings the most influential include American Power and the *New Mandarins, Human Rights and American Foreign Policy* and *Fateful Triangle: the United States, Israel and the Palestinians.* Chomsky continues to write actively in both linguistics and politics.

Chomsky's work in linguistics is predicated on a rationalist theory of mind, which posits, in defiance of the empiricist tradition emanating from **Locke** – and in the ascendant prior to Chomsky's work – that the mind is very far from being a blank slate or

A renowned political activist and critic of US foriegn policy, Chomsky travelled to Hanoi as part of an anti-Vietnam war campaign in 1970.

Chomsky's work in linguistics and cognitive function has had a widespread impact on approaches to teaching.

'tabula rasa' at birth, but instead, is constrained in its operations by certain innate structures. Chomsky's concern, of course, is with language learning and the 'syntactic structures' that underlie different languages. In Chomsky's view, all languages share, at a fundamental level, a universal structure, or grammar, and this universal grammar is 'hardwired' in our brains, rather than something that is learnt through teaching and experience.

The notion of a universal grammar is relatively simple. There are something like 5,000 known varieties of human language. According to Chomsky, despite their many surface differences, they are all constrained by certain parameters and principles that are innate, and unique, to the human mind. A significant argument for this conclusion rests on what some have called the 'productivity' argument. Experimental psycho-logists will often attest to the speed at which grammatical ability develops in children around the age of two or three, an ability that goes far beyond the meagre input of language they've been exposed to. Consequently, it would seem plausible to suppose the child has a head-start. The grammatical rules do not need to be learnt, they are hardwired in the mind: early exposure to language merely acts as a trigger,

and the child develops his linguistic competence at an accelerated rate.

This hardwiring is, like other cognitive faculties, an aspect of our human nature. Chomsky sees this as having positive political implications. Rather than being the blank sheet of Lockean empiricism, or the unconstrained free agents of existentialism, our very nature prevents us from being subjugated by extreme and wayward forces.

52

Our nature determines that there are only certain possible political structures that we can tolerate. Oppressive political systems, as in say Orwell's *1984* or Huxley's *Brave New World,* cannot completely mould our minds. Our thoughts are not, as the behavioural psychologists earlier in the 20th century had supposed, merely conditioned responses to repeated stimuli. The concept of being a 'free agent' is as hardwired into our nature as the constraints that act on our forms of speech.

This reveals a further development of Chomsky's linguistic theory. For Chomsky the nature of the human mind is revealed by the nature of language. Not only because language is a uniquely human activity, but also because language 'is the vehicle of thought' and therefore uniquely placed to illuminate the essence of the human mind. It should be understood that by 'mind', Chomsky means the cognitive principles and processes that underlie human behaviour and that Chomsky firmly holds to an 'innatist' theory reminiscent of

Language 'is the vehicle of thought' and therefore uniquely placed to illuminate the essence of the human mind

Leibniz and others. According to this theory, the human mind is endowed – 'hardwired' as we have said – with certain innate properties that constrain what we are like and what we can know.

Chomsky is as well known now for his numerous political writings as he is for his work in linguistics. He has been a constant critic of US foreign policy and of US involvement in Vietnam, Cambodia and the Gulf Wars. He remains an active supporter of radical social change in the US, as well as continuing his work as a linguist and theoretical philosopher. He describes his political view as 'libertarian socialist' – a blend of socialism and anarchism.

53

‖ ESSENTIAL READING ‖

Syntactic Structures (1957)
Chomsky's highly influential book is regarded by many as a landmark in the field of linguistics. In it he puts forward his idea of 'transformational grammar' in which each sentence in a language has a 'deep structure' and a 'surface structure'. The deep structure contains properties common to all languages which are mapped onto the surface structure via 'transformations'.

Aspects of the Theory of Syntax, Language and Mind (1965)
In this work, Chomsky introduces a hierarchy, which he calls 'Levels of Adequacy', as a means of judging grammars and 'metagrammars' (theories of grammars) according to their elegance and effectiveness.

CICERO, MARCUS TULLIUS

106–43BC

For much of his life Cicero was known as a Roman politician, lawyer and orator, who despite his humble origins, rose to pre-eminence among the conservative Roman aristocracy. As a youth he had travelled and studied in Greece and maintained a firm interest in philosophy throughout his public life. He maintained friendships with philosophers from all the leading schools but it was not until his retirement, finding himself in the political wilderness, that he devoted his final years to translating large parts of the Greek corpus into Latin. Much of our knowledge of Greek thought is due to Cicero's translations and he remains a primary source for students of Hellenistic philosophy.

Of Cicero's many works the most important include his *Academica,* on the impossibility of certain knowledge, the *De Finibus* and *De Officiis,* in which he discusses the ends of human action and the rules of right conduct, the *Tusculan Disputations,* concerning the problems of happiness, pain, the human emotions and death, and *On the Nature of Gods* and *On Divination,* both concerned with theological matters.

Mostly produced in the last two years of his life, Cicero's philosophy comprises a

Cicero was a Roman polymath: a senior politician, orator, historian, philosopher and Hellenistic scholar.

mixture of scepticism in the theory of knowledge and stoicism in ethics. He was largely critical of all things Epicurean. Although he maintained a claim to some originality in his thought, Cicero's dialogues are principally a 'pick and mix' of the three leading Greek philosophical schools. This was neither by accident, nor disguised. Cicero felt that the more modern Latin language could resolve and clarify the problems of Greek philosophy, as well as make it more appealing to a modern audience.

> *Cicero's philosophy comprises a mixture of scepticism in the theory of knowledge and stoicism in ethics*

In this aim Cicero is largely judged to have been successful. The philosophical vocabulary invented by him is responsible for Latin becoming the primary philosophical language over Greek: despite the invention of modern languages, Latin remained the primary language of philosophy right up until the Renaissance. Even **Descartes**' hugely influential *Meditations on First Philosophy,* published in 1641, was written first in Latin and only later translated into French. Its most famous conclusion 'Cogito ergo sum' (popularly translated as 'I think, therefore I am') is still today referred to in philosophical schools by its Latin name, 'the Cogito'.

Although philosophy no longer uses Latin as its first language, many of Cicero's philosophical terms are still in common employment today. Latin phrases

In 63BC, Cicero exposed a plot by the politician Cataline to overthrow the Senate of Rome. His addresses to the ruling body of Rome became known as the Cataline Orations.

such as *a priori* (meaning 'prior to experience'), *a posteriori* (derived from experience), *a fortiori* (even more so), *reductio ad absurdum* (reduction to absurdity), *ceteris paribus* (a caveat meaning 'other things being equal'), are not just in common philosophical usage but also, in some cases, set the agenda for the philosophical debate. For example, the great debate between empiricists and rationalists (see **Locke** and **Leibniz**, respectively) is primarily a debate over whether there can be such a thing as a priori knowledge – as the rationalists

Cicero's dialogues are principally a 'pick and mix' of the three leading Greek philosophical schools

maintain – or whether all knowledge is *a posteriori*, in other words, derived from experience. In both logic and philosophical logic, Latin terms remain in current and widespread use.

‖ ESSENTIAL READING ‖

Academics (45BC)

In this work, which takes the form of a dialogue, Cicero puts forward and refutes the positions of different philosophical schools on the question of how we perceive and understand the world and whether we can ever know the truth.

On Ends (45BC)

In this dialogue, Cicero sets out the positions of different philosophical schools on the question of the end, or purpose, of human life. As with *Academics,* Cicero does not offer his own viewpoint, but leaves it to the reader to decide.

Tusculan Disputations (45BC)

Here, Cicero refutes the idea that death and pain are evil; he argues that a wise man does not suffer from excessive emotion, be it joy or suffering, and that virtue, found through philosophy, is the route to true happiness.

On Duties (44BC)

Written in the form of a letter to his son, this work looks at the topic of duty: how do we define what our duties are, and how should they be performed. He looks at honourable actions and how to judge the honourableness of an action. What if what is honourable conflicts with what is expedient? Cicero asserts that these two may seem to conflict, but actually never do.

COMTE, AUGUSTE

1798–1857

An unusual and perhaps unbalanced character, Comte had an early career characterized by academic brilliance punctuated by events in which he became a student rebel, mental patient and failed suicide. In his lifetime he never held a professorship at any university, despite the helpful intervention of friends on his behalf, amongst them, J.S. **Mill**. Nonetheless, this French philosopher became the posthumous hero of the 20th century positivist movement and inspiration for the trend towards 'scientism' (that view which claims science is, in **Quine**'s immortal words, 'the final arbiter of truth'). Comte was also the self-professed founder of sociology, familiar to sociology students the world over, and the first to apply the methods of science to the study of people and society. His most important work in which these ideas are set out, *Course on Positive Philosophy*, would later be contradicted by his more mature but romantic ideas which tried to find a place for religious sentiment in a secular world.

In his early work, Comte held that theological and metaphysical speculations should be abandoned in favour of a rigorous ordering of confirmable observations that alone should constitute the realm of human knowledge. The ordering of 'positive science' begins with mathematics and progresses in degrees of complexity through astronomy, physics, chemistry and biology. After biology comes the new science of sociology, which is the study of the 'statics and dynamics' (terms borrowed from engineering) of society. Statics, the science of forces in equilibrium, as applied to social phenomena, engenders the view that no part of the 'social consensus' can be overhauled without radically affecting the whole. As a result, Comte insists, economic, cultural and social conditions all affect each other according to the state of knowledge in each arena. In dynamics, the science of change, the development of society mirrors the development of intellectual progress. Thus, according to Comte, just as historical knowledge began with theology and metaphysics before arriving at positivism, so social orders have progressively moved through stages of theocracy, monarchy, anarchy and arrived at, or were due to arrive at in Comte's vision, a new social order led by science.

No part of the 'social consensus' can be overlooked without radically affecting the whole

It was the working out in detail of this final stage of the social order that saw Comte soften his earlier views. He professes a new 'Religion of Humanity', in which he recognizes the important, cohesive, social role played by religious and ideological beliefs. In professing this new 'religion', however, Comte envisages himself as the High Priest of a new cult. Unsurprisingly, it is generally felt that at this point Comte had passed from the detached objective view of epistemology, which had informed his earlier work, into the realm of the absurd.

In trying to explain Comte's later writings, commenatators have cited his involvement with Mme Clotilde de Vaux, who by his own admission, apparently taught him the importance of 'subordinating the intellect to the heart'. In his later writings, such as *The Catechism of Positive Religion*, Comte makes room for a morality that he sees implicit in the scientific endeavour itself. The truth revealed by science maintains man's humility and imposes a naturalistic kind of law or justice. Echoing **Hume**, Comte now professes that the intellect should be, not the slave of the passions, but the servant of the heart. Needless to say, it is in his earlier rather than later writings that Comte has exerted his widest influence.

Comte declared himself to be the founder of sociology, and found posthumous recognition among 20th-century positivists.

‖ ESSENTIAL READING ‖

Course on Positive Philosophy (1830–1842)

This six-volume work was Comte's magnum opus and encapsulates his positivist philosophy. He explains the three stages of human intellectual development (theological, metaphysical and positivist) and shows how with each stage there is a corresponding development in the sciences, each dependent on the previous stage. So, without mathematics, there can be no astronomy, and without astronomy there can be no physics, etc. The culminating science, which he claimed to have invented, was sociology. The study of sociology would, he believed, bring about a reorganization of society along positivist (scientific) lines.

COPERNICUS, NICOLAUS

1473–1543

Born in Poland and graduate of Cracow University, Copernicus studied Greek philosophy, mathematics, medicine, astronomy and theology before becoming a canon of the cathedral at Frauenberg, where he finally settled. Inventor of modern astronomy, Copernicus did more to revolutionize man's conception of himself and his place in the universe than perhaps any other thinker, before or since. Even if his work would have a profound and negative impact on the Church, he was a man of impeccable orthodoxy. Although he delayed publication of his findings for fear of censure by the Church, it is clear that he believed his views were not inconsistent with his theology.

Prior to Copernicus, astronomers had favoured the view, following both **Aristotle** and Ptolemy, that the earth was at the centre of the universe, with both the stars, sun and the moon revolving about it. Known as the Ptolemaic system, this view was wholly in keeping with many theological teachings, in which the universe is seen to be created by God for the express purpose of man. The effect of Copernicus' work was to turn all this on its head.

Probably first posited by Aristarchus of Samos around 340BC, Copernicus revived the idea that the earth and planets revolve around the sun, which remains in a fixed position. Moreover, he

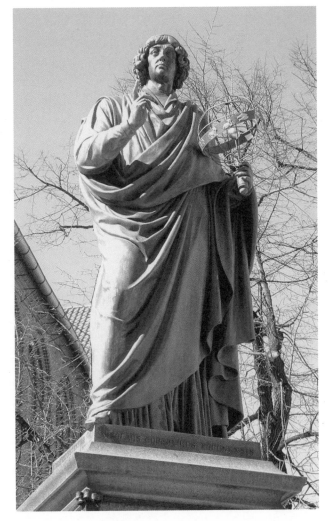

Copernicus' discoveries brought about a profound shift in religious and scientific thought: they were nothing short of world-changing.

The two great revolutionary thinkers of the Renaissance, Copernicus and Galileo, preside over globe and atlas.

proclaimed that in this system the earth has a twofold motion. On the one hand it turns on its own axis, rotating one full turn every twenty-four hours, and on the other it completely circumnavigates the sun every 364 days. This heliocentric (sun-centred) system was vigorously resisted by the Church, which saw it as usurping man's central place in creationist stories of the universe. By using Pythagorean

COPERNICUS, NICOLAUS

calculations, however, Copernicus managed to predict and account for various astronomical observations with amazing accuracy. Although Copernicus claimed his work was no more than hypothetical, eventually the weight of evidence would be too great to be resisted, and before long Copernicus would famously be supported by Galileo **Galilei**, Johannes Kepler and Isaac **Newton**, amongst others. Though still not widely accepted during his lifetime, by the end of the following century Copernicus' idea would have been refined to the point of irrefutability.

The heliocentric theory would soon be condemned by the Church, but Copernicus was careful during his life not to incur its wrath, unlike Galileo after him. Indeed Copernicus even dedicated the work in which he proclaims the heliocentric theory, the *De Revolutionibus Orbium Celestium*, with apparent sincerity, to the Pope. It was only later, in Galileo's time, that the Church condemned Copernicus' work as heretical.

So great and profound was the effect of Copernicus' hypothesis on the intellectual world that philosophers and scientists have since coined the phrase 'Copernican Revolution' to describe world-changing ideas. The effect of the original 'Copernican Revolution' on the development of

The earth and planets revolve around the sun, which remains in a fixed position

Western thought, both philosophical and scientific is difficult to exaggerate. It gave birth to the scientific age and helped to remove many of the superstitious and ignorant beliefs that were so widespread at the time. It would, for better or worse, lead the decline of the power of the Church, and to a new age of scientific inquiry and invention.

∥ ESSENTIAL READING ∥

De Revolutionibus Orbium Celestium (1543)

Copernicus began work on his six-volume masterpiece (translated as *On the Revolutions of the Heavenly Spheres*) as early as the 1520s, and actually first developed his heliocentric system in about 1510. The book took so long to write because of the massive amount of research that went into it, incorporating astronomical observations going back a thousand years. It contains 300 pages and over 100 pages of tables. The book was finally published just before his death in 1543. Remarkably the original manuscript, in Copernicus's own hand, still survives.

DARWIN, CHARLES ROBERT

1809–1892

The young naturalist's voyage aboard the *Beagle* in 1831 provided Darwin with observational material to put forward the most influential theory of modern times, the theory of evolution. Set out in detail in his *Origin of Species* and later *The Descent of Man,* the simplicity of Darwin's theory does nothing to detract from either its power of explanation nor its influence on almost every intellectual discipline.

Prior to Darwin, the received wisdom inherited from **Plato** and only partially modified by **Aristotle**, was that every natural kind, be it gold, silver, animal or plant, can be thought of as having essential qualities that make it what it is, and accidental qualities, that it may gain or lose without suffering a change of identity. Applied to the natural world, what makes an individual a member of one species rather than another is that it is an instance of a particular kind, a dog or horse, rose or nettle. Clearly there are differences amongst different types of dogs as there are between individual dogs. But these are 'accidental differences'. All dogs share certain fundamental qualities which make them dogs and not cats or horses. Call these fundamental qualities the 'essence' of a kind.

Philosophers had long wondered how to account for essences. From where did they appear? The

obvious answer had always been they were the work of a grand designer. God designed the forms of things which are used as blueprints for the

Prolific and hard-working, Darwin suffered from seasickness aboard the *Beagle* and from recurring bouts of ill health throughout his life.

production of individuals. Darwin's work would show that complex design could arise naturally without the need to posit either a designer or a blueprint.

The background to evolutionary theory lies in the work of Thomas Malthus on population explosion. Malthus noted that in order to avoid extinction a population must continually expand. However, there will inevitably come a time when population outstrips available resources. Necessarily, some will die and others survive. Darwin's theory begins by asking, in the lottery of who will survive and who will perish, what determines the winners from the losers? He notes 'If…organic beings vary at all in the several parts of their organization…I think it would be a most extraordinary fact if no variation had ever occurred useful to each being's own welfare…if variations useful to any organic being do occur, assuredly individuals thus characterized will have the best chance of being preserved in the struggle for life; and from the strong principle of inheritance they will tend to produce offspring similarly characterized. This principle of preservation, I have called…Natural Selection.'

Natural selection thus has two components. First, the minor differences that exist between individuals, and second the principle of inheritance

This 1882 cartoon parodies Darwin's last work *The Formation of Vegetable Mould Through the Action of Worms*, showing a metamorphosis of worm to man.

that passes these differences down through the generations. Aboard the *Beagle*, Darwin noted how topological and geographical features could magnify these differences. A major geological or climatic event might make some minor feature the difference between life and death in that region. Accordingly, any individuals without that feature would become extinct.

The so-called 'essential' differences between species is nothing more, Darwin showed, than 'descent by

Complex design arises naturally without the need to posit a designer

modification'. Descendants are modified by time and environment to the point where what looks like 'design' is merely the survival of inheritable qualities. What qualities survive are not pre-ordained by a divine creator, but depend on the vicissitudes of circumstance.

Thus Darwin's *Origin of Species* solves the problem of 'the origin of essences', in his own words, because, 'it will be seen that I look at the term species, as one arbitrarily given for the sake of convenience to a set of individuals closely resembling each other, and that it does not essentially differ from the term variety, which is given to less distinct and more fluctuating forms'.

Critics have complained that evolutionary theory is scientifically vacuous because it is incapable of refutation. If true, Darwin's idea would be less of a theory and more of a blind faith. However, Darwin himself was clear about what could falsify the theory. 'If it could be demonstrated that any complex organ existed, which could not possibly have been formed by numerous, successive, slight modifications, my theory would absolutely break down'. So far, no alternative theory has provided the required demonstration to meet Darwin's challenge.

‖ ESSENTIAL READING ‖

The Origin of Species (1859)

This book is the seminal work in evolutionary biology and a landmark of scientific literature. It introduced the theory that species evolve over a period of generations through a process known as natural selection. Darwin first began to develop the theory in 1838, and wrote the book over the course of the next 20 years. He only felt compelled to publish it after hearing, in 1856, that the naturalist Alfred Wallace was proposing a very similar idea himself. The book was published in 1859 and quickly became a bestseller, going through six editions in Darwin's lifetime.

The Descent of Man (1871)

In his second important work, Darwin applied his theory of natural selection to human evolution, explaining how our physical and mental traits evolved and showing how natural selection still applies in civilized society. He explains his theory of sexual selection in which the frequency of traits can increase or decrease depending on the attractiveness or fertility of the bearer.

DEMOCRITUS

c. 460–370BC

Although it is said that in Athens Democritus was hardly recognized by the intellectual elite, he nevertheless can be seen as representing the pinnacle of Presocratic thought and his atomist metaphysic has been much admired for its distinctly modern flavour.

According to Democritus, the fundamental nature of the universe consists of indivisible atoms in constant motion and travelling in an infinite void. Material objects are temporary concatenations of these atoms, made and destroyed as atoms come together or disperse according to natural forces, whilst the atoms themselves are eternal and indestructible. In answer to **Zeno**, Democritus held that whilst atoms could be geometrically divided, it is only matter containing spaces – literally, parts of the void between the atoms – that can be physically divided. An atom itself could not be physically divided since it is perfectly solid, completely excluding the void, and thereby indivisible.

Democritus' atomism represents a cogent attempt at unifying the thought of earlier philosophers. With **Heraclitus**, the atomist philosophy agrees that change and motion are both possible and necessary states of nature. But there is also a certain sympathy with **Parmenides**' claim that non-existence or non-being is problematic. For Democritus, anything that

Democritus is often referred to as the 'laughing philosopher' for the emphasis he placed on the value of cheerfulness.

exists is a concatenation of atoms, even thoughts in the mind. Yet along with both Parmenides and Zeno, Democritus agreed that motion would be impossible if the universe consisted of nothing but matter. The universe would be an immense solid where change is impossible, just as Parmenides had claimed. To account for motion Democritus postulated that the only true non-being is the infinite void, the absolute space in which atoms are eternally in motion. One might suppose that Parmenides would have objected to this on logical grounds: to say that there is a void is to say the void exists, so one can only claim on pain of contradiction that the void is the absence of being or of existence. Democritus' solution, ingenious for its novelty even if not entirely convincing, was to abandon the old idea (an idea ironically reinvented in **Einstein**'s relativistic physics) that the void or space must be conceived of as a property of matter. Rather, Democritus held that the infinite void was merely the absence of matter and materially independent of the existence of atoms.

This problem, of the relationship between the void and matter, or in philosophical parlance, on the ontological status of space, would reappear much later in the protracted debates between Isaac **Newton** – who would uphold Democritus' idea of absolute space as a kind of receptacle for matter – and **Leibniz**, who thought of space as merely a relation between physical objects. The history of the debate is interesting in its own right, for until Einstein, the general opinion amongst philosophers and scientists was that Democritus and Newton were correct, whereas it now seems that Parmenides, Leibniz and Einstein have the better of the argument.

The fundamental nature of the universe consists of indivisible atoms in constant motion

Democritus' atomic theory has other modern connotations. For he also held that every event in the universe is causally determined by preceding events, on account of the fact that material objects behave according to the impacts of atoms upon each other, much as one billiard ball striking another causes each to alter its course. A more sophisticated version of this view, called 'determinism', has been both vigorously defended and denied in the recent history of modern philosophy and remains a live issue to this day.

‖ ESSENTIAL READING ‖

No more than fragments of Democritus's writings have survived beyond the Middle Ages, and most of what we know of his philosophy are from citations found in the works of others, including **Aristotle** and Diogenes Laertius. Democritus appears to have written works on a number of subjects, including ethics, physics, music, mathematics, geometry and cosmology. Two works, the *Great World System* and the *Little World System,* have been credited to Democritus, although Theophrastus claimed that the former was by Leucippus.

DENNETT, DANIEL

1942–

'Some of the most beautiful and deep ideas of the 20th century come from engineering,' declared American philosopher Daniel Dennett in a 2004 interview. Indeed, his lifelong respect for engineering and design may well have been the inspiration for many of his theories about consciousness, the mind and the universe.

Dennett spent his early years in Beirut, before moving to Boston. He studied philosophy at Harvard under **Quine**, a strong early influence, and received his doctorate in philosophy at Oxford, where he was tutored by the ordinary language philosopher Gilbert **Ryle**.

Throughout his career, Dennett has been concerned with the question of how meaning, design and morality arose in a universe that began as a meaningless, formless void. He has sought answers to this problem not only in the writings of other philosophers, but also in the fields of evolutionary biology, cognitive science and artificial intelligence.

At the heart of Dennett's philosophy is the idea that everything in the universe, including consciousness, developed from natural processes, rather than from anything supernatural. Unlike **Descartes**, he does not believe in a separate, disembodied mind. Every

aspect of ourselves, he argues, including our personality and intelligence, can be explained by looking at the engineering involved in our brains.

The brain is a 'semantic engine', a mechanism that can extract meaning from the world

Dennett describes the brain as a 'semantic engine', a mechanism that can extract meaning from the world. For many of his critics, consciousness cannot be explained in such simple, mechanistic terms. If it could, then the physical structure of individual neurons should be able to show how the brain can think and extract meaning, just as the physical structure of DNA – the double helix – reveals how it can copy information. Dennett is not concerned by this issue. What matters, according to him, is not what the brain is made of (neurons) but what it does – its work as a semantic engine.

Dennett downplays the notion of consciousness as something mysterious. If something acts as if it were conscious, then we have no reason to say that it isn't conscious. He predicts that the whole debate about consciousness will soon appear antiquated. As computers advance into areas that were once the preserve of humans – when they can tell funny jokes and write decent novels and offer good companionship – it will become harder and harder for philosophers to keep up this distinction between 'conscious' and 'non-conscious' beings.

This philosophy places Dennett firmly among those who see the brain as nothing more than a sophisticated computer. In fact he is famous for his extreme views about artificial intelligence, claiming that even thermostats have beliefs about the world. He is not claiming here that a thermostat is conscious, only that its behaviour embodies assumptions about the world and these cannot be distinguished, in their effects on the world, from beliefs.

Dennett is perhaps best known for his views on artificial intelligence and its similarities to the human brain, which he sees as a sophisticated computer.

But getting back to Dennett's central question, how did such a sophisticated design as the human brain arise in a universe that was originally without meaning or design? To answer this, Dennett turned to evolutionary biology and Darwinism. Through his theory of natural selection, Charles **Darwin** revealed the essential mechanism for creating design out of chaos. Most importantly, from a philosophical point of view, Darwin showed that this was possible without the aid of a mind (natural selection being 'mindless'), answering John **Locke**'s age-old question about what came first, mind or matter?

Dennett believes that Darwin's theory, originally intended only as a theory of biological evolution, has profound implications for other areas of science and philosophy. If biological evolution could be the result of natural selection, is it not possible that other aspects of ourselves developed this way also, including our own minds? In this respect, Dennett is a leading proponent of the theory of neural Darwinism, in which it is argued that human intelligence and consciousness can be explained by Darwinian selection.

Many philosophers and scientists are resistant to Dennett's 'ultra-Darwinism'. Noam **Chomsky**, for example, argues that language is hard-wired into the human brain in a way that cannot easily be explained by step-by-step evolution. He calls Darwinism a 'place holder' until a true explanation for human language capacity is found. Dennett counters that the more intricately 'designed' a feature appears to be (and our capacity for language certainly fits this description) the more certain it is to have evolved through natural selection. The fact that we don't yet know how it happened is no reason to reject the theory. The only other possible explanations, he adds, are God and chance. If Chomsky is not arguing for either of these, then all that is left is Darwinism.

Dennett also argues that Darwinism operates at the level of the cosmos. In this regard, Dennett is sympathetic to the views of cosmologists such as Lee Smolin, who suggest that our universe may be one of many, born from black holes, and that this 'multiverse' is subject to the principles of natural selection, just as much as we are.

‖ ESSENTIAL READING ‖

Content and Consciousness (1969)
In this work, based on his dissertation, Dennett broke up the problem of explaining mind into the need for a theory of content and the need for a theory of consciousness.

Brainstorms (1978)
This next book made Dennett's reputation. In it he reflects on the early achievements of artificial intelligence as a means of building a new theory of consciousness.

Consciousness Explained (1991)
Dennett's controversial work attempts to show how consciousness arises from the interaction of physical and cognitive processes in the brain. He argues against the idea of a 'Cartesian theatre', a place in the brain where conscious experience takes place.

Darwin's Dangerous Idea (1995)
In this book, Dennett argues that Darwinism is the central organizing force in the universe, accounting for everything from the laws of physics to human consciousness.

Breaking the Spell (2006)
In this work, Dennett uses the principles of Darwinism to try to explain the origins of religion. He uses empirical evidence to answer questions such as whether religion makes us moral and gives meaning to our lives.

DERRIDA, JACQUES

1930–2004

Algerian-born French philosopher, Derrida is most famous for his 'deconstructionist' development of postmodernist themes found in **Saussure**, **Levi-Strauss** and **Foucault**. His most significant works to date include *Voice and Phenomenon, Of Grammatology* and *Writing and Difference.* His impact on modern thought is reflected in the fact that by 1999 he had reportedly been cited more than 14,000 times in journal articles throughout the previous seventeen years.

Derrida's work takes as its starting point Saussure's structuralist approach to language, in which the sense of a sign is constituted by its relations to and differences from other signs in the conceptual scheme. Unlike Saussure, however, Derrida insists that the distinction between signifier and signified cannot legitimately be made; for him, the means of expression is inseparably bound with its content. How something is expressed is just as important as its conventional 'meaning' in determining those ideas to which it is connected and those from which it should be distinguished, as devices such as poetry, rhetoric and irony make clear. Consequently, there is, Derrida claims, no fixed conceptual order amongst signifiers.

If Derrida is right about this then it follows that meaning is something that can only be distilled or

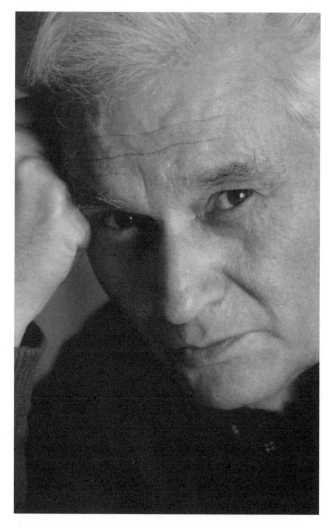

Derrida contended the structuralist view of language championed by Saussure, becoming known as the 'father of deconstructionism'.

Derrida was a prominent figure in literary and philsophical circles, shown here attending the welcome of Bangladeshi writer Taslima Nasreen at feminist publishers Editions des Femmes.

interpreted from any particular situation: there is no objective 'structure' as the structuralists had supposed. Indeed, Derrida goes further, for in his view a sign always signifies things other than which the author might suppose. There is an indeterminable network of associations stretching through time and use in which any given sign 'circulates'. What meaning it has for any given person at any given time can only be interpreted by that person at that time, but they cannot claim any authority or objectivity for their interpretation.

This dissolution of objective meaning infects every concept and has a significant impact on our conception of the world and of ourselves, especially when we apply it to traditional metaphysical concepts such as 'self', 'substance' and 'idea'. Derrida argues that as they have been used in the metaphysical works of philosophers, all such concepts have been implicitly defined by opposition and cannot be articulated independently. For instance, 'subject' implies 'object', 'self' implies 'other', 'substance' implies 'quality' and so on.

The concept of self is itself a linguistic construction

Since the concept of 'self' cannot have conceptual independence from the concept of 'other', it is illegitimate to suppose that the self is in any sense metaphysically prior to the concept of other. In fact, Derrida claims the concept of self is itself a linguistic construction, inescapably part of the 'text' of human language, but which has no metaphysical or ontological necessity. The human subject is, Derrida insists, 'a function of language' and that 'there is no subject who is agent, author and master of language'. Precisely what Derrida envisages as an alternative is not clear, since he is the first to admit that his own theories are bound by the same principles. He can be neither the author nor the authority of his own works.

This perhaps accounts for Derrida's style of writing, which one commentator describes as not so much philosophical theory building, as 'guerrilla warfare' in which Derrida strikes, retreats, punctures and parodies the theses of traditional philosophy. Certainly he is an extension of the postmodernist tradition which rejects the so-called 'transcendental pretence' of humanism, the idea that the conscious subject is a rational, autonomous being in charge of its own language, meaning and ultimately, it has to be concluded, thought.

Undoubtedly Derrida's work is controversial. It is presently very much in vogue in both literary theory and continental philosophy, but has encountered resistance amongst analytic philosophers. However one values Derrida's work, it is hard to contest the fertility of his ideas, which have led to extensive re-examination on the part of philosophers and literary critics of fundamental philosophical ideas such as identity, self-evidence, and the objectivity of the dichotomies – fact/fiction, rational/irrational, legitimate/illegitimate, observation/imagination – by which we live.

▌ ESSENTIAL READING ▌

Of Grammatology (1967)
In this his most famous work, Derrida examines the idea put forward by thinkers such as **Plato, Rousseau,** Saussure and Levi-Strauss that the spoken word is far closer to a person's thoughts than the written word, and that speech therefore preceded writing. Derrida attacks this view and the presuppositions of its proponents, demonstrating, for example, that Saussure's suggestion that writing is derivative can equally be applied to speech.

Speech and Phenomena (1967)
This is essentially a critique of the philosopher **Husserl** and his assertion that language is founded on logic rather than on rhetoric. Derrida takes issue with this idea, claiming that meaningful language is limited to expression because expression alone conveys sense.

Writing and Difference (1967)
This is a collection of essays written between 1959 and 1967 on Levi-Strauss, Artaud, Bataille, **Freud** and Foucault. It demonstrates Derrida's deconstruction method and was published as a reader to accompany the other two works of the same year.

DESCARTES, RENÉ

1596–1650

French philosopher and mathematician, Descartes is often called the father of modern philosophy. Known to physicists as the discoverer of the law of refraction in optics, Descartes' most famous work is

'cogito ergo sum', 'I think therefore I am'

in philosophy. *Meditations on First Philosophy* set the agenda for speculation in the philosophy of mind and epistemology for at least the next 300 years. He raised problems of such radical scepticism about our knowledge of the world that he suggests that the only thing one can be certain of is the fact of one's own existence, an insight summed up in his famous maxim 'cogito ergo sum', popularly translated as 'I think therefore I am'.

Descartes' program in the *Meditations* is to put the edifice of human knowledge upon secure foundations. Reviewing his beliefs, he finds that many are contrary. Some are more or less justified than others; some, such as the propositions of mathematics, seem certain; others readily turn out to be false. He resolves to put some kind of order into this jumble of beliefs so that justification of one proposition may follow from another. In order to do

that he needs to begin with whatever is most certain and infallible. The question is, where to start?

Descartes comes up with an ingenious program. Rather than attempt to examine and order each

An illustration from Descartes' work *Optics*, illustrating the interaction between mind, body and eye.

perception. He notes that the senses, however, can often mislead. A stick may look bent viewed half submerged in water, the true size of the sun and the moon is many times greater than would appear from sight and so on. One can even

Descartes rejects any information obtained through the senses as being uncertain and fallible

suffer hallucinations such that what one thinks to be there does not exist at all. Descartes resolves not to trust completely that which has deceived him once, and therefore rejects any information obtained through the senses as being uncertain and fallible.

Even so, one might think that although the senses may deceive from time to time, Descartes can be sure, at least, that he is sitting in his study, or is a Frenchman with an interest in philosophy and so on. But he recognizes that there is no clear and distinct way of telling the difference between reality and dreaming. How does he know that the life he thinks he is leading is not just part of a dream? There are no clear ways of distinguishing between waking life and a life merely dreamt.

So, rejecting all perceptual knowledge, Descartes turns to what he believes on account of his own internal reflections. Surely he knows that $2 + 3 = 5$, that a mother is older than her daughter, that a triangle has three sides? But it could be the case, reflects Descartes, that he is the subject of a massive deception. Now Descartes imagines a scenario

Descartes' most famous legacy is that of Cartesian Dualism, for which he has been called 'the father of modern philosophy'.

belief in turn, a task impossible to contemplate, he decides to examine his beliefs against a method of doubt. The method of doubt consists in questioning the source of his beliefs and asking whether that source is infallible. If not, he can be sure that any belief from that source cannot be relied upon to provide the foundations of knowledge.

To begin with, Descartes notes that many of his beliefs are derived from his senses, or from wherein he might be deceived by a divinely powerful, but malignant being; a demonic being that could manipulate his thoughts, as God might if he were not supremely good, into thinking anything the demon might choose. This idea of wholesale radical deception has been the subject of recent popular films such as *The Matrix* and *Twelve Monkeys*. Descartes realizes, however, that there is one proposition that neither the evil demon nor even God could ever make false. This is that at any time when he thinks, it must be the case that he exists. For he must exist in order to be able to think. By such reasoning Descartes is led to the cogito as the one certain, infallible rock of knowledge.

For Descartes, the cogito was the beginning of a project in which he attempted to prove the existence of God, in order to guarantee the rest of human knowledge. His commentators, unimpressed by his weak version of **Anselm**'s ontological argument or his own 'trademark argument' to prove the existence of God, have taken the *Meditations* to be the definitive work of epistemological scepticism.

▌ ESSENTIAL READING ▌

The World (1633)

In this treatise on physics and cosmology, Descartes defends the Copernican heliocentric view of the solar system. Knowing this to be contrary to the then Catholic orthodoxy and wishing to avoid condemnation by the Church, he decided not to publish the book. It was only published posthumously.

Discourse on Method (1637)

Autobiographical in style and very easy to read, the *Discourse* forms the preface to a collection of essays on optics, meteorology and geometry. It is here that Descartes expresses his famous dictum: 'I think, therefore I am'. On this basis, he builds a theory of knowledge and a scientific method, and lays the foundations of modern philosophy.

Meditations on First Philosophy (1641)

This book covers much the same ground as the *Discourse*. Starting from a position of total scepticism, Descartes again satisfies himself of his own existence, and the existence of God and the world. The book also contains a discussion of what is known as Cartesian Dualism, the view that mind and matter are distinct substances.

Principles of Philosophy (1644)

This is the last of Descartes' three main books on epistemology, physics and metaphysics, restating some of the conclusions of the *Meditations*. There is a discussion of the relationship between mind and body, and on the structure of the universe.

DEWEY, JOHN

1859–1952

When Bertrand **Russell** wrote his retrospective analysis of philosophical thought in 1946, *The History of Western Philosophy*, he concluded it by claiming that Dewey is 'generally admitted to be the leading living philosopher of America'. Undoubtedly Dewey's influence is present in the work of **Quine**, who subsequently held that mantle until his death at Christmas, 2000, and Russell's epithet is testament to the influence of pragmatist thought both then and now on American philosophy.

Dewey was a pragmatist philosopher, psychologist and educational reformer.

habits of behaviour that have proven successful in action. However, when habitual behaviour is disrupted by novel or unexpected experiences, the organism must engage in reasoning or 'intellection'. Dewey characterized five different states of the reasoning process.

First, when the organism's habitual patterns of action are disturbed, it will nevertheless continue to act in order to resolve the situation. Since its principle of action (belief) has proven unsuccessful it must begin a process of 'intellection'. The second stage then, is to extract the significant elements of the situation in order to formulate it as a problem-solving exercise. The next step involves 'hypothesis construction', the creative use of imagination to provide possible answers. The fourth stage that Dewey identifies is the use of reason to weigh up and order the alternative hypotheses. This consists in reckoning up the different experiences each hypothesis might actually result in. Finally, 'testing' or experiment is the process by which hypotheses are eliminated as they are tried out in the court of experience.

Dewey's pragmatism consisted in replacing the notion of truth as 'correspondence to reality' with truth as successful rules for action. He went beyond his predecessors, however, in developing his pragmatism as an instrumentalist theory of both logic and ethics in which the notion of 'warranted assertability' does all the same work as the notion of 'truth' but without the metaphysical baggage.

Following **Peirce**, Dewey upheld the idea that knowledge is a state of the human organism which consists in the settling of beliefs, understood as

The end result of this process is a successful resolution of the problem with the adoption of a new hypothesis that works. This led to Dewey's famous remark that 'the true is that which works'. We are warranted in asserting an hypothesis only on the condition that it works, any further claim of it 'corresponding to reality' is, in Dewey's view, a 'metaphysical' claim that adds nothing either to what we already know about or to what we can do with the hypothesis.

Dewey was keen to extend the instrumentalist approach beyond the theory of knowledge and into ethics, education and social theory. Societies, like individuals, are characterized by habitual patterns of action. When such patterns break down, they too must be repaired in light of the five stages mentioned above. For Dewey, what is ethically 'good' is 'a unified orderly release in action' of conflicting tensions and impulses that arise out of moral conflicts. The good, like the true, is ultimately what works.

Dewey's instrumentalism shares certain affinities with the existentialist work of **Heidegger**, a connection explored in depth by the contemporary philosopher, Richard **Rorty**. Both Dewey and Heidegger reject the prevailing philosophical emphasis on the subject as an isolated spectator in an external world in favour of a being embedded in an environment which it must manipulate, adapt and control.

'the true is that which works'

The organism is nothing more than 'the organization of a material system in space-time', and whose features and capacities (psychological, social, ethical and so on), 'their emergence, development and disappearance', are wholly 'determined by changes in such organizations'. Clearly, Dewey's work falls within the scientific paradigms of the modern age and represents a sustained attempt to work out the philosophical implications of that framework.

‖ **ESSENTIAL READING** ‖

The School and Society (1899)
One of Dewey's most influential books, this sets out his theories on education.

How We Think (1910)
This work gives an outline of Dewey's theory of inquiry, the means by which we can formulate beliefs and ideas that will allow us to respond appropriately to new situations.

Democracy and Education (1916)
This is a fuller statement of Dewey's philosophy of education. It also provides a good introduction to other aspects of Dewey's philosophy.

Human Nature and Conduct (1922)
In this book Dewey attempts to establish a theory of ethics based on the study and analysis of human nature, informed by the principles of psychology. The analysis is reminiscent of **Aristotle**'s ethics.

The Public and Its Problems (1927)
This books contains a defence of participatory democracy against the views of those who had argued that complex modern societies can only allow for a very limited form of democracy.

Logic: The Theory of Inquiry (1938)
Logic is Dewey's definitive statement of his logical theories. It contains a further exposition of his theory of inquiry, and of pragmatism, and a new theory of propositions. It is still considered an important work in the field of logic.

DIDEROT, DENIS

1713–1784

Along with **Rousseau** and **Voltaire**, Diderot is considered the third great figure of the Enlightenment. The 'Enlightenment' refers to the currents of ideas and attitudes that appeared in

Europe in the late 17th and 18th centuries. Whilst there are various disunited strands of Enlightenment thought, they all share a drive to break the power of dogmatic religion and throw off the shackles of superstition, appealing instead to the power of reason. Feudal social relationships and political absolutism were also rejected.

An illustration from the *Encyclopédie*, showing a foundry for casting iron products. The furnace is being tapped to allow molten metal to run into moulds.

Diderot embraced the Enlightenment ideals of reason and progress through human inquiry, as exemplified in the *Encyclopédie*.

Inspired by the new science of **Galileo** and **Newton**, the Enlightenment was the beginning of the so-called 'Age of Reason'. At its heart was a conflict between the Church's domination of intellectual life, and the inquiring mind, struggling to know and understand the world through reason. Enlightenment thinkers believed truth could be arrived at by a combination of reason, empirical observation and a healthy dose of systematic and critical doubt. However, underlying all this was a fundamental belief in the universe as an essentially rational progression.

Diderot, born to a cutler in Langres, France, was educated by the Jesuits in Paris. In 1745 the publisher André Le Breton commissioned him to translate an English encyclopaedia into French. What actually happened was that Diderot and his co-editor for a time, Jean d'Alembert, along with a team of like-minded 'litterateurs', scientists and even clergy (not to mention of course, Voltaire), re-wrote the whole work. Many of the articles were written exclusively by Diderot

Diderot was arrested and imprisoned for espousing a version of materialist atheism

himself. What they created was an encyclopaedia that brought out the essential principles and applications of every art and science then known, underpinned by a modern, rationalist philosophy and a belief in the progress of human inquiry.

Like the writings of Voltaire, Diderot's would not go without censure, and Diderot too was arrested and imprisoned for espousing a version of materialist atheism. Despite three months incarceration, Diderot completed and published the first volume of the *Encylopaedia* in 1751. Throughout the next twenty years a further 16 volumes of writings, accompanied by 11 volumes of plates would appear, despite numerous attempts by the authorities to suppress it. Diderot's co-editor resigned upon publication of the seventh volume in 1758, for fear of censure. Even the publisher, Le Breton, without Diderot's knowledge, secretly edited out certain

material in the final corrected proofs. Diderot, however, was undaunted, although deeply wounded when he learnt of Le Breton's deceit.

Diderot wrote a number of other pieces in his lifetime, in which he espoused his materialist philosophy and presented some remarkable insights in biology and chemistry which foreshadowed later developments. In particular, his speculations on the origin of life, which dispensed with the need of divine intervention were a remarkable precursor of **Darwin**'s evolutionary theory. He also pre-empted **Freud** by suggesting that childhood experiences were influential in the development of moral values.

Despite its huge impact on the development of Western thought, the Enlightenment period eventually failed because of the over-emphasis on reason and rationality at the expense of other human characteristics. Both **Hume** and **Kant** criticized it in this respect. Reason, Hume famously declared, is merely the slave of the passions. In other words, it is instrumental in bringing about our desires, but is not the fundamental driving force of mankind, let alone the universe at large.

‖ ESSENTIAL READING ‖

Encyclopédie (1751–1766)

Originally commissioned as a translation of Chambers' *Cyclopedia* into French, under the editorship of Diderot, *Encyclopédie* became a different work entirely. The final product comprised 35 volumes containing 71,818 articles and 3,129 illustrations. Diderot edited the first 28 volumes. *Encyclopédie* is a grand summary of the full extent of human knowledge in the era of the Enlightenment. It had a profound influence on the intellectual life of the times, and its emphasis on reason and scientific method as opposed to belief and faith was seen as a none-too-subtle attack on the Catholic Church.

DIOGENES OF SINOPE

400–325BC

Contemporary of **Aristotle**, Diogenes' style and method of philosophy could not have been further removed from that taught at **Plato**'s Academy. Diogenes was a charismatic and enigmatic character and inspiration for the Cynics, a school of thought that rejected the complications and machinations of civic life. Whether Diogenes ever actually wrote down his ideas is open to question, but if so they are all lost and it would seem out of keeping with his lifestyle and philosophy for him to have done so.

Diogenes professed a simplistic lifestyle, foregoing the trappings and distractions of civic life in favour of a devotion to the mastery of the self. Equally he reviled metaphysics and the intellectual pretensions of philosophers. Diogenes claimed that happiness could only be achieved by living 'according to nature'. This meant satisfying only the most basic requirements

of the body by the simplest means possible. Nicknamed 'the dog' for his vagrant lifestyle, Diogenes was allegedly described by Plato as 'a **Socrates** gone mad'. He made his living by begging, refusing to wear anything but the simplest of

Diogenes was an itinerant philosopher who eschewed the comforts of civic life in favour of 'self sufficiency'.

82

DIOGENES OF SINOPE

This woodcut shows Diogenes mocking Plato's definition of humans as featherless, two-legged animals by holding up a plucked chicken.

cloth and was renowned for outrageous public stunts – once reputedly masturbating in front of a crowd to show how easily and trivially sexual desires can be sated.

According to Diogenes, mastery of the self, or 'self-sufficiency', leads to both happiness and freedom but requires constant practice and training in the face of adversity. His uncompromising philosophy requires that one should abandon all property, possessions, family ties and social values in order to minimize the distraction of 'illusory' emotional and psychological attachments. But to avoid such distractions is not enough. One must aggressively attack society to help liberate others, and purposefully open oneself up to ridicule and abuse in order to remain emotionally detached. Though more radical and uncompromising, Diogenes' philosophy has its counterpart in the teachings of the oriental schools of Buddhism and Taoism. However, critics complain that Diogenes' lifestyle is self-indulgent, relying on the generosity and productivity of others to support his vagrant lifestyle. There is a philosophical point here, not just a pragmatic one, concerning the universalizability of ethical prescriptions. If everyone were to follow Diogenes' example society would collapse, making it economically impossible for anyone – including Diogenes – to concentrate on the mastery of the self. Therefore Diogenes' philosophy is elitist – it cannot be universally followed.

Mastery of the self, or 'self-sufficiency', leads to both happiness and freedom

Such criticism hardly troubled the Cynics, the loose collection of philosophers who followed in Diogenes' footsteps. It must be noted that the term 'Cynic' had a different connotation from the modern one, being derived from the Greek word 'Kyon' meaning 'dog', Diogenes' nickname. In Ancient Greece and Rome, where a resurgent Cynicism also enjoyed brief popularity around AD1, the term stood for what we would now understand as asceticism. As such it would be over simplistic to pass off the Cynics' philosophy as merely self-indulgent or elitist. The Cynics' popularity coincided with times of economic turbulence and social unrest. Their ideas, which taught that the one thing of real value – which was neither family, friends, cultural values or material goods, but the mastery of the self – was the one thing that could not be taken away no matter how calamitous a misfortune one might suffer. As a general philosophic principle it has merit and was highly influential upon the later Stoic philosophers.

‖ **ESSENTIAL READING** ‖

No writings of Diogenes have survived, although he is believed to have written several books. What we know of his life and philosophy has come down to us through stories and sayings found in a variety of classical sources, in particular the third-century Roman biographer Diogenes Laertius.

83

DUNS SCOTUS, JOHN

1266–1308

A Franciscan scholar and Scholastic philosopher, Duns Scotus was born in Scotland but travelled widely, teaching in Oxford, Paris and Cologne, where he died prematurely. Known as the 'Subtle Doctor' in his time, Duns Scotus is immortalized in the English language for giving his name to the term 'dunce'. While the term may now refer to stupidity, or slow learning, the Dunses were schoolmen who, following Duns Scotus, opposed many of the classical teachings. They insisted that nothing can be known without divine illumination.

> ## Duns Scotus is immortalized in the English language for giving his name to the term 'dunce'

Duns Scotus maintained that there are, with the help of divine illumination, but three modes of knowing that do not require further proof. First, there are principles known by themselves; following **Cicero**'s vocabulary, these would be called a priori. Second, there are things known immediately by experience and third, there is knowledge of our own actions. A follower of **Augustine** in many respects, particularly in his Platonism, he nevertheless disputed Augustine's rejection of Pelegianism, and upheld a belief in free will. Against **Aquinas**, Duns Scotus also affirmed the immaculate conception, much to the pleasure of Rome.

His greatest influence, however, concerns certain logical and linguistic debates. Though begun in medieval times, they have become the centrepiece of many modern controversies in the philosophy of language. Amongst these there is the concern over the principle of individuation – a matter later taken up in detail by **Leibniz**. According to Duns Scotus, that which individuates one thing from another depends on form rather than on matter. The distinction, between something's form and its substance, is borrowed from **Aristotle** and constitutes a firm rejection of Platonism in this regard.

Duns Scotus held that two things cannot be individuated merely by claiming they are different substances occupying different spatial (and possibly temporal) locations. The reason this idea is insufficient, claims Duns Scotus, is that substance is never identified by itself per se (in this regard he is a precursor of **Hume**). For any object is only identified by means of its attributes or qualities. Strip all these away – extension, solidity, opaqueness, and so – and one is left with a nothing rather than a something. So what is it, exactly, that is supposed to be the bearer of these qualities, situated as it is, in space and time?

Duns Scotus' answer was that what individuates one thing from another is not its place in space and time, since we cannot clearly identify what the 'it' is over and above the exhibition of certain qualities, but rather the particular combination of qualities exhibited. In other words, the form of the thing itself. This leads immediately to the objection that two things may possess all the same qualities, two genetically cloned apples for instance, but clearly they are not one and the same object, but two. Duns Scotus' reply is to make space and time themselves qualities of an object, in other words, part of a thing's form. After all, no one in any school of thought has (yet) claimed that space and time are part of the substance of a thing. Therefore they must be part of its form, in other words, part of the combination of qualities that makes a thing what it is. According to Duns Scotus, no two objects can ever have the same combination of qualities, and that it is only by means of form and not substance that we tell two things apart. If we maintain that space and time are part of the qualities or form of an object, then of course, Duns Scotus is quite correct to say no two things could ever have exactly the same combination of qualities.

This detail from a 13th-century medieval illuminated manuscript shows Duns Scotus with his pupils.

‖ ESSENTIAL READING ‖

Little is known about the details of Scotus' life or the chronology of his writings. Much of what survives of his work takes the form of lecture notes; some of it is of dubious authenticity, while other material is in a disorderly state and in need of editing. Furthermore, Scotus' philosophy is not easily discerned from any single work because of the excursive, inconclusive and frequently obscure style of his writing.

Ordinatio

Ordinatio is generally regarded as his most significant work. It was begun after he left Oxford for Paris in 1302 and he continued to work on it up to his death in 1308. It is his revised version of notes for the lectures he gave at Oxford University.

DURKHEIM, EMILE

1858–1917

Generally regarded as the father of sociology and the founder of a rigorous empirical method for the social sciences, Durkheim nevertheless considered himself a social philosopher first and foremost. As he wrote, 'Having begun from philosophy, I tend to return to it; or rather I have been quite naturally brought back to it by the nature of the questions which I met on my route'. His most important work is undoubtedly *The Division of Labour in Society*, which provides the theoretical framework for several lesser works, including *Suicide* and *The Elementary Forms of the Religious Life*.

Durkheim's principal task in *The Division of Labour* is to show that the fabric of all human societies is bound together by moral rules. These rules serve a central function in the organization of society. Durkheim insists we must undertake a thorough investigation in order to understand them. However, unlike **Kant**'s deontological theory or **Mill**'s utilitarianism, the investigation should be an historical one, inquiring into moral rules as they have actually operated in societies. Following **Comte**, he demands a 'science of morality' to undertake this task.

What Durkheim finds, in treating morality according to a scientific methodology, is that in the evolution of societies from primitive to modern, there is a weakening of collective conscience and a move towards individualistic conscience. In traditional societies with strong religious symbolism pervading the culture, there is a notable conformity

The trend towards individualism is itself a moral phenomenon which exhibits a collective conscience

amongst the individual's moral beliefs. In other words, the moral beliefs of each individual in a traditional society tend to be identical. Such beliefs also, remarks Durkheim, tend to be held with a certain intensity, such that divergence from the norm will elicit strong condemnation and penal sanction. By contrast, in modern individualistic societies, there is a marked difference amongst the moral beliefs held by individuals in society concomitant with a more tolerant attitude towards non-conformist behaviour, precisely because what is non-conformist is as diverse as the variety of moral beliefs.

The originality of Durkheim's thesis, however, is in showing how the increasing trend towards individualism is itself a moral phenomenon

After several years working in the first teacher training centre in France, Durkheim assumed the influential position of chair of education at the Sorbonne in 1902.

which exhibits a collective conscience no less than before, albeit transformed into a new expression. In order to see this, one must make the crucial distinction between 'individuation' and 'individualism'. Individuation is just that phenomenon already discussed whereby individuals in society develop a variety of beliefs independent of any dominant moral authority. But individuation has as a consequence moral individualism, or what Durkheim calls 'the cult of the individual'. The cult of the individual is a new moral code which places emphasis on the equal right of every individual to develop their own faculties in accord with their own beliefs. In Durkheim's own words: 'In the same way as the ideal of the less developed societies was to create or maintain as intense a shared life as possible, in which the individual was absorbed, our ideal is constantly to introduce greater equality in our social relations, in order to ensure the free unfolding of socially useful forces'.

The upshot of this idea is that it turns out individualism, rather than reflecting an erosion of moral values in society, is merely the expression of new moral values in line with – and hence the title of the book – the division of labour. In modern societies there is no longer a strict and simple economic order, but diverse economic relations whose proper functioning require a diversity of beliefs and values. Hence the 'cult of the individual', a new moral code reflecting a new social and economic order.

Durkheim goes on to argue that the cult of the individual has been misconstrued as the cult of the self-interested ego. He maintains that a collection of purely egotistical individuals could not form a society at all, that indeed, there has to be the recognition of others' interests, expressed in 'moral individualism' by the importance of equality and rights.

This provides only the barest outline of Durkheim's work, but from this framework he went on to discuss how both religious belief and social issues such as suicide are formed by this moral individualism. His work is significant for both social philosophy and sociology.

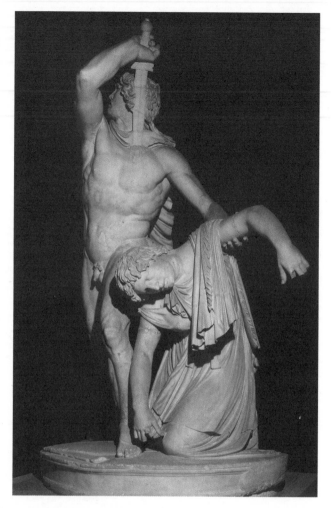

In *Suicide*, Durkheim argued that suicide was not purely a self-interested, personal act, but one determined by manifold sociological factors.

‖ ESSENTIAL READING ‖

The Division of Labour in Society (1893)

In this his most important work, Durkheim proposes the idea that societies evolved from a simple, non-specialized form, called 'mechanical', to a highly complex, specialized form, called 'organic'. In its organic state, with its division of labour, social bonds loosen as people become more individualistic, causing a breakdown of social norms known as 'anomie'. In this state, people are no longer sure of their place in society, without clear rules to guide them, leading to dissatisfaction, conflict and deviant behaviour. Anomie, he says, increases in times of economic depression.

EINSTEIN, ALBERT

1879–1955

German-born physicist of Swiss parentage, Einstein became a naturalized American in 1935, after leaving Hitler's Germany to avoid persecution as a Jew. After an unpromising start to his academic career, at one time declaring, 'I have given up the ambition even to get to a university', he accepted a job in the Bern patent office, where he conceived the theories of general and special relativity which were to found modern physics. Einstein was also politically active, both in the cause of world peace and Zionism. In 1952 he was offered the presidency of Israel but declined, claiming he was too naïve in politics. On the relation between his scientific and political interests he once said, 'Equations are more important to me, because politics is for the present, but an equation is something for eternity'.

The philosophical import of Einstein's work is enormous. His theory of relativity assigns an unprecedented importance to the role of the observer in his description of the physical world, threatening the received notions of space and time, as found in **Newton**, **Locke**, **Kant** and others. The central aspect of Einstein's works is that the speed of

Einstein's famous formula, published in the 'miracle year' of 1905, expresses the equivalence of mass and energy.

light is constant. It gives rise to the two most famous ideas of relativity physics: the equivalence of mass and energy expressed in the equation $E = mc^2$ (where E is energy, m is mass and c is the speed of light), and the law that nothing can travel faster than the speed of light.

These ideas have at least two philosophically important consequences. First, it follows from relativity that one cannot speak of an event occurring at precisely the same time for different observers. Each observer's time frame is relative to himself. Imagine an observatory on Jupiter looking at an observatory on earth. In each

Space and time are not independent dimensions, but form a four-dimensional unity, space-time

an astronomer looks through his eyeglass at the other at, we might suppose, exactly the same time. Since light takes 35 minutes to travel from Jupiter to earth, the event on Jupiter in which the astronomer

In 1932, Einstein left Germany for good and moved to the United States, becoming an American citizen in 1940.

looks through his telescope must have taken place 35 minutes before the astronomer on earth observes the event. Equally, the same applies to the astronomer on Jupiter: as he observes the astronomer on earth he is observing an event that took place 35 minutes prior to his own time frame. It is tempting to think there is some absolute position in which the two events could be observed as simultaneous, but this is exactly the possibility ruled out by relativity theory. Space and time are not independent dimensions, but form a four-dimensional unity, space-time, in which every event can only be recorded relative to a local time-frame.

The second philosophically interesting consequence of relativity is that although the speed of light is constant, its frequency (the number of waves of light per second) varies closer to massive objects like planets. This means time appears to run slower near a massive body than farther away. In

> ## It follows from relativity that one cannot speak of an event occurring at precisely the same time for different observers

1962 physicists confirmed this prediction by using two very accurate clocks, one at the base and one at the top of a water tower. The clock at the base was found to run slower than the other. This gives rise to the famous 'twins paradox'. Suppose one twin goes for a lengthy journey into space while the other stays on earth. When he returns he would appear to be much younger than his twin. The paradox arises from the assumption of an absolute time frame. The relativity thesis means that each body carries around its own personal time scale which does not, in general, agree with the time scale of other entities. Relative to each other, fifty years near a massive gravitational body is a shorter duration than fifty years far away from a massive body. Thus while fifty years might have passed on earth the space travelling twin might find he has only been away in space for thirty five years. The exact difference depends on the gravitational influences on the two twins throughout their lives.

The philosophical consequences of Einstein's *Theory of Relativity*, like the empirical consequences, are yet to be fully known. Issues such as time-travel, the passage or 'flow' of time, the asymmetry between past and future and between cause and effect – all require an understanding of Einstein's momentous work.

▌ ESSENTIAL READING ▌

Einstein's major works included four papers he produced in his 'miracle year' of 1905, and his 1916 paper on General Relativity.

Photoelectric Effect (1905)

In this paper, Einstein used quantum theory to explain the photoelectric effect (the process by which light rays dislodge electrons from the atoms on a metal surface). Einstein showed that light was made up of energy particles called photons, which could knock electrons from their atoms.

Brownian Motion (1905)

In his second paper of 1905, Einstein provided a theoretical explanation for Brownian motion, the movement of tiny particles suspended in liquid. The paper was important for providing further evidence of the existence of atoms.

Special Relativity (1905)

His third paper of that year, 'On the Electrodynamics of Moving Bodies' outlined his Special Theory of Relativity, which proposed that space and time are relative to the observer – they change depending on the position and speed of the object experiencing them. The only absolute is the speed of light, which is always the same, and is the upper speed limit of the universe.

$E=MC^2$ (1905)

In a fourth paper of that year, Einstein showed that mass is energy in a different form, and from this he derived his famous equation.

General Theory of Relativity (1916)

Einstein spent the next ten years trying to extend his Special Theory of Relativity to include gravity. The paper, when finally submitted in 1916, proposed that gravity was not a force, but a distortion in space-time created by the presence of mass.

EMPIRICUS, SEXTUS

c. AD100–200

Nothing is known of Sextus Empiricus' biography, only that his name is attached to some of the most important surviving works of the Roman era, the eleven volumes of *Arguments against the Dogmatists and Mathematicians* and the *Outlines of Scepticism,* in which Sextus Empiricus sets forth the doctrine of the Pyrrhonian Sceptics. It is solely due to the survival of his works that we know anything of the Sceptics and a great deal more than we otherwise would about many of the earlier Greek philosophers. Founded by Pyrrho around the third century BC, the Pyrrhonian Sceptics expounded a formidable counter-philosophy to contemporary schools of thought, principally the Aristotelians, the Epicureans and the Stoics. Pyrrho, like **Socrates** and several other philosophers of the Ancient world, wrote nothing himself nor took much care to elucidate his philosophy for others, so far as we can tell. Nonetheless, this did not stop his followers from documenting and developing his philosophy which seems to have culminated in the voluminous works of Sextus Empiricus.

The philosophy of the Sceptics is at once both simple and far-reaching. It is simple in that it turns on one principal claim, which is that one cannot assert any proposition with any better justification than one can assert its contradictory. Thus Pyrrho's philosophy is said to be summed up in the dictum

'No more this than that', meaning that one is no more justified to assert a proposition 'X' than its negation, 'not X'. It is far-reaching because the intention of sceptical philosophy is not to simply

> *The sceptic, by suspending all judgement of what is good or bad, right or wrong, true or false, remains indifferent*

checkmate the intellect into philosophical apathy, a result common amongst philosophy students who are rarely taught the deeper import of scepticism. Rather, the intention is to bring about a kind of therapeutic apostasy, which Sextus clearly shows will lead to tranquillity and peace of mind, the ultimate ambition of sceptical philosophy.

Sextus offers a battery of sceptical arguments to back his claim that for any proposition its contradictory can be asserted with equal justification. Clearly, the same object can look very different from a distance than it does from nearby, but why should we think the closer inspection more truthful than the other? Sometimes it is only by standing back that something can be seen clearly. To someone who claims snow is white, it could be pointed out that snow is only frozen water, and that water is colourless. Of course, we can give explanations as to why snow 'appears' white and water 'appears' colourless, but to do so is only to favour one way of looking at things over another. Someone could equally give an alternative and incompatible explanation to account for the same appearances. Because of the logical gap between reality and appearance, a gap we cannot close because knowledge of reality is always mediated by the fallible bodily senses, there is no way of proving that things are really one way rather than another.

How does this lead to tranquillity rather than intellectual anxiety? Sextus argues thus: suppose someone asserts that things are assuredly either good or bad. Such a person will remain troubled throughout life, feeling hard done by insofar as they lack the good things and are recipients of the bad. On the other hand, if they are fortunate to benefit from a bounty of good things, they will remain anxious not to lose them, living in fear of a change of fortune. But the sceptic, by suspending all judgement of what is good or bad, right or wrong, true or false, neither pursues nor avoids anything with any passion or intensity. He remains indifferent to the vicissitudes of life, and hence achieves tranquillity.

Critics have complained that sceptical philosophy is not a possible way of life, that passing judgement is a natural and unavoidable psychological function. Moreover, the sceptical claim is self-defeating. If it is true that one cannot justifiably assert a proposition over its negation, then this applies to the sceptical claim itself. Paradoxically, this seems only to add merit to the sceptical view. If one cannot conclusively pass judgement on scepticism one way or the other, perhaps one should indeed avoid passing judgement at all, just as the sceptic recommends.

Sextus Empiricus' works expound the philosophy of scepticism, founded by Pyrrho around the third century BC.

‖ ESSENTIAL READING ‖

Arguments against the Mathematicians

This detailed exposition of the principles of Pyrrhonian Scepticism is made up of 11 volumes. It is possible that at least one, but as many as five volumes are missing from the beginning of the work. Each volume has a different title, for example, *Against the Grammarians, Against the Rhetoricians and Against the Geometricians.*

Outlines of Scepticism

This book is the fullest description of Sextus's philosophy that still exists and is also one of the best sources of information about the other Hellenistic philosophies. It has been described as a manifesto of scepticism and its argumentative approach revolutionized the study of philosophy when Sextus's works were rediscovered in the 16th century.

ENGELS, FRIEDRICH

1820–1895

Friend and collaborator of **Marx**, Engels is largely responsible for developing and expounding the concept of 'dialectical materialism' within the Marxist framework. Along with Marx, Engels is

> *'Everywhere barbarous indifference, hard egotism on one hand, and nameless misery on the other, everywhere social warfare...'*

credited with being the first to argue that the working class and its demands will drive capitalist economics to its necessary outcome, socialism. His book *The Condition of the Working Class in England*, written whilst living in Manchester in the 1840s, is a masterpiece of social observation and an important historical record. **Lenin** describes it as 'a terrible indictment of capitalism and the bourgeoisie... written in absorbing style and filled with the most authentic and shocking pictures of the misery of the English proletariat.'

Unlike many like-minded contemporaries, however, Engels did not view the working class as a problematic outcome of capitalism. Many of those who objected to the social horrors created by the industrial revolution thought that what was needed was a way of running the economy that did not generate a proletariat. Marx and Engels, however, took the opposite view. The more workers there are, the greater their strength as a force for revolution. The increasing size of the proletariat only hastens the advent of socialism. Moreover, it is the very condition of the working class which will drive it to help itself once they realize that socialism is, and should be, their political ideal.

It is generally thought that it was Engels, rather than Marx, who developed **Hegel**'s idea that the universe is undergoing a constant process of change and development into the doctrine of 'dialectical materialism'. Unlike Hegel, Engels was a materialist – what was undergoing the dialectic process of thesis, antithesis and synthesis was not ideas but matter. Just as material causes underlie natural phenomena, so the development of society is conditioned by the development of material forces, which he construed as the forces of material production. Since productivity depends on the relations people enter into in order to effect the production of goods, it seemed that this single fact could explain all social phenomena, including laws, aspirations and ideals.

94

ENGELS, FRIEDRICH

The social conditions of the working class were so appalling, it seemed to Engels, that the dialectic process could have but one possible outcome, namely socialism. He writes, 'What is true of London, is true of Manchester, Birmingham, Leeds, is true of all great towns. Everywhere barbarous indifference, hard egotism on one hand, and nameless misery on the other, everywhere social warfare, every man's house in a state of siege, everywhere reciprocal plundering under the protection of the law, and all so shameless, so openly avowed that one shrinks before the consequences of our social state as they manifest themselves here undisguised, and can only wonder that the whole crazy fabric still hangs together'.

Engels records that starvation was a common phenomenon amongst the unemployed. But even the employed should not rest content, thinks Engels. 'True, it is only individuals who starve, but what security has the working-man that it may not be his turn tomorrow? Who assures him employment, who vouches for it that, if for any reason or no reason his lord and master discharges him tomorrow, he can struggle along with those dependent upon him, until he may find some one else "to give him bread"? Who guarantees that willingness to work shall suffice to obtain work,

The statue of Karl Marx (sitting) and Friedrich Engels (standing) in Alexanderplatz in Berlin – perhaps the most influential philosophers of all time.

that uprightness, industry, thrift, and the rest of the virtues recommended by the bourgeoisie, are really his road to happiness? No one. He knows that he has something today and that it does not depend upon himself whether he shall have something tomorrow'.

Of course, by combining such erudite polemics with philosophy, Marx and Engels would become the philosophical fathers of the communist revolution across half the world. For that reason alone Marx and Engels might justifiably be thought as the most influential philosophers of all time. The republics that would be realized in response to their philosophy would put an end to the fear of unemployment, but how far they satisfied the other, immaterial, needs of their citizens may only be judged by history.

The *Communist Manifesto* called on the proletariat to rise up and overthrow the old order.

▌ ESSENTIAL READING ▌

The Condition of the Working Class in England (1844)

This book is a detailed description and analysis of the condition of the industrial working class in England in the mid 1840s. It was written during Engels' stay in Manchester between 1842 and 1844 and is widely regarded as the definitive study of the working class in Victorian England.

The Communist Manifesto (1848)

Co-written with Karl Marx, this is arguably one of the world's most influential political tracts. Commissioned by the Communist League, it sets out the League's program of action, calling for a proletarian revolution to overthrow the bourgeoisie, ultimately to bring about a classless society.

The Origin of the Family, Private Property and the State (1884)

In this key work, Engels attacks the institution of the family. He regards the primary unit of the family as an unnatural development, born out of capitalism and designed to 'privatize' wealth and human relationships in a way that goes against the natural pattern of human and animal evolution. He looks at the history of the family in relation to class, gender inequality and private property.

EPICURUS

341–270BC

Born to a poor Athenian colonist in Samos, Epicurus was neither wealthy nor aristocratic and apparently suffered from ill health for much of his life. His philosophy represents a creative blend of the metaphysical interests of the Presocratics with the ethical concerns of **Socrates**. In line with **Democritus**, Epicurus espoused an atomistic metaphysics but combined and justified it with a brand of therapeutic hedonism, in which the anxieties of contemporary life were salved by the pursuit of pleasure without fear of divine punishment.

In essence, Epicurus follows Democritus' atomism but with one important modification. According to Epicurus, atoms in the void originally moved in undisturbed parallel lines. However, some atoms swerved from their course by a spontaneous act of free will. The resulting collisions giving rise to the myriad forms of things and the phenomenal world as we now know it. This important modification of atomism allowed Epicurus to proclaim mechanism but reject determinism as an explanation of human behaviour, one of the primary reasons for dissatisfaction with Democritus' philosophy. Although he kept to the idea that the soul was itself nothing but the movement of atoms in the material body, some atoms could freely 'swerve in the void'. This mysterious and wholly unaccounted for

property allowed Epicurus to maintain a concept of human free will against the critics of earlier atomic theories.

> *Epicurus' ethical teaching consisted in the pursuit of happiness, which he conceived of as the elimination of pain*

It is clear, however, that Epicurus' real interest was not in speculative metaphysics but with a practical philosophy of life which required atomism only for its theoretical underpinnings. His ethical teaching consisted in the pursuit of happiness, which he conceived of as the elimination of pain, both mental and physical. Of the two, Epicurus taught, mental pain is the worse, for severe physical pain either soon abates and can be brought under control of the mind, or results in death. Death was not to be feared, since there is no afterlife and no avenging gods, the soul being, in accordance with the doctrine of atomism, merely the concatenation of atoms which will be dispersed upon bodily death. Mental anguish, on the other hand, in the form of anxiety and fears, could continue unabated and result in distraction, depression and other psychological ills.

Although thought of as a hedonist because of his emphasis on the pursuit of pleasure, it would be a mistake to think of Epicurus as condoning a promiscuous or decadent lifestyle, an accusation unjustly levelled at him by the stoic philosopher, Epictetus. On the contrary, he was aware that many of the bodily pleasures brought with them pain or had painful consequences. He himself was a man of little means and of poor health, given which it is perhaps unsurprising that central to his philosophy were both prudence and temperance. Epicurus also taught that wisdom was the greatest virtue, for through it we could learn which pleasures to seek and which to avoid. Moreover, he professed that no one could be completely happy unless they lived a virtuous life, not because virtue was good in itself, but because it led to pleasurable consequences and the absence of pain and fear.

Like Democritus and other Presocratics before him, Epicurus rejected the idea of anthropomorphic gods who were cognizant of human affairs. Indeed, he was the first to formulate an argument that later became called 'the problem of evil' for those who maintain that there is an all-loving, all-knowing, all-powerful deity. Noting the many ills suffered by people in the world, Epicurus complained, 'Is God willing to prevent evil, but not able? Then he is not omnipotent. Is he able, but not willing? Then he is malevolent. Is he both able and willing? Then how can there be evil?' Even so, Epicurus was not an atheist, since he believed there were gods, but that these gods had no interest in human affairs, which would only have distracted them from their own pursuit of pleasure in contemplation.

Epicurus' philosophy represents a curious mix of opposing ideas. He is at once a hedonist who preaches prudence and temperance, a theist who rejects divine intervention and the survival of the soul, and an atomist who upholds both mechanism and free will. His followers became known as the Epicureans, the most famous of whom was Lucretius. Epicurean philosophy enjoyed almost six hundred years of popularity, remaining faithful to the teachings of its founder throughout, before being eclipsed by the Roman interest in Stoicism.

Epicurus' philosophy promoted a virtuous life, free from pain.

‖ ESSENTIAL READING ‖

The only surviving complete works by Epicurus are three letters and two sets of quotes, the *Principle Doctrines,* preserved in Book 10 of Diogenes Laertius's *Lives of Eminent Philosophers.* There is also another group of quotes, the *Vatican Sayings,* found in a manuscript from the Vatican Library. Much of what we know about Epicurus and his philosophy comes from other writers such as Lucretius, **Cicero**, Horace, Plutarch and Diogenes Laertius.

ERASMUS, DESIDERIUS

1466–1536

Dutch humanist philosopher and theologian, Erasmus was the illegitimate son of a priest and was himself forced into a monastic life by his guardians. In the monastery at Steyr his lifelong passion for Latin began, and he quickly outstripped the ability of his tutors. He escaped the monastic life in his late twenties and proceeded to travel and study widely.

Erasmus' *In Praise of Folly*, first published just a few years before the Protestant Reformation, was hugely influential in its satirizing of the Roman Catholic Church.

> *Erasmus believed in religion as a worship 'from the heart' that has no need of the offices and intermediaries supplied by the Church*

He eventually came to England and struck up a friendship with Thomas **More**, which lasted until the latter's death at the hands of Henry VIII. It was whilst making his way to England on a subsequent visit from Italy that he conceived his best known work, *In Praise of Folly*. Arriving at More's house in London, he quickly committed it to paper and published it, with More's support, in 1509.

In Praise of Folly has a dual purpose. On the one hand, Erasmus uses it to satirize and inveigh against the offices and institutions of the Church, for which he had developed a deep hatred during his time at Steyr. He attacks the monastic orders and their conception of worship as consisting in 'the precise number of knots to the tying on their sandals'. With more venom he goes on, 'It will be pretty to hear their pleas before the great tribunal: one will brag how he mortified his carnal appetite by feeding only upon fish: another will urge that he spent most of his time on earth in the divine exercise of singing

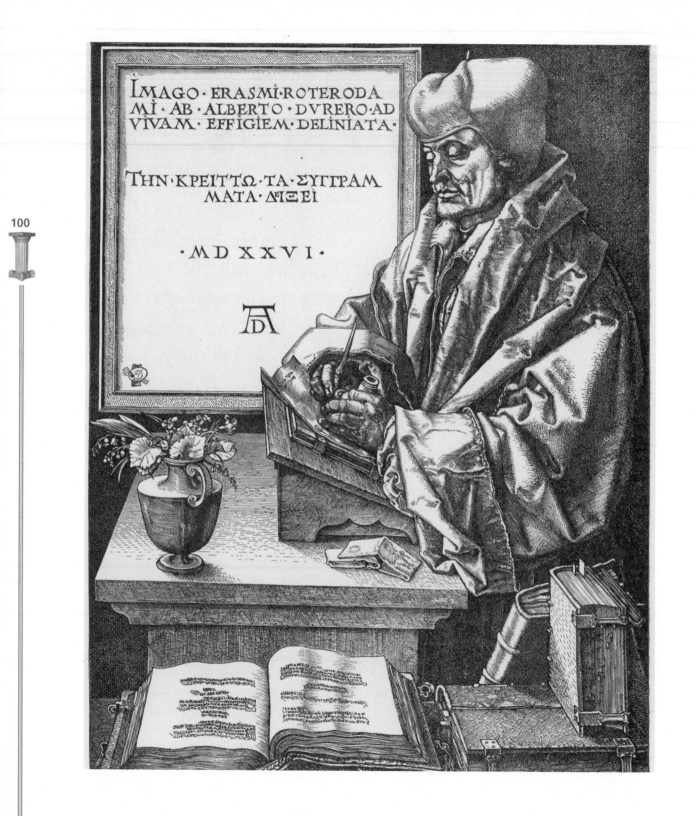

IMAGO · ERASMI · ROTERODA
MI · AB · ALBERTO · DVRERO · AD
VIVAM · EFFIGIEM · DELINIATA ·

ΤΗΝ · ΚΡΕΙΤΤΩ · ΤΑ · ΣΥΓΓΡΑΜ
ΜΑΤΑ · ΔΙΞΕΊ

· M D X X V I ·

Erasmus, scholarly, well-travelled and powerful, was one of the first great humanists of the Renaissance.

psalms... but Christ will interrupt: "Woe unto you, scribes and Pharisees, ...I left you but one precept, of loving one another, which I do not hear anyone plead that he has faithfully discharged."'

Erasmus's hero was Augustine, from whom he took the doctrine that reason must be the servant of faith

This introduces the central theme of Erasmus's *Folly*, namely his concern with religion as a worship 'from the heart' that has no need of the offices and intermediaries supplied by the Church. True religion, Erasmus insists, is a form of Folly, in the sense that it is simplistic and direct, not convoluted with unnecessary sophistications and dogmatic doctrine. For Erasmus, religion is based on a thorough-going humanism, understood in its classical sense as a confidence in human reason to know and worship God.

In similar vein, Erasmus was no friend of scholasticism, nor indeed of the philosophical fathers of his day, **Plato** and **Aristotle**. Erasmus's hero was **Augustine**, from whom he took the doctrine that reason must be the servant of faith. Apart from *In Praise of Folly* and his later *Colloquia* much of his work consisted in Greek and Latin translations of the Bible.

Erasmus had enormous influence on ushering in the Reformation, but surprisingly, in the struggle between the Catholics and the Protestants, the latter of whom were undoubtedly closer to Erasmus' religious ideas, he eventually sided with the Catholics. This apparent contradiction reflects his somewhat timid nature. He could not condone the violence of the Lutherans, preferring to attack the Catholics with words rather than actions. When More was executed by Henry VIII for refusing to accept his supremacy over the Pope as head of the Church of England, Erasmus is quoted as saying, 'Would More have never meddled with that dangerous business, and left the theological cause to the theologians'. A quote that brings into sharp relief the difference between his character and the uncompromising, incorruptible nature of More.

‖ ESSENTIAL READING ‖

In Praise of Folly (1511)

Erasmus's famous work was originally written in the space of a week while he was visiting Sir Thomas More at his estate in Bucklersbury. He later revised and extended the work and it was printed in 1511, with woodcuts by Hans Holbein the Elder. The narrator of the work is Folly, the daughter of Money and Freshness. It is sometimes light and humorous and at other times a harsh critique of the pious yet superstitious abuses of the Catholic Church. The book was a bestseller in Erasmus's lifetime, and was even enjoyed by Pope Leo X.

FEYERABEND, PAUL

1924–1994

Philosopher of science, Feyerabend became notorious in the 1960s and 1970s for his 'epistemological anarchism', which attacked the prevailing assumption that science was underscored by a rational methodology. Once enamoured of both logical positivism and Karl **Popper**'s 'falsificationism', he came to reject both and became popular with the 1960s alternative movements which rejected the hegemony of scientism. Feyerabend's classic work in this regard is his *Against Method*.

> *'There is only one principle that can be defended under all circumstances and in all stages of human development. It is the principle: anything goes.'*

Feyerabend's disillusionment with Popper began under the influence of **Kuhn**'s thesis of 'incommensurability'. However, Feyerabend goes beyond Kuhn's idea that science oscillates between periods of 'normal science' and 'revolutionary science'. Rather, he suggested, science is always revolutionary, since scientific practice is characterized by a plurality of concurrent hypotheses which are incommensurable with each other. Indeed, he argues that Kuhn's idea of theoretical monism, in which only one theory is accepted as fruitful at any given time, would be detrimental to the development of science. For according to Feyerabend, what drives scientific research is the competition provided by a plurality of alternative theories. Even if we are confident in the adequacy of a theory, Feyerabend maintains it is healthy to encourage alternatives to challenge it, which will aid both our understanding of the favoured theory and increase our justification for it.

This view, which Feyerabend calls 'theoretical pluralism' moves him towards relativism and anti-realism. For Feyerabend abandons the traditional conception that a theory is good just insofar as it 'fits the facts'. There are no facts, Feyerabend maintains, since all factual statements are theory-laden. By this Feyerabend has in mind a certain theory of meaning, influenced by the later work of Wittgenstein. On this view, the meaning of any factual statement can only be explained by reference to the 'language-game' of which it is a part – that is, the social practices and rules that are counted as criteria for the employment of the terms in the statement. But if this is so, then it looks like the meaning of factual statements is embedded not in the truth of some independent reality but in the conventions of social and linguistic activity, which in turn, are reflections of what we believe about the world. So 'facts' depend, ultimately, Feyerabend maintains, on what people believe.

Given this as a background, Feyerabend proposes to do away with the old untenable model of corroborating a theory against such 'facts'. Instead, we should encourage as many competing theories as possible and compare them with one another. We choose that theory which best contributes to our understanding. Empirical observation must enter into this picture somewhere, but does so in a more indirect way than in the traditional realist model.

Feyerabend's theoretical pluralism extends into a methodological pluralism, or as he called it 'epistemological anarchism'. He argues that in the quest for a plurality of theories, there is no one single guaranteed method we can rely on to produce good results. Indeed, of scientific practice

he says 'there is not a single rule, however plausible...that is not violated at some time or other...there are always circumstances when it is advisable not only to ignore the rule, but to adopt its opposite'. Since there are no sets of rules, it follows that science is anarchic in nature. Feyerabend goes on, 'There is only one principle that can be defended under all circumstances and in all stages of human development. It is the principle: anything goes.'

Interestingly, Feyerabend's anarchism received at first harsh criticism and then was ignored, principally because scholars refused to take his extreme relativism seriously. On the other hand, his audience outside of academic circles grew precisely because the anarchic message of his work struck a chord with certain alternative movements in society. However much disdain academics might have toward his work, he has probably reached a wider audience than any other philosopher of science.

Educated at the University of Vienna, Feyerabend went on to become emeritus professor at Berkeley in the United States.

‖ ESSENTIAL READING ‖

Against Method (1975)

In this celebrated work, Feyerabend proposes the idea that there are no rules governing scientific method. A set of rules, he says, would restrain scientific activity and retard progress. He suggests that science could benefit from a more anarchic approach. He cites historical examples of scientific progress, such as the Copernican Revolution, showing that at these times the commonly held rules of scientific method were ignored. [One of the rules he attacks is the 'consistency criterion', which insists that new theories be consistent with earlier theories, which Feyeraband insisted gave too much advantage to existing theories. Another is 'falsificationism', that a theory must agree with all known facts. He argues that no interesting theory is ever consistent with all relevant facts.]

FOUCAULT, MICHEL

1926–1984

Founder of a new French tradition in philosophy. Foucault's 'postmodernism' places the emphasis in philosophy on the subject of experience as situated in an external world. With the advent of 'the linguistic turn', that emphasis stressed the meanings of concepts rather than the impact concepts have had upon the world. It is with this historical retrospective, or 'archaeology', that Foucault is concerned. His most important works are *Madness and Civilization, Discipline and Punish: the birth of the prison* and *The History of Sexuality*.

The theme that underlies all Foucault's work is the relationship between power and knowledge, and how the former is used to control and define the latter. What authorities claim as 'scientific knowledge' are really just means of social control. Foucault shows how, for instance, in the 18th century 'madness' was used to categorize and stigmatize not just the mentally ill but the poor, the sick, the homeless and, indeed, anyone whose expressions of individuality were unwelcome. 'Madness' became the antithesis of 'reason' and was ascribed promiscuously not from an ignorance of medical science, but from the knowledge of its efficacy as a means of social control.

Foucault continues the theme of knowledge usurped in the service of authority in his study of the birth of the prison. He records how prisons replaced public executions in France and argues that this reflected a realization by the authorities that controlling the mind is a more effective means of social control than punishing the body. The concept of an extended, dehumanizing punishment holds greater terror than that of a quick, if brutal, release into the freedom of death through execution.

In his *History of Sexuality*, Foucault argues that this new emphasis on controlling the mind, as a more effective technique of domination than controlling the body, is continued in the psycho-analytic method of **Freud**. Whereas in the Middle Ages sex was wholly a bodily concern, Freud redefines it as a psychological feature of the mind.

Foucault used Jeremy Bentham's panopticon prison design to illustrate how not just detainees, but all citizens, are subjugated by processes of surveillance.

Now the emphasis is not on people's sexual behaviour, but on their sexual intentions. Sexual behaviour is controlled by focusing on people's attitudes towards sex, which are seen as representing a fundamental facet of their identity. Though the individual is encouraged to speak

Controlling the mind is a more effective means of social control than punishing the body

more freely about his or her sexual inclinations than ever before, this freedom is tempered by the fear that their inclinations reveal something fundamental about their personality. As a means of control its effectiveness is unsurpassed.

The overall intent of Foucault's work is to highlight how both what we take to be knowledge and the concepts through which we understand ourselves – those such as 'reason', 'normality', 'sexuality' – are contingent, mutable and 'ahistorical'. That is, they do not evolve along some 'path of progress' or represent a

Foucault's postmodernist philosophy upheld that society, and all social interaction, is maintained through relations of power.

sustained development, but rather change in response to the needs of authority to control and regulate the behaviour of the individual.

Though Foucault's work is dark and pessimistic in outlook, there is some room for optimism. He reasserts the value of philosophy, as a discipline conceived according to his method, as a means of redressing the balance of authority over the individual, through an exposure of the power structures intended to control us. In the light of these, we must strive to build social structures that minimize the risk of domination, and to re-examine what we think we know in light of the effect that knowledge has on our lives.

▌ ESSENTIAL READING ▐

Madness and Civilization (1961)

In this book, Foucault analyses the perception and treatment of madness from the Middle Ages to the present time, the creation of asylums and the treatment of the mentally ill, and the origins and development of modern psychology, which he sees as less benign than it thinks itself to be.

Birth of the Clinic (1963)

This book traces the development of the medical profession and shows how the development of medical science led to the human body being treated as an object, something to be analysed, labelled and cured. A key concept is that of the 'medical gaze'.

The Order of Things (1966)

A best-seller in France when first published, this book is concerned with the human sciences – psychology, sociology and cultural history – and presents an analysis of the 'episteme', a system of thought and knowledge which is the 'apparatus which makes possible the separation … of what may from what may not be characterized as scientific' at any given period of time in history.

The Archaeology of Knowledge (1969)

This contains a systematic formulation of the 'archaeology' Foucault used in his earlier work. The premise of the 'archaeological' method is that systems of thought and knowledge ('epistemes' or 'discursive formations') are governed by rules that individuals are not consciously aware of and which determine the boundaries of what can be thought in any given period of time.

Discipline and Punish (1975)

Discipline and Punish is a study of the development of the modern penal system, from the time when corporal punishment and public execution were standard punishments through various forms of prison such as **Bentham**'s Panopticon to a discussion of the modern prison system and why it fails.

The History of Sexuality (3 volumes: 1976, 1984, 1984)

Comprising part of a study that was incomplete at the time of Foucault's death, these three volumes trace the history of Western attitudes to sexuality. The first volume deals mainly sexuality since the 18th, the second and third volumes with sexuality in ancient Greece and Rome.

FREGE, GOTTLOB

1848–1925

A German philosopher whose work went unnoticed in his own lifetime, Frege has become one of the greatest influences on 20th-century philosophy for his work in logic and the philosophy of mathematics. That philosophy took the so-called 'linguistic turn' – the prefacing of ontological and metaphysical reflections with a prior analysis of how such commitments arise in language – is largely due to Frege. His invention of 'quantificational' logic was the greatest development in that subject since **Aristotle** and has now completely replaced Aristotelian 'syllogistic' logic in university courses.

Frege's contributions to modern philosophy and logic begin with his rejection of the Aristotelian analysis of sentences as being fundamentally of subject/ predicate form. According to the classical analysis, a sentence such as '**Socrates** is wise' can be analysed into two distinct parts. First, the subject of the sentence, 'Socrates', and second a property ascribed to the

Mathematician, logician and philosopher, Frege spent his entire career in the mathematics department at the Univeristy of Jena.

subject, namely 'being wise'. This had been the received wisdom for over two thousand years and gave rise to some notoriously intractable philosophical puzzles, not least concerning the notion of substance and the ontological status of universals and particulars.

Frege swept all this away by analysing sentences on a mathematical model of function and argument. In his view, the sentence 'Socrates is wise' contains a function, '( ) is wise', with 'Socrates' taking the place of argument for that function; in other words, filling the gap in the incomplete functional expression, '( ) is wise'. This view is taken directly from mathematics, where sentences such as '2 + 3' may be analysed in terms of a function '( ) + ( )' being completed by the arguments '2' and '3'.

This allowed Frege to inaugurate some profound developments in the philosophy of language. Since neither the functional expression nor the argument assert anything individually, but only when they are combined to form a complete expression, it follows that the meaning of a term can only be given in the context of the sentence (Frege's 'context principle'), by deducing what contribution it makes to the sense of the whole expression ('the compositionality of meaning'). This combined thesis has been Frege's most enduring legacy to the philosophy of language.

Meaning is primarily a property of sentences, and only derivatively of single words

Having argued that meaning is now primarily a property of sentences, and only derivatively of terms, Frege could then apply a distinction in meaning between the sense and reference of an expression. Respectively, these are the thought the sentence expresses and the objects being referred to or talked about by the sentence. For instance, it is clear that 'the Commander-in-Chief' and 'the President' are talking about, or referring to, one and the same person. It is equally clear, however, that the two expressions express different ideas. Being Commander-in-Chief is not the same thing as being the President.

The sense/reference distinction has become a centre-piece of many modern theories of meaning. It lies at the heart of philosophical projects which try to show how language is connected to reality. Since, according to Frege, the sense of an expression determines what it refers to, it has seemed to some philosophers that there must be some essential connection between what we say and what there is. This is the idea that informed the logical atomism of both Bertrand **Russell** and the young Ludwig **Wittgenstein** (a view Wittgenstein would later reject), and continues to feature in a number of important contemporary philosophical projects.

⦀ ESSENTIAL READING ⦀

Concept Notation (1879)

In this landmark work, Frege introduces his new logical language, which he called 'Begriffsschirift' (concept notation).

The Foundations of Arithmetic (1884)

Frege uses the logical language he developed to prove that the laws of arithmetic are true and that they existed prior to experience.

Function and Concept (1891); *On Sense and Reference* (1892); *On Concept and Object* (1892)

In these influential articles, Frege looks at the nature of language, functions and concepts, and logic, and develops a new theory of meaning based on the distinction between 'sense' and 'reference'.

FREUD, SIGMUND

1856–1939

Austrian psychologist and inventor of 'psychoanalysis', Freud has had a monumental impact on Western thought and philosophy. His best work is contained in *The Interpretation of Dreams*, *The Psychopathology of Everyday Life*, *Three Studies on Sexuality* and *Future of an Illusion*. Though trained as a physician rather than a philosopher, Freud famously said, 'when I was young, the only thing I longed for was philosophical knowledge, and now that I am going over from medicine to psychology I am in the process of attaining it'.

Freud's couch, where a patient would be encouraged to relive early experiences, represented an entirely new method of treatment.

The key to understanding Freud's work is two-fold. On the one hand psychoanalysis is predicated on the view that certain early childhood experiences, are 'repressed' by the Ego into the Unconscious. Typically, these are experiences that the child feels would elicit disapproval, and crucially for Freud, are tied in with the child's sexual identity in relation to one or both of its parents. The second element of Freud's theory concerns the separate, empirical claim, that such repressed memories are the cause of physiological disruptions, particularly nervous illness. Thus, Freud defines psychoanalysis as 'a procedure for the treatment of the medically ill'.

As one commentator has pointed out, however, it is an entirely unusual kind of medical treatment, in that nothing passes between the doctor and patient except conversation. The doctor's 'treatment' consists in eliciting repressed memories from the patient by interpreting the responses to his questions. This has led critics, notably **Popper**, to question the scientific status of Freud's procedure. Since the interpretation by the doctor is neither objective nor 'testable', in the ordinary scientific sense, and is moreover protected from scrutiny by the ethos of doctor-patient confidentiality, there is no objective way of measuring the results of psychoanalytic practice.

Despite such philosophical concerns, the popularity of psychoanalytic treatment is apparent and such popularity, its supporters would maintain, must surely be an indicator of its success. However, it is important to distinguish several logically independent claims. That personalities can be understood by interpreting an account of childhood experiences is one claim; that the interpretation given of such an account represents some objective truth about the patient is another; and that this process of 'conversation and interpretation' can effectively treat nervous illnesses is a third. The popularity of psychoanalysis could be attributable to the truth of any, all or none of these claims.

In purely theoretical terms, Freud's division of a publicly responsible Ego suppressing the impulses of the Unconscious also invites criticism. In particular, it attributes conflicting intentional

Freud with his daugher Anna, also a psychoanalyst, on holiday in the Dolomites in 1913.

Freud proposed an entirely unusual kind of medical treatment, in which nothing would pass between the doctor and patient except conversation

or purposive agency to distinct realms of the mind. **Sartre** criticized Freud's psychology for incoherently proposing that the conscious censor, the Ego, suppresses unconscious desires. If the Ego is not conscious of the unconscious ideas or desires, how could it be in a position to know that they must be repressed?

Despite this, philosophy in general has reacted well to Freud's theoretical principles. Freud himself suggested that his psychology represented a new 'Copernican revolution'. Just as **Copernicus** had shown that the earth is not at the centre of the universe, as **Darwin** had shown that man is not lord and master over the animal kingdom, but merely a continuous extension of it, so Freud claims to have proven that the conscious mind, or the self, is not 'master of its own house', as all rationalist and Cartesian philosophies presuppose.

111

⦀ ESSENTIAL READING ⦀

The Interpretation of Dreams (1899)
In this book, Freud introduces the Ego and describes his theory of the unconscious by means of dream interpretation. He explains that dreams are all forms of wish-fulfillment, and illustrates this a number of examples, both his own dreams and those of his patients. [He also discusses what later became the theory of the Oedipus Complex.]

Three Essays on the Theory of Sexuality (1905)
In the *Three Essays*, Freud put forward his theory that a person's sexual development begins not at puberty but in early childhood. He argues that the repression of sexuality is the source of neuroses. He introduces concepts such as penis envy, castration anxiety and the Oedipus Complex.

The Future of an Illusion (1927)
Here Freud puts religion on the couch, examining first its origins and development and then psychoanalysing it. He describes religion as an illusion, by which he means that it is derived from human wishes. He believes religion was necessary to society because it helped to restrain human nature's anti-social, sexual and destructive tendencies. [He sees God as a child-like 'longing for a father' to 'exorcize the terrors of nature ... reconcile men to the cruelty of Fate ... and compensate them for the sufferings [of] civilized life.']

GALILEI, GALILEO

1564–1642

Italian philosopher, astronomer, scientist and mathematician, Galileo is probably best remembered for his work in support of **Copernicus'** heliocentric theory of the solar system. For the sake of his life, Galileo recanted his views in 1633, admitting that the earth did not spin on its own axis. It is unlikely that the recantation was sincere and he nevertheless remained under house arrest.

Galileo's belief in science based on observation led him into conflict with the Church, who felt their authority was under threat.

In 1608 the Dutchmen Lippershey invented the telescope. Within two years Galileo used it to dramatic effect, showing by his astronomical observations that the Ptolemaic or geocentric theory which held that the earth was at the centre of the universe, was seriously flawed. Galileo also observed that the Milky Way was in fact made up of many millions of individual stars. He observed the phases of Venus and discovered the moons of Jupiter, which had theological experts up in arms. Indeed, Galileo's findings attracted such sharp criticism, both from secular and ecclesiastical quarters that he felt compelled to offer, both in his defence and in reply to his critics, the *Letter to the Grand Duchess Christina* in 1615. In the *Letter*, Galileo argues that scientific and theological matters should not be confused. Science could not cast doubt on religious doctrine, only strengthen it. Nonetheless he was condemned by the Inquisition, first in private communication in 1616 and later in 1633, when he publicly recanted.

Although his work was instrumental in bringing the Copernican system into prominence, Galileo was far more than just an astronomer. Much of his important work lay in dynamics and the principles of movement. He was the first to discover the law of falling bodies, or constant acceleration, published after his recantation and whilst still under house arrest in 1638, in his *Discourse on Two New Sciences*. Moreover, what would later be **Newton**'s celebrated First Law of Motion was directly taken from Galileo's principle of inertia, namely that a body moves in a straight line with uniform velocity unless acted upon. This principle was important in helping to support the Copernican theory. Critics of Copernicus had claimed that if the heliocentric theory were true, then a falling body should not fall in a straight line, but in fact land somewhat to the west of the point from which it was dropped, on account of the eastwise rotation of the earth. It had been proven by experiment that this was not

> *Far more than just an astronomer, much of Galileo's important work lay in dynamics and the principles of movement*

the case, a result which led many to dismiss Copernicus as wrong even if they did not share the religious reasons for dismissing him. It took Galileo's work in dynamics to show why the

Frontispice du IV.ᵉ Tome.

Dessiné et Gravé par J. P. Le Bas.

LA LUNETTE DE HOLLANDE
apliqueé a l'Astronomie,
en 1609.
Voyez l'explication fin du Tome II.

This engraving shows Galileo demonstrating a telescope to the Venetian Doge and the senators of Venice.

prediction was not fulfilled. Simply put, the falling stone retains the rotational velocity of the Earth.

Philosophically, Galileo held that 'the book of nature is written in the language of mathematics'. He was heavily influenced by Greek philosophy and a great admirer of Archimedes. He also maintained, like **Locke**, that there was a metaphysical distinction between the primary and secondary qualities of bodies. The former are essential and inherent in objects, whereas the latter exist only insofar as they cause certain effects in the minds of observers. Undoubtedly, Galileo was a great thinker who risked much in the pursuit of truth, helping to set free the quest for knowledge from the chains of religious dogmatism.

This illustration shows Galileo's observations of the phases of the moon, as the earth's shadow moves across it.

‖ ESSENTIAL READING ‖

The Starry Messenger (1610)

In this short treatise, Galileo recorded the results of his observations of the night sky with his telescope. He wrote of his discovery that the moon had mountains, contradicting **Aristotle**; that the Milky Way was in fact a vast collection of stars; and that he had observed four moons of Jupiter.

Letter to the Grand Duchess Christina (1615)

In 1613, Galileo's former student, Benedetto Castelli, wrote to him about a recent dinner conversation between Castelli, a professor of philosophy and Christina, widow of the Grand Duke of Tuscany, in which arguments were put for and against the heliocentric theory. This prompted Galileo to write a long letter to Christina stating quite explicitly his view that the earth rotated around the sun. The letter was later printed as a book and led the Inquisition to accuse Galileo of heresy.

Discourse on Two New Sciences (1638)

This work was the culmination of thirty years of Galileo's experiments on the the physics of motion and force. His 'law of falling bodies' anticipated Newton's laws of motion and was the first to offer a mathematical equation for the displacement of a falling object, starting from rest, under the influence of gravity over time. The accuracy of the experiments from which he deduced this law were far ahead of his time. As such, this work laid the foundations of the new science of experimental physics.

GÖDEL, KURT
1906–1978

Famous Czech mathematician and logician, Gödel produced theories that would have major repercussions in both these subjects as well as in philosophy. Though he contributed a great deal to various developments in mathematics, particularly in the 1930s, it is for what is now known as 'Gödel's Theorem' that he became most famous.

The human mind is capable of working out truths that no formal or mechanical procedure can decide

What is often referred to as 'Gödel's Theorem' is really two related theorems of incompleteness. The first theorem states that in any formal (mathematical or logical) system that is internally consistent (i.e., contains no contradictions), there will be some well-formed proposition that cannot be proven either true or false, in other words, that will be formally undecidable. In fact, Gödel shows that such a proposition is equivalent to an instance of the 'liar paradox', a statement such as 'This sentence is not provable', which if true, is false, and if false is true. The second incompleteness theorem shows that one cannot prove within the system that the system actually is internally consistent.

The upshot of these two proofs had a remarkable effect. First, in mathematics, it effectively put an end to the 'formalist' programme – derived from **Kant**'s metaphysics by the mathematician David Hilbert – which attempted to show that classical mathematics consists not in the description of an independently real but abstract realm of entities, 'numbers', but rather in a system of signs constructed out of perceptual experience. Key to the formalist programme was the ability to give an account of infinite quantities, which are never part of experience but are nevertheless indispensable to mathematics. Hilbert had worked out a theory whereby infinite quantities could be taken as assumptions adopted for their instrumental value. Since Hilbert needed a means of distinguishing and justifying valid assumptions from invalid ones, he made consistency a condition of adoption. In other words, no instrumental assumption should lead to a contradiction in the total system. Gödel's work showed that the demand for a proof of consistency could never be met, and thereby wrecked Hilbert's programme.

In philosophy, Gödel's works was seen as a reaffirmation of Platonism and, more recently a proof of the impossibility of artificial intelligence. Platonism in philosophy and mathematics, is just that idea, derived from **Plato**, that abstract objects

Gödel (second from right) receives the first Albert Einstein Award for Achievement in the Natural Sciences, from Einstein himself, in 1951.

exist independently in a 'third realm' – they are neither mental nor physical, but occupy a distinct and eternal world described by mathematics, logic and geometry and glimpsed, at times, by effort of the intellect. Gödel himself was a strong believer in Platonism. Now clearly the Gödel statement 'this sentence is not provable' in the finite system is true. It is the very fact that it is true but unprovable within the system that establishes Gödel's Theorem. Therefore it follows, according to Gödel and indeed

more recently the famous physicist and mathematician Roger Penrose, that the human mind is capable of working out truths that no formal, or mechanical procedure can decide. According to Penrose and others, this scuttles hopes of artificial intelligence programs, since all such machines, however complex, are formal finite systems.

What is clearly wrong with this argument, as Alan **Turing** was one of the first to point out, is that although it is correct that there is a limitation to the power of any machine that uses a formal language, it assumes without any kind of proof that the human intellect does not suffer from just the same kind of limitation. Perhaps for this reason Gödel's work has clearly not stemmed the tide of research into artificial intelligence, nor done much to resurrect Platonism outside of mathematics. However, within that discipline, Platonism has the status of orthodoxy. Given the centrality of mathematics to science, this must have repercussions on our philosophical reflections. We would seem obliged to either oust Platonism from mathematics or make some kind of room for it in our general conceptions of the nature of reality, as suggested by Gödel, Penrose and others.

Gödel proved that in all logical or mathematical systems there would always be some propositions that could not be proven either true or false...

‖ ESSENTIAL READING ‖

Incompleteness Theorems (1931)

Godel's incompleteness theorems, published when he was just 25, had a powerful impact on science and philosophy in the 20th century. He proved that in all logical or mathematical systems there would always be some propositions that could not be proven either true or false, using the rules of that system. You can only prove all propositions by going outside that system, creating a larger system with its own unprovable propositions.

An Example of a New Type of Cosmological Solution to Einstein's Field Equations of Gravitation (1949)

In this article, Godel found a new solution to his friend Einstein's equations of General Relativity, one in which the universe is not expanding, but rotating, with the centrifugal force caused by this rotation balancing out gravity to keep everything stable. The most extraordinary aspect of this rotating universe is that it's geometry mixes up space and time, allowing the possibility that a person going on a sufficiently long journey in a rocket ship, could travel back to any point in his or her own past.

HEGEL, GEORGE WILHELM FRIEDRICH

1770–1831

German idealist born in Stuttgart, Hegel produced perhaps the most difficult and yet influential works of any philosopher since **Kant**. His most important are *The Phenomenology of the Spirit*, an early work, and the more mature *Philosophy of Right*. Taking up where Kant left off, Hegel attempts to construct a grand metaphysic that will close the gap between appearance and reality that Kant's 'transcendental idealism' seemed to have left wide open.

By the early 1800s, Hegel was established as a major philosopher, attracting students from far and wide.

In Kant's metaphysics, since the mind imposes certain categories on experience, all that human knowledge can attain to is a complete and systematic knowledge of the phenomena presented to the mind. This leaves the reality behind those appearances, what Kant called 'the noumenal world', utterly beyond any possible human conception. It was a result Kant saw as inevitable, but which Hegel found unacceptable.

In Hegel's philosophy, ultimate truth is slowly uncovered through the unfolding evolution of the history of ideas. There is an absolute truth which, Hegel claims, is not propositional truth but rather conceptual. This difficult idea is best approached by first understanding Hegel's views on the development of history and of thought.

According to Hegel, the fundamental principle of the understanding mind is the commitment to the falsehood of contradictions. When an idea is found to involve a contradiction, a new stage in the development of thought must occur. Hegel called this process 'dialectic'. Hegelian dialectic begins with a thesis, initially taken to be true. Reflection reveals that there is a contradictory point of view to the thesis, which Hegel calls the 'antithesis', that has an equal claim of legitimacy. Faced with two incompatible ideas, thesis and antithesis, a new and third position becomes apparent, which Hegel calls the 'synthesis'. The synthesis now becomes a new thesis, for which an antithesis will sooner or later become apparent, and once more generate yet another synthesis, and so the process continues.

Europa's Wiedergeburt durch den grofsen Herrscherverein zu Wien 1814.

1. Kaiser Franz 2. Kaiser Alexander 3. König von Preufsen 4. Lord Castlereagh 5. König v. Dänemark 6. König v. Baiern 7. König v. Würtemberg 8. Churfürst v. Hefsen 9. Herzog v. Braunschweig 10. Talleyrand 11. Mediatisirte Fürsten und Staatsminister.

bey Martin Engelbrecht.

Hegel saw his ideas played out at the Congress of Vienna in 1814, as conflicting positions were overcome through progressive debate.

Ultimate truth is slowly uncovered through the unfolding evolution of the history of ideas

This gradual, and in Hegel's view, necessary unfolding of thought is a progression towards absolute truth, indeed towards an absolute universal mind or spirit. But truth for Hegel is not propositional. In other words truth does not belong to assertions that say the world, or reality, is of such and such a nature. Rather, attainment of truth in Hegelian philosophy is the attainment of completeness, or the transcendence of all limitation. Ideas, or to use Hegel's terminology, concepts, are that which are capable of being false rather than assertions or propositions. Falsehood is merely limitation, the incomplete understanding of the absolute. This entails that for Hegel falsified scientific theories are not in themselves wholly wrong, but

HEGEL, GEORGE WILHELM FRIEDRICH

merely do not tell the whole story. They are limited conceptions of a more all-embracing truth.

Hegel's dialectic process concludes with a grand metaphysical conception of universal mind. He tells us: 'The significance of that 'absolute' commandment, 'know thyself', whether we look at it in itself or under the historical circumstance of its first utterance – is not to promote mere self-knowledge in respect of the particular capacities...of the single self. The knowledge it commands means that of man's genuine reality – of what is essentially and ultimately true and real – of spirit as the true and essential being'.

The complexities of Hegelian philosophy are manifold and so too, perhaps as a result of both this and the obscurity of his writings, are the many schools and philosophical influences that arose from his work. Perhaps the most significant influence exerted by Hegelian philosophy, however, is in the work of Karl **Marx**.

▐ ESSENTIAL READING ▐

The Phenomenology of Spirit (1807)

Hegel's most brilliant, most celebrated and most difficult work, the *Phenomenology* had, in spite of its difficulty of interpretation, a huge influence in philosophy during the following century. In it, Hegel describes the unfolding of Being through history, that is, the evolution of the mind/spirit from mere consciousness through successive stages of self-consciousness, reason, morality and religion to absolute self-knowledge.

The Science of Logic (1812–16)

This is a detailed and systematic exposition of Hegel's system of metaphysical logic, using his dialectical method.

Elements of the Philosophy of Right (1821)

Here, Hegel sets out his social and political philosophy, advocating a constitutional monarchy as the ideal society and analysing the contradictions inherent in unconstrained capitalism.

Lectures on the Philosophy of History (1833–36)

Compiled from lecture notes after Hegel's death, this is an easier introduction to Hegel's philosophy than the other books listed here. Hegel regards history as a process moving towards the realization of human freedom, and he traces its progress over time and in different societies, both in Europe and in India and China.

HEIDEGGER, MARTIN

1889–1976

German existentialist, born in Messkirch, Baden. After studying theology and then philosophy, Heidegger went on to study under **Husserl**, to whom he dedicated his main work, *Being and Time*, at the University of Freiburg. He founded existentialist phenomenology under the influence of both **Nietzsche**'s and **Kierkegaard**'s work. Notoriously, Heidegger praised Hitler in a speech of the 1930s, an act for which he was widely criticized and which would do his career lasting harm. It is generally thought that he was at least a sympathiser with national socialism, if not an outright supporter. After the war he claimed it had been a massive social experiment that had gone drastically wrong.

His contribution to philosophy, fortunately, is not politically orientated and, for better or worse, has been highly influential. Heidegger saw the history of philosophy as concerned with the wrong kind of questions. Ever since **Plato**, Heidegger complains, philosophers have been asking about what there is and what they can know about what there is. For Heidegger, these questions presuppose too much. They notoriously presuppose a number of dualisms, in particular the Cartesian one of subject and external world. Like Nietzsche, Heidegger rejects this division, rejects the notion of a world as external to some conscious spectator.

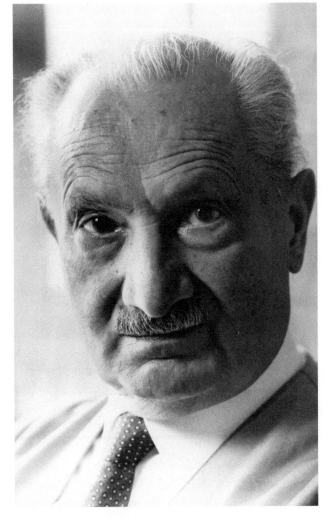

Heidegger's existentialism maintained that modern man had become alienated from his primitive oneness or 'Being'.

Heidegger attends an election rally of German academics in 1933 – the year in which Hitler's National Socialists were voted into power.

In place of such dualisms, Heidegger focuses on the question 'What is Being?', by which he intends that before we can ask about what sorts of properties objects might be said to have, we have first to look and examine, in a priori fashion, what it means for something to 'be'. The question can be seen as arising from the most basic philosophical puzzle of all: 'Why is there something, rather than nothing?' Few philosophers or philosophies have ever addressed this question, yet for Heidegger an

> *It is only in full and uncompromising awareness of our own mortality that life can take on any purposive meaning*

answer is essential before any other philosophical questions can be engaged.

For Heidegger, the question 'what is Being?' in general narrows down to considering what type of being one is oneself. He gives Being the deliberately vague name of *Dasein* – 'being-there'. 'Being-there' is supposed to denote what we ordinarily might call the human subject, but of course Heidegger rejects the subject-object distinction. For him 'being-there' is a perspective, which, it turns out, is a locus of action extended through time. In sum, *Dasein* is a perspective from which action originates.

In Heidegger's phenomenology, *Dasein*'s first comprehension of objects is not of determined and independent material things to be measured, analysed and classified. Rather, *Dasein*'s first comprehension of things is as tools: whether they are useful, whether anything can be done with them, and if so, what? What about *Dasein*'s comprehension of itself? Heidegger insists that what is characteristic of *Dasein*, as a temporal, self-conscious phenomenon, is that it knows its own fate. Dasein knows that it is finite and mortal. This generates what he calls angst or dread. But it is only in full and uncompromising awareness of our own mortality that life can take on any purposive meaning, insists Heidegger. Properly understood, self-awareness leads to the 'authenticity' of a life created out of nothing, in the face of dread, by reference only to one's own deliberate purposes.

Accordingly, on Heidegger's view, the question of why there is something rather than nothing comes back to the choice of 'being-there'. *Dasein* chooses to make something out of nothing and so, without *Dasein*, according to Heidegger there would be nothing. Due to the obscure language and often undefined concepts which Heidegger uses, it is not clear if the thesis is really just that without self-consciousness there would be no-one to be aware of the existence of anything. That is not a position Heidegger ought to take, for it would show that his previous rejection of the 'mind – world' distinction had been presupposed all along. Nonetheless, it is not clear what other sense we can make of Heidegger's proposal.

123

‖ ESSENTIAL READING ‖

Being and Time (1927)

This long treatise on the nature of being and its relationship to time is not easy reading, but it is one of the most important works of 20th-century philosophy, in which ontology is investigated by means of phenomenology.

HERACLITUS

c.?600–?540BC

Everything is in a state of flux, or change, and war and strife between opposites is the eternal condition of the universe. So claimed Heraclitus, whilst famously condemning his fellow citizens of Ephesus as so witless they should hang themselves and leave the city to the rule of children. An antagonist of the first order, Heraclitus ridiculed Homer, claiming he should have been turned out and whipped, and further poured scorn on the ideas and intellectual integrity of both **Pythagoras** and **Xenophanes**, amongst others.

Seeking to understand the basic structure of the universe, Heraclitus thought the three principal elements of nature were Fire, Earth and Water. However, Fire is the primary element, controlling and modifying the other two. 'All things are an exchange for Fire, and Fire for all things…the transformations of Fire are, first of all, sea; and half of the sea is earth, half whirlwind'.

The cosmic fire has its counterpart in the human soul, which in weak men is tainted by the 'watery' elements of sleep, stupidity and vice. The virtuous soul can survive the death of its physical body and eventually rejoin the cosmic fire. However, the process of separation and unity is continual. Mirroring the Oriental concepts of yin and yang, Heraclitus believed the dynamism between opposites was the driving force and eternal condition of the universe. 'Men do not understand that being at variance it also agrees with itself, there is a harmony, as with the bow and the lyre'. Heraclitus continues to tell us that 'God is day and night, winter and summer, war and peace, fullness and hunger'. Strife and opposition are both necessary and good, for the concept of universal tension ensures that whilst opposites may enjoy periods of alternating dominance, none shall ever completely extinguish or vanquish the other: 'The sun may not overstep his measure; for the Erinyes, the handmaids of Justice, shall find him out'.

This universal tension ensures that change is continual, that everything is in a state of flux. Permanence does not exist in the universe, only the permanent condition of change as a result of the transformations of Fire. This implies that whilst nothing remains changeless within the universe, the universe itself is eternal. The universe 'was ever, is now, and ever shall be, an ever-living Fire'.

Heraclitus, unlike the emerging rationalist philosophers of his period, chose not to explain the reasons behind his thinking in very great detail. Indeed, the fragments of his works that survive are so obscure that even those who followed in his footsteps, principally the Stoics, nicknamed him

Permanence does not exist in the universe, only the permanent condition of change

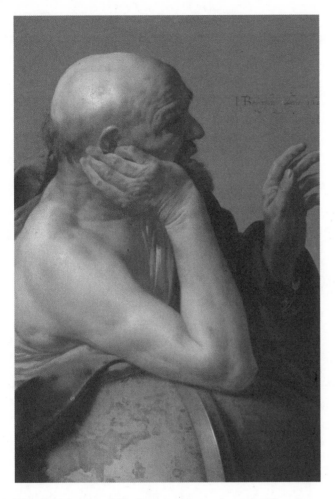

Heraclitus' doctrine of flux has been taken up by many philosophers, such as Henri Bergson, down the centuries.

'the riddler'. His works are written in aphoristic and prophetic style, with a clear contempt for those that cannot see what is clearly before them. Heraclitus is undoubtedly a mystic and there are strong affinities between his writings and the Chinese classic Tao Te Ching supposedly written by Lao Tzu ('Old Master') at around the same time. Whether Heraclitus had any contact with the oriental tradition, or vice versa, is impossible to determine.

Heraclitus conception of reality as a process, an ever-changing flux, stands in stark contrast to almost the entire subsequent development of metaphysics emanating from **Aristotle**. Two thousand years of metaphysical speculation has consisted in reflecting on the nature of substances and the qualities that they can, do or must possess. Only closer to our own times, in the works of **Bergson** and **Whitehead**, is metaphysics once again conceived not as the study of substances, but as the study of a process.

▌ ESSENTIAL READING ▌

In his *Lives and Opinions of Eminent Philosophers*, Diogenes Laertius informs us that Heraclitus wrote a book. Subsequent philosophers, such as Plutarch and Clement also refer to this book. Today, however, his writings survive only in fragments quoted by other authors.

HOBBES, THOMAS
1588–1679

British philosopher and author of the famous political treatise *Leviathan*. Although Hobbes made important contributions in a number of other fields, including geometry, ballistics and optics, it is for his work as a political thinker that he is best known. Like both **Bacon** and **Descartes**, Hobbes sought to underpin his inquiries not by finding out more facts but by finding and using a new methodology. Unlike Descartes, his concerns were more political than epistemological, but he borrowed from him, and other contemporaries such as **Galileo** and **Newton**, the idea that if the natural sciences could be underpinned by axiomatic laws of nature, then this should also be the case for the social sciences. Hobbes' method was to apply the rule of natural law to the realm of politics.

Hobbes' new political science first appeared in his *Elements of Law* in 1640, a treatise not intended to be published, but rather for use by supporters of King Charles I to justify the king's actions to an

The frontispiece of Hobbe's most famous work *Leviathan*, published in 1651.

increasingly hostile Parliament. Hobbes spent the next ten years in self-imposed exile in France, where he made a name for himself as a serious thinker.

His *De Cive,* published in Paris in 1642, develops the themes of the *Elements,* but his thought is exhibited at its best in his masterpiece, the *Leviathan.* According to Hobbes man acts according to certain natural laws. In an analogy reminiscent of Newton's first law of motion, which says matter will behave in a uniform way unless acted upon, Hobbes believes the natural state of man is one of war and strife, unless acted upon and governed by the rules of social living. Only a covenant kept by the rule of the sword can keep man from falling back into his natural state. Without the covenant, Hobbes tells us, society would disintegrate and it would be 'a war of every man, against every man' and the result would inevitably be that the life of man would be 'solitary, poor, nasty, brutish and short'.

Accordingly, Hobbes advances the notion of a social contract by which we are kept – and keep each other – from falling into this dark, natural state of war and strife. Every man operates, says Hobbes, according to a natural law of self-preservation. We each naturally want what is good for ourselves, and the covenant ensures that this can only be gained by taking into account the good of others.

> *The natural state of man is one of war and strife, unless acted upon and governed by the rules of social living*

Hobbes' social contract is premised upon the naturalistic forces that drive human beings. It is unsurprising, therefore, that Hobbes turns out to be a materialist, for whom everything in the universe is corporeal, ruling out the existence of such things as incorporeal spirits or souls. Even God is merely matter. Not since the presocratic Greeks had a philosopher advanced such an unremitting materialism.

Hobbes spent much of his life in the employment of the third Earl of Devonshire, a patron who shared his interests.

Although in the spirit of his times, many of his contemporaries hesitated to make so bold as he, fearing the censure of the Church.

This materialism, however, had to make way for some element of free will without invoking the incorporeal soul or mind. For although Hobbes made much of the natural state of man, he had to give some account of how societies came about according to a covenant. For Hobbes, free will and determinism were not mutually exclusive, but compatible notions. Just as water is unconstrained and yet will always flow to earth, so is man free but constrained by natural law. So long as a man is free to follow his natural inclinations, which ultimately are to survive and multiply, he is free to act. That man's inclinations are determined by his nature presents no problem for Hobbes.

▌ ESSENTIAL READING ▌

De Cive or The Citizen (1642)
Based on Hobbes' earlier work *The Elements of Law*, *The Citizen* develops his defence of a king's right to rule as an absolute monarch. Although less well known than *Leviathan*, it presents a clear exposition of Hobbes' moral and political philosophy.

Leviathan (1651)
This is Hobbes' masterpiece, and the work for which he most well known. Starting from the view that human beings are all selfish seekers after their own individual good, Hobbes argues that, if left unchecked, this would lead to perpetual fighting. To prevent this state of affairs, Hobbes argues, people surrender their individual rights to the authority of a 'sovereign' (either a monarch or a governing assembly) who in return ensures their security and well-being.

The ideas expressed in Hobbes' early treatise *The Elements of Law* led him to be labelled as a royalist supporter of King Charles I (above). Hobbes fled the political turmoil of the Civil War, moving to Paris for 11 years.

HUME, DAVID

1711–1776

David Hume is the philosophical hero of modern day sceptics and empiricists, renouncing all knowledge except for that which can be gained from the senses. Alas, as **Quine** would later famously say, echoing Hume, what can be garnered from the senses is, after all, not much.

There is no justification for believing that there is any causal necessity in the ordering of events

From **Locke**, Hume drew the conclusion that all human knowledge is based on relations amongst ideas, or 'sense impressions'. Anything not given in experience is mere invention and must be ruthlessly discarded. As a result he denies the existence of God, the self, the

Hume's rigorous empiricism rejected *a priori* reasoning as unreliable, dismissing it as nothing more than a tendency to search for order in events.

objective existence of logical necessity, causation, and even the validity of inductive knowledge itself. His aim is twofold: at once demolitionary – to rid science of all falsehoods based on 'invention rather than experience' – and constructive, to found a science of human nature. Much impressed with how Isaac **Newton** had described the physical world according to simple mechanical laws, Hume had a mind to do something similar for the nature of human understanding. His *Treatise on Human Nature* is a painstaking study in experiential psychology in search of general principles. In this Hume can be seen as having failed spectacularly, primarily because his whole taxonomy of 'impressions' and 'ideas' is derived from the much discredited Cartesian model. Nevertheless, Hume's negative program is a devastating example of the power of logical critique. His sceptical results, especially regarding induction, remain a problem for modern philosophers.

Hume observes that we never experience our own self, only the continuous chain of our experiences themselves. This psychological fact leads Hume to the dubious metaphysical conclusion that the self is an illusion, and that in fact personal identity is nothing but the continuous succession of perceptual experience. 'I am,' Hume famously says, 'nothing but a bundle of perceptions'. Following a similar line of thought, Hume notices that the force that compels one event to follow another, causation, is also never experienced in sense impressions. All that is given in experience is the regular succession of one kind of event followed by another. But the supposition that the earlier event, the so-called 'cause', must be followed by the succeeding event, the 'effect', is merely human expectation projected onto reality. There is no justification for believing that there is any causal necessity in the ordering of events.

Hume's scepticism does not stop there, and human belief in causation is just a special case of a more general psychological trait: inductive reasoning. Inductive reasoning is the process that leads us to make generalizations from observing a number of similar cases. For example, having observed many white swans but no black swans, one might seemingly be justified in the conclusion that 'All

During his lifetime, Hume was recognized as one of the leading figures of the Enlightenment.

swans are white'. Equally, being aware that men often die, we conclude 'All men are mortal'. But such generalizations go beyond what is given in experience and are not logically justified. After all, black swans were found in Australia, and there is always the logical possibility of coming across an immortal man. Hume claimed that inductive reasoning could not be relied upon to lead us to the truth, for observing a regularity does not rule out the possibility that next time something different will occur. Since all scientific laws are merely generalizations from inductive reasoning, this so-

Personal identity is nothing but the continuous succession of perceptual experience

called 'problem of induction' has been an urgent one for philosophers of science. Trying to show how induction is justified has taxed them throughout the 20th century. Karl **Popper** is notable for offering the most promising solution to Humean scepticism.

‖ ESSENTIAL READING ‖

Treatise of Human Nature *(1739)*
Although this is Hume's major philosophical work, it received almost no attention during his lifetime. It was intended as a complete analysis of human nature, and is divided into three parts dealing respectively with understanding, the passions, and morals.

An Enquiry Concerning Human Understanding *(1748)*
This is a shortened version of the *Treatise of Human Nature*, more accessible than the larger work but, as Bertrand **Russell** said, perhaps unfairly, 'leaving out the best parts'. It is an attempt to define the principles of human understanding, and discusses, amongst other things, causality, induction, and belief in miracles (which he argues against). Hume's scepticism affirms that while we cannot have certainty, we cannot avoid having beliefs.

An Enquiry Concerning the Principles of Morals *(1751)*
This is a rewriting of a section of the *Treatise of Human Nature*, and Hume considered it his best work. In it, he attempts to build a system of morality on the basis of sentiment: approved moral qualities are grounded in people's feelings, on the basis of either their utility or their agreeableness.

Dialogues Concerning Natural Religion *(1779)*
This book was considered so controversial that it was published posthumously. In the dialogues, Philo, a sceptic, puts forward objections to all the main arguments that claim to demonstrate the existence of God.

HUSSERL, EDMUND

1858–1938

German philosopher and founder of 'phenomenology', the descriptive analysis of subjective processes and events that lies at the heart of all existentialist philosophies. Husserl insisted that philosophy must proceed like science, from real issues and problems and not merely from the consideration of other philosophers' works. Nevertheless, Husserl also conceived this 'scientific' enterprise as a non-empirical one. Rather, it is a conceptual exploration of perception, belief, judgement and other mental processes. Like **Descartes**, Husserl believed in philosophy as essentially a rational enterprise beginning with the self-evidence of one's own subjectivity. It is a view that would famously be rejected by Husserl's follower and intellectual heir, Martin **Heidegger**.

Husserl's phenomenology begins with the concept of 'intentionality', as conceived by Brentano. According to Brentano, all conscious states refer to a content, though that content may or may not exist, may be abstract or particular. For instance, take someone who is afraid of ghosts. That person's fear is directed towards something, namely ghosts, and yet this is true whether we believe in ghosts or not. Similarly, if one believes that tomorrow it will rain, one's belief is directed towards, or refers to, tomorrow – a possibility rather than an actuality.

Husserl, following Brentano, suggested that the intentionality of the mind entails that one cannot separate the conscious state (fear, for example) from the object of that state (a ghost, say) in an ontological sense. They can only exist together, as two aspects of a single phenomenon, the intentional act. This leads Husserl to claim that consciousness is 'directedness towards an object'. The mental state and the object of that state exist together in consciousness without implying that there is any 'material' object answering to the call. Pursuing this idea, Husserl thought that philosophy's aim should be to understand all the various ways in which this 'directedness' or intentionality, manifests itself.

This constitutes Husserl's 'non-empirical science' – a pure investigation into the very elements of mental processes. Husserl believed that stripping away all the 'contingent' or unnecessary aspects of conscious experience could fulfil such an investigation. Consequently, the inquiry does not need to consider what, if anything, lies behind appearances. Speculation about what exists beyond appearance is open to doubt and scepticism, and Husserl, like Descartes before him, sees himself as being involved in a foundational inquiry whose task is to discover certainties. Since all 'knowledge-of-things' is acquired through the intentional objects of consciousness, any science of knowledge must begin with the intentional, with what can be known without doubt. Only those phenomena that form, to borrow a Kantian phrase, 'the necessary preconditions of experience' can satisfy such an inquiry.

Beyond an inquiry into the very elements of conscious experience, Husserl realizes that he faces the same obstacle as Descartes' 'cogito' (the conclusion popularly translated as 'I think, therefore I am'), namely that it is impossible to say anything very certain about 'the external world'. However, Husserl is less concerned with scepticism about 'knowledge of things' and more with scepticism regarding 'knowledge of self'. For Husserl has identified consciousness with the intentional act, and yet the self is not the act, but is the observing subject of the act. But this subject is never given in experience, is never, in Husserlian terms, the object of an intentional act. Accordingly, Husserl endorses a view akin to **Kant**, that the subject of experience is transcendental – outside of the spatio-temporal causal order. That conclusion is rejected by Heidegger but taken up again by **Sartre** in his *Being and Nothingness*, in which consciousness is portrayed as a unique phenomenon able to negate, through denial and imagination, what is real. Consequently it must stand outside of the ordinary causal order, as Husserl, Descartes and an extended line of 'dualist' philosophers, have long agreed.

Consciousness is 'directedness towards an object'

The founder of phenomenology, Husserl greatly influenced later philosophers such as Merleau-Ponty and Heidegger.

∥ ESSENTIAL READING ∥

Logical Investigations (1900–01)
In this work, Husserl criticizes 'psychologism', the attempt to base logic on psychology, and introduces the key themes in phenomenology.

Ideas (1913)
Not an easy book to read, *Ideas* is an exposition and development of the main themes in phenomenology. Husserl introduces terms such as 'noesis', the act of consciousness; 'noema', the object of an act of consciousness; and 'epoche', suspension of judgement with regard to the actual existence of the objects of consciousness.

Formal and Transcendental Logic (1929)
Another difficult book, this deals with the phenomenological foundations of formal logic.

Cartesian Meditations (1931)
Based on a series of lectures given at the Sorbonne, this is an easier work to understand than the preceding ones. It is primarily concerned with the phenomenology of the ego.

Crisis of European Sciences and Transcendental Phenomenology (1936)
This is something of a departure from Husserl's previous work, through which he extends phenomenology into the realm of the social sciences.

JAMES, WILLIAM

1842–1910

Born in New York and brother of Henry James (the novelist), James graduated from Harvard in medicine but later became a professor of psychology and philosophy. He is most famous for his 'pragmatist' philosophy which is captured by his dictum 'there can be no difference anywhere that doesn't make a difference elsewhere'.

Something is either true or right just insofar as it has a successful application to the world

According to James, empiricism has laid too much emphasis on the elements and origin of experience, without attending to the importance of how those elements, or 'sense-data', are related and used to predict future experience. James insists all knowledge is pragmatic – in other words, something is either true or right just insofar as it has a successful application to the world. Moreover, philosophical questions can be settled by attending to the difference competing answers would make to the lives of people who chose one option over another. If two competing theories offer no immediate practical differences, then the best theory may still be found by considering what effects believing in one or the other might have, and whether the mere belief in a theory would contribute to successful living. This idea, in particular, informs James' view of religion, found in his two most famous works, *The Will to Believe* and *The Varieties of Religious Experience*.

According to James, some questions require that we take a stand, that a sit-on-the-fence attitude is not possible with what he calls 'forced' issues. A forced issue is one in which a neutral stance or the refusal to commit is ruled out. Unlike having the choice of calling something true or false a forced issue is, James says, akin to being asked 'either accept this truth or go without it'. No middle ground is possible. James thinks the choice whether to believe in God or not is a 'forced' issue of this kind. To back agnosticism or scepticism in this case is tantamount to telling others that 'to yield to our fear of being in error is wiser and better than to yield to our hope that it may be true'. But this is mere dupery, he tells us, asking the question, 'what proof is there that dupery through hope is so much worse than dupery through fear?' The point is that an agnostic attitude is just as much a choice as believing.

If an issue is forced, James considers that we then have to ask if it is 'momentous' or not. By this he means whether it is a unique, life-changing, opportunity. Is it a decision that is afforded to us only once, and which will have far-reaching

James used his philosophy of pragmatism to recommend the tangible benefits of religious belief in improving quality of life.

consequences if taken? James claims the issue of religion is both forced and momentous.

In line with his pragmatism, however, James does not attempt any rationalistic proofs of the existence of God. Equally, he accepts that there is no straightforward empirical evidence that can settle the matter one way or another. However, there are good reasons, both empirical and pragmatical, that justify 'the will to believe'.

First, James reiterates the point that religious belief is both 'forced' and 'momentous' – for certainly momentous things follow if it is true. Now, if we must decide, then in the spirit of pragmatism and empiricism we should consider what difference opting to believe will have on our lives compared to not believing. Since a life of religious belief has a positive effect of bringing discipline, motivating force and strength into our character, James considers that it does indeed have a pragmatic effect: to make our lives better than if we do not believe.

Although James was an orthodox Protestant, he was perhaps unaware that his argument, if sound, is applicable not just to his own religious beliefs, but to any kind of religious belief. Commentators have noticed that this would widen the scope of 'religion' to include any kind of 'over-beliefs' by which people organize and motivate their lives. These might include such varied passions as science, sport, communism, capitalism or hedonism, as well as traditional and fundamentalist ideology. Whether or not James is right that living one's life in accordance with some doctrinal beliefs can instil qualities we might otherwise lack, the argument seems too weak to justify all the claims that one is committed to by a religious life.

'There can be no difference anywhere that doesn't make a difference elsewhere'

‖ ESSENTIAL READING ‖

The Principles of Psychology (1890)
This monumental work discusses consciousness, mind and thought. James argues that thought has developed as part of the process of evolution and is an instrument in the struggle for survival, and that consciousness can be characterized as a 'stream of thought'. He also discusses free will.

The Will to Believe and Other Essays in Popular Philosophy (1897)
Here, James discusses such concepts as rationality, belief, morality and the meaning of life. He argues that it is both right and sometimes necessary to make choices and adopt beliefs on the basis of insufficient evidence.

The Varieties of Religious Experience (1902)
In this book, James discusses various types of religious experiences and behaviour, such as mysticism, saintliness and conversion.

Pragmatism (1907)
This book consists of a number of lectures outlining the principles of pragmatism with regard to knowledge, truth and meaning, and pragmatism as a method of resolving philosophical disputes.

JUNG, CARL GUSTAV

1875–1961

Swiss psychologist and therapist, Jung was for a time the disciple of **Freud**, but he would go on to outline a theory very different from Freud's materialistic psychoanalysis. His works are numerous, but his most accessible are *Man and his Symbols,* and the autobiographical *Memories, Dreams, Reflections.*

Unlike Freud, Jung would divide the psyche into the ego, the personal unconscious and the collective unconscious. His reading of Freud, interjected with ideas from mythology, religion and philosophy, led him to posit a universal unconscious that revealed itself in symbolic form through dreams, mysticism and religion.

The collective unconscious determines that our experience is conceived according to certain organizing principles, the archetypes

The key to Jung's idea of a collective unconscious lies in the notion of an 'archetype'. According to Jung, the collective unconscious determines that our experience is conceived according to certain organizing principles, the archetypes. There are any

Despite its mystical, imprecise nature, Jung's philosophy has practical applications in modern personality profiling techniques.

number of archetypes, too many to be fully classified, claimed Jung. However, he did outline some of the most powerful archetypes that shape our lives and account for our behaviour.

One such archetype is the 'mother' archetype. Although it is clear that having a mother is a necessary biological relationship, Jung's mother archetype amounts to more than just the common relation that we all bear to some other human being. The mother archetype reflects a psychological need. What is significant about the mother archetype, Jung tells us, is that we all expect something or someone in our lives to fulfil the role of nurturing us and providing us with comfort in times of stress. This is an evolutionary need so it should come as no surprise that Jung says we come into the world ready to want mother, to seek her, to recognize and to deal with her. Ordinarily we project this need on to our biological mother. However, where Jung's theory comes into action in psychotherapy is in revealing the patterns of behaviour people exhibit when the biological mother has not fulfilled the archetypal role. For instance, someone whose biological mother did not fulfil the archetypical role may find themselves attracted to 'mother-substitutes', the church, the army, national patriotism and so on.

Jung went on to distinguish between a number of different personality types, and invented the terms 'introvert' and 'extrovert' to describe two of the

Jung's theory of archetypes pinpointed the crucial role of the mother in nurturing a child both physically and emotionally.

most basic. These have become synonymous with being shy or being an exhibitionist, but Jung's explanation of these ideas was far more sophisticated and not judgemental as regards either one being 'better' than the other. According to Jung, introverted personalities were those, such as himself, whose 'ego' was turned more towards the internal and unconscious, whereas extroverts were orientated more towards outer reality and external activity.

The distinction plays an important role in Jung's notion of the self. The self is the master archetype, that principle by which we structure our whole lives. Jung thought the self was in a constant process of development, which became fully realized when all aspects of our personalities are equally expressed. Thus to be overly introvert or overly extrovert represents an immaturity in development. However, if we develop normally, as we get older we tend to balance out the different aspects of our personality. Ultimately, Jung claims, the self is fully realized in death.

Critics have found Jung's psychology overly mystical and in parts unscientific, inasmuch as the emphasis, as with Freud's theory, is on subjective interpretation which appears to be incapable of falsification. However, it has been enormously popular and practically fruitful. Jungian psychology has led to the development of highly accurate personality profiling, such as the Myers-Briggs Type Indicator, and contributed to the development of psychometric testing, the use of which is now widespread in human resources departments for assessing the suitability of candidates for employment.

Jung's synthesis of Freudian psychology with mysticism is the first reputable attempt to bring Eastern philosophical principles into arena of modern Western thought. As such it represents a return to the mysticism found in the Ancient Greek philosophers from **Pythagoras** onwards, but which has since been overlooked due to the emphasis placed on materialism and rationalism.

‖ ESSENTIAL READING ‖

Symbols of Transformation (1911)
The publication of this book marked Jung's decisive split with his former mentor, Freud. In it Jung introduces his concept of the collective unconscious as well as different kinds of dream and other mystical symbols, which he interprets.

Psychology and Alchemy (1944)
In this book, based on a series of lectures he gave in 1935–6, Jung compares dream symbols with the imagery of ancient and medieval alchemists, showing that alchemy was based on collective archetypal images. The book inspired many scholars to re-examine alchemical symbolism.

Memories, Dreams, Reflections (1961)
In 1957, aged 81, Jung embarked on his autobiography, continuing to work on the manuscript until his death in June 1961. The result is a very personal and revealing account of his formative experiences, ideas and beliefs.

Man and his Symbols (1964)
Published posthumously, this accessible work is an attempt by Jung to explain his theory of dream symbolism to the layperson.

KANT, IMMANUEL

1724–1804

Probably the most influential philosopher since **Aristotle**, Kant spent almost the whole of his life exclusively in his birthplace, Königsberg. Popular myth has it that the Königsberg professor, an inveterate bachelor, was so regular in his daily constitutional that housewives would set their clocks by the time at which he passed their windows. Undoubtedly apocryphal, the story nevertheless highlights the fact that Kant was a very unadventurous fellow, with little interest in music or the arts but with a passion for mathematics, logic and science. Kant claimed in his work to have discovered and laid out universal principles of thought applicable to the whole of mankind and for all time.

Kant's influence stems largely from the first two of his three *Critiques* – the mammoth and cryptic *Critique of Pure Reason* (1781), in which he sets out to discover and justify the principles underlying objective judgements about reality; and the shorter, more lucid *Critique of Practical Reason* (1788), in which he attempts to give a rational justification for ethical judgements. *The Critique of Judgement* (1790), principally concerned with ideas of beauty and purpose, has received considerably less attention.

Despite never leaving his home town of Königsberg, Kant's influence on philosophical thought was unparalleled.

In the first of his *Critiques*, Kant was concerned to justify metaphysics as a legitimate subject of inquiry. In Kant's eyes, it had been brought into disrepute by the impasse between the rationalists (see **Leibniz**) and the empiricists (see **Hume**). The former claimed that metaphysical judgements – the fundamental principles upon which all knowledge is based – are known and justified purely by the intellect. The empiricists on the other hand, claimed that the human mind is like a blank sheet or tabula rasa waiting to be written upon by the world of experience.

Kant's genius was finding a way to synthesize these two opposing views. His fundamental insight sprang from posing the question, 'what are the necessary preconditions for having any experience at all?' He argued that in order for human beings to interpret the world the human mind had to impose certain structures on the flux of incoming sense-data. Kant attempted to define these in terms of twelve fundamental judgements he called the Categories (substance, cause/effect, reciprocity, necessity, possibility, existence, totality, unity, plurality, limitation, reality and negation) which could only be applied within a spatial and temporal framework. Thus Kant claimed both the Categories and space and time, which he called 'forms of intuition', were imposed on phenomenal experience by the human mind in order to make sense of it. This idea Kant proudly called his 'Copernican revolution'. Like **Copernicus**, who had turned the traditional idea of the sun orbiting the earth on its head, Kant had solved the problem of how the mind acquires knowledge from experience by arguing that the mind imposes principles upon experience to generate knowledge. This idea was later to have great influence on the phenomenologists and gestalt psychologists of the 20th century.

Just as Kant had laid down laws of thought in his first *Critique*, so in his second he claimed to have discovered a universal moral law which he called 'the categorical imperative'. He gave several formulations of this law, the first of which was 'act by that maxim which you can at the same time will as a universal law'. In essence, this categorical imperative is an expression of the oft-heard moral remonstration: 'what if everybody did that?' Kant realized that taking this seriously entailed that some moral rules could not be rationally broken. Suppose an agent is about to break a promise but stops first to consider Kant's imperative: 'could I will that promise-breaking become a universal law?' According to Kant the answer is no, for it is only because some people keep promises that the practice of promising makes any sense. Thus one cannot rationally assert that everyone should break their promises and hence, argued Kant, we have a duty as rational creatures to keep them.

Kant thought this kind of reasoning could be applied to many of our most cherished moral imperatives and would entail the obedience of any rational creature. Versions of Kant's theory of moral duty, often called deontological theories, have been widely upheld and defended by philosophers up to and including the present day.

The mind imposes principles upon experience to generate knowledge

‖ ESSENTIAL READING ‖

Critique of Pure Reason (1781)
This is Kant's greatest work, and one of the most impressive books on philosophy ever written, though it has also been described as 'overwhelmingly difficult and impenetrably obscure'. Seeking to solve certain fundamental problems in metaphysics, Kant sets out to determine the limits and correct use of reason.

Critique of Practical Reason (1788)
This book seeks to deal with problems of ethics. It discusses the relationship between morality and reason, desire, moral obligation, duty, God and immortality.

Critique of Judgement (1790)
This book contains a discussion of aesthetics and the nature of judgements about what is beautiful.

KEYNES, JOHN MAYNARD

1883–1946

Trained initially as a mathematician, and influenced by the work of **Russell** and **Whitehead**, Keynes gave up working on probability theory in order to pursue economics. He founded a school of thought, Keynesian economics, the only one in that subject to bear an author's name. His best known works are *The Economic Consequences of Peace*, in which he predicted that the high levels of reparation being levied on Germany after the First World War would result in political instability, and his *General Theory of Employment, Interest and Money*. It is the second of these works that has had such a massive effect in social, political and ideological terms.

Keynes showed how government intervention could lead to a stable free market economy

In his *General Theory*, written in the depression years of the 1930s, Keynes optimistically argues that downturns in the economy are short-term problems stemming from a lack of demand. Keynes offered a simple if radical solution: the government should boost short-term demand through public spending. Once the economy returns to buoyancy the government reclaims its budget deficit by increasing taxes and reducing public spending.

The underlying principle is straightforward enough: government spending should be inversely proportional to private trade. When trade is booming, government should spend little, when the economy slumps, public spending should go up. But what was radical about this proposal was the general principle that the government should intervene in the economy to control demand, an idea that has come to be known as 'demand management policy'.

Keynes' theory was seen at the time as the answer to **Marx**'s prediction that the boom and bust cycle of capitalism would inevitably lead to socialism. Keynes showed how government intervention could lead to a stable free market economy. However critics deplored the idea of government intervention in the trade cycle. It encouraged the anti-liberal idea that social problems should be solved by government, and indeed that government should look to academics to show them how to solve such problems. Nothing could have been more repugnant to the supporters of the classical 'laissez-faire' economics of Adam **Smith** and J.S. **Mill**. On the classical view, the economy functions best when there is no interference from government. Smith and Mill believed that the natural economic order will, so long as it is not disturbed by governmental meddling, tend towards the maximum well-being of both the individual and society. This kind of controversy still rages today, both in politics, economics and philosophy.

Keynes' theories were followed for much of the subsequent years in the UK until around the 1970s, with controversial results. Although supporters are quick to point out that the practical interpretation of his ideas has rarely been agreed upon, critics will retort that Japan and Germany, two powerhouses of post-war world economics, both refrained from adopting Keynesian policies. Ethical issues concerning globalization also have a Keynesian dimension, anti-globalization supporters should note: the two ethical pariahs of world trade, the International Monetary Fund and the World Bank, were both Keynesian inventions.

Ultimately, economic thought has moved on from Keynes, but his work remains the yardstick with which all other theories are measured. Although his work began in probability theory as a response to Russell and Whitehead, his ideas were to have a dramatic effect on the world as we know it.

Keynes' influence as a leading economist was at its greatest in the aftermath of the two world wars.

‖ ESSENTIAL READING ‖

The Economic Consequences of Peace (1919)
In this book, which established Keynes's reputation as a leading economist, he attacks the Versailles Treaty which marked the end of the First World War. He claims that the high reparations imposed on Germany in the treaty were unfair and endangered economic recovery for the whole of Europe. The book was an immediate bestseller in both Europe and America.

General Theory of Employment, Interest and Money (1936)
Keynes's magnum opus, with its advocacy of government intervention in the economy in times of depression, ushered in a revolution that would shape the economic agenda of much of the Western world for the rest of the 20th century.

KIERKEGAARD, SØREN

1813–1855

Danish philosopher born in Copenhagen, Kierkegaard is often considered the father of existentialism, (see, for example, **Sartre**). He was the youngest of seven children, five of whom, along with their mother, had already died by the time he was twenty-one. He himself only lived to be 42. His early work *On the Concept of Irony* proved a masterful criticism of the philosophy of **Hegel**, whilst his later works offered sustained criticism of the State Church, which he found to be incompatible with his own Christian beliefs.

Kierkegaard's work once more returns ontological prominence to the Cartesian individual as opposed to either the species or the whole, as seen in the works of **Spinoza**, Hegel and **Marx**, for whom the individual is, more or less, an irrelevance. Against this conception Kierkegaard rails: 'Each age has its characteristic depravity. Ours is perhaps not pleasure or indulgence or sensuality, but rather a dissolute pantheistic contempt for individual man'. However, Kierkegaard is anything but Cartesian in every other respect. His work is probably best summed up by his own famous epigrams, that 'the conclusions of passion are the only reliable ones' and 'What our age lacks is not reflection but passion'. For Kierkegaard, the whole history of thought has been preoccupied by the wrong concerns.

Since the Greeks, philosophy has concentrated on architectonic metaphysical schemes, venerating reason or experience in order to comprehend and make sense of the world. But none of these systems take into account the fundamental

'Each age has its characteristic depravity. Ours is perhaps not pleasure or indulgence or sensuality, but rather a dissolute pantheistic contempt for individual man'

human condition. We are, at every turn, faced with the need to make decisions. Choice is our starting point, constant companion, and heaviest burden. In his *Journals* Kierkegaard complains, 'What I really lack is to be clear in my mind what I am to do, not what I am to know... the thing is to find a truth which is true for me, to find the idea for which I can live and die'. The burden of decision making is a theme that recurs throughout all existentialist thought, and is what justifiably identifies Kierkegaard as 'the first existentialist', though he would not have recognized the label himself.

Fearing the ethical commitment of the institution of marriage, Kierkegaard remained a scholarly bachelor throughout his life.

The answer is religious belief, which Kierkegaard holds to be a matter of passion not reason. Reason can only undermine faith, never justify it. For even though one might indulge in rationalistic proofs of God's existence, in the manner of **Anselm** or **Aquinas**, these nevertheless have nothing at all to do with a belief in God. One must choose to believe in God passionately and personally, not as a mere intellectual exercise. An authentic belief acquires its force from within, as a 'leap of faith' without the guidance of reason to reassure us that what we are doing is 'right' or 'true'. Such reassurances would, after all, maintains Kierkegaard, remove the need for faith if God's existence were simply a matter of common-sense or rational reflection.

Kierkegaard's later works frequently attack the institutions of the Christian Church, which he claims are the very antithesis of Christianity. Going through the motions of a Christian life – attending church, following ordained ethical precepts, reciting scripture and so on – has nothing to do with the religious life if it does not involve a personal and direct confrontation with the divine.

Towards the end of his life Kierkegaard's reputation suffered considerably for both his conflict with the Church and a long running public feud with the Press. He nevertheless enjoys a reputation today not just as a forerunner of the influential existentialist movement, but as a masterful essayist with great persuasive style.

‖ ESSENTIAL READING ‖

Either/Or (1843)

This book contrasts two of the three modes of existence that Kierkegaard distinguishes in his philosophy: the 'aesthetic' and the 'ethical'. (The third mode of existence is 'religious'.) The aesthetic mode of existence is based on pleasure and immediate gratification, while the ethical mode is built on responsibility, obligation and duty.

Repetition (1843)

Repetition is concerned with the ethical mode of existence. It is the story of a young man who is in love but who cannot bring himself to commit to marriage because he fears the ethical commitment involved, which would require him to dedicate himself to that one person. The book closely resembles Kierkegaard's own situation.

Fear and Trembling (1843)

Illustrated by the biblical story of Abraham and Isaac, this book discusses the conflict between the ethical mode of existence and the religious. As instructed by God, Abraham is prepared to sacrifice his own son, his religious commitment obliging him to act (or be prepared to act) in a way completely contrary to normal conceptions of moral behaviour.

The Concept of Anxiety or The Concept of Dread (1844)

This book discusses the concept of 'anxiety' or 'dread', also commonly referred to as 'angst'. For Kierkegaard, this anxiety is caused by the individual's awareness of their freedom of action with nothing to guide them in making a choice out of all the possible actions they could take.

KRIPKE, SAUL

1940–

American philosopher Saul Kripke has made a number of original and highly influential contributions in the fields of logic and philosophy of language. Born in Omaha, Nebraska, the son of a rabbi and university lecturer, Kripke showed a prodigious intellect from an early age, writing a series of groundbreaking essays on the semantics of modal logics while still in his teens.

Kripke proposed replacing descriptivism with a new theory of 'direct reference'

Kripke is perhaps best known for his series of lectures at Princeton in 1970, which went under the title of *Naming and Necessity*. In the course of three lectures, Kripke offered a revolutionary new approach to the philosophy of language and metaphysics. The lectures were an attack on the descriptivist theory about the meaning of names, championed by Gottlob **Frege** and Bertrand **Russell**. According to this theory, a name refers to an object because of the name's association with a description of that object. In other words, a name is best seen as an abbreviated form of that description. But Kripke saw a problem with this theory. If, for example, the name 'Norman Greenbaum' means 'the composer of "Spirit in the Sky"', then there is

Kripke's groundbreaking work on modal logic and the truth theory has established him as a leading philosopher of our time.

no possible world in which Norman Greenbaum did not compose that song. But this must be false: even if Norman Greenbaum had never written this or any other song, he would still be Norman Greenbaum.

Kripke proposed replacing descriptivism with a new theory of 'direct reference'. According to this theory, a name 'rigidly designates' its referent (the object to which it refers) in every possible world in which it exists. In other words, a name is simply a 'tag' attached to its referent and has no descriptive content whatsoever. Furthermore, Kripke put forward a new theory for how names are transmitted, which he called the 'causal theory of names'. According to this theory, the parents of a

There is a part of Mary – that which is referred to by her name – which is essential to her

newborn baby call it a name, such as 'Mary'. Those who witness the naming now know the new baby's name. A 'causal chain' then passes from the namers and those who witnessed the naming to everyone else who uses the name. By this proposition, Kripke resurrected the theory, unfashionable at the time, known as 'essentialism', which states that for any entity (for example, Mary), it is at least theoretically possible for there to be a set of characteristics which that entity cannot fail to have. In other words, there is a part of Mary – that which is referred to by her name – which is essential to her in every possible world.

In 1975, Kripke proposed a theory of truth, showing that it may be possible to create a sentence in a natural language, such as English, that contained its own 'truth predicate' without giving rise to a contradiction or paradox. A truth predicate is a phrase such as *is true* in the sentence *This sentence is true.* It can give rise to a contradiction or paradox in the sentences such as *The following sentence is true. The previous sentence is*

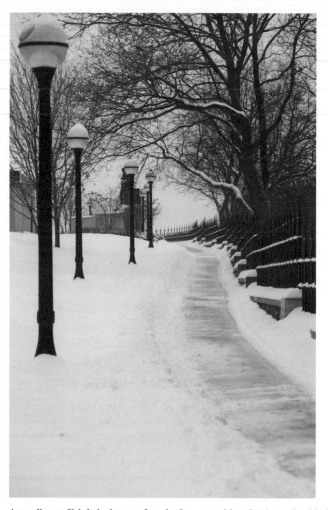

According to Kripke's theory of truth, the proposition that 'snow is white' can be formulated in English without giving rise to a contradiction.

false. With this claim, Kripke contradicted the Polish logician Alfred **Tarski**, who contended that no natural language could contain its own truth predicate. According to Tarski, the expression *is true* could only apply to sentences in some other language, which he called an 'object language'. Kripke showed how to build a sentence with its own truth predicate in a natural language, as follows: Start with a sentence that does not contain the predicate 'is true' or 'is false', such as 'Snow is white.' Next, define the truth predicate for that sentence. Then add the truth predicate to the sentence i.e. '"Snow is white" is true'. Next, define the truth predicate for this sentence as a whole. For example: '"*Snow is white* is true" is true'. Imagine this process repeated infinitely. With Kripke's method, because sentences like *This sentence is false* were not included in the original subset, the truth never gets defined for them and so they are neither true nor false. This resolves the 'liar paradox' inherent in such sentences (if they are true, then they are false, and vice versa).

Kripke published another highly influential work called *Wittgenstein On Rules and Private Language* (1984), a critique of the Austrian philosopher's discussion of rules as they are observed among solitary individuals or isolated communities. Kripke's starting point is a sentence by **Wittgenstein**: 'This was our paradox: no course of action could be determined by a rule, because every course of action can be made out to accord with the rule.' Later, Wittgenstein modifies this when he says: 'there is a way of grasping a rule which is *not an interpretation*'. Kripke disagrees. He argues that, in a small community, all that matters is that rules are followed correctly. Whether or not they are being followed correctly is determined, he says, not by what might be right or true in a universal sense, but by what the individual or community believes to be right or true. In such situations, claims Kripke, two plus two need not necessarily equal four, if the community, or experts appointed by that community, believe otherwise. Kripke's argument offered a new form of scepticism, known as 'meaning scepticism', and provoked a great deal of debate. However, several scholars criticized him for misrepresenting Wittgenstein. Indeed, some referred to the hybrid philosopher whose views are presented in the book as 'Kripkenstein'.

‖ ESSENTIAL READING ‖

Saul Kripke is famous for rarely setting words to paper. He lectures without notes. The talks are later transcribed, and Kripke edits and revises them before approving them for publication.

Semantic Considerations on Modal Logic (1963)
A highly influential paper, based on ideas he had first proposed as a teenager, which helped to transform the study of modal logic.

Naming and Necessity (1980)
This revolutionary book, based on a series of lectures he gave in 1970, attacked the descriptivist theory of names and replaced it with a new theory of direct reference.

Wittgenstein on Rules and Private Language (1984)
A study of the views of the later Wittgenstein that proposed a new theory, dubbed 'meaning scepticism'.

KUHN, THOMAS

1922–1996

Although he wrote five books and many articles during his career as a philosopher, Kuhn is best known for his seminal work *The Structure of Scientific Revolutions*, written as a graduate student in theoretical physics at Harvard. Dismayed by the somewhat simplistic accounts philosophers gave of the history of science as a continually progressive subject edging always closer to the truth, Kuhn argued that there are radical and incommensurable discontinuities between different periods of scientific investigation which make the idea of continuous progress untenable.

The history of science, Kuhn argued, is punctuated by violent intellectual revolutions that overturn long periods of conservative puzzle-solving. Periods of so-called 'normal' science are characterized less by independent and objective research than by adherence to agreed assumptions and expected outcomes. During periods of normal science, anomalous or unexpected findings get brushed aside as either irrelevant or problems to be solved another time. Original research that questions the current assumptions of accepted theory are often debunked as wild and useless speculation. This gives rise to Kuhn's notion of a paradigm. The current paradigm is a web of interwoven assumptions and beliefs shared by a particular community which underlies and sets the agenda for current research.

According to Kuhn, only results which tend to strengthen the current paradigm get accepted during periods of normal science. The paradigm itself is never questioned or criticized. However,

> *The history of science is punctuated by violent intellectual revolutions that overturn long periods of conservative puzzle-solving*

from time to time paradigms are overthrown by intellectual revolutions. When the paradigm fails to provide adequate models for observed phenomena, or a new, more powerful model has greater explanatory force but requires a 'paradigm-shift', a revolution takes place. Examples of such revolutions might be, for instance, **Copernicus**' heliocentric theory of the Solar system which replaced the Ptolemaic idea that the sun revolves around the earth; or **Einstein**'s replacement of **Newton**'s theory of gravity, space and motion.

Kuhn also popularized the notion of 'incommensurability' which defied the notion that science is on an advancing path of progress towards ultimate truth. According to Kuhn, the rejection of

Kuhn's formulation
of scientific
paradigm-shifts
dispenses with the
notion of continuous
progress in the
history of ideas.

KUHN, THOMAS

a previous paradigm in favour of a completely different one rules out the possibility of comparison. Kuhn argues that the scientists' view of the world is so radically altered by the acceptance of a new paradigm that old and new are qualitatively and quantitatively incomparable. Kuhn argues that scientists operating at different historical periods with different paradigms live in psychologically different worlds. Kuhn says, 'After Copernicus, astronomers lived in a different world'. His idea is that the world of Ptolemy is not the same world as Copernicus, for when Ptolemy observes the sun he observes an object that moves around the earth, whereas Copernicus sees the central star of the solar system.

The idea of absolute truth is one we can do without

This subjectivism in science makes the idea of absolute truth a questionable notion and, according to Kuhn, one we can do without. Since it is impossible to investigate the nature of reality without operating with some paradigm or other, we should see science as the evolution of ideas in response to the world. If we think of the evolution of ideas in much the same way as the evolution of organisms, then according to Kuhn, there is no more reason to believe ideas are evolving towards some ultimate truth than there is to think that organisms are evolving towards some ultimate being.

▌ ESSENTIAL READING ▌

The Structure of Scientific Revolutions (1962)
As a graduate student at Harvard University in 1947, Kuhn first became interested in the history of science and asked himself why **Aristotle**'s ideas about matter and motion were so very different from Newton's. This was the genesis of his landmark work. Kuhn's book argues that scientists work within the intellectual framework of their time, and their ideas cannot be described as erroneous if they are based on prevailing perceptions. From this he concludes that science does not advance through the straightforward accumulation of facts but through changing intellectual circumstances and possibilities. Kuhn's book has been highly influential, encouraging philosophers such as **Feyerabend** to call into question the basic assumptions of science, and used by those, such as creationists, who wish to attack the scientific establishment.

The dominant Ptolemaic theory of a universe centred around the earth (top) was overthrown by Copernicus' proposal of a heliocentric system (bottom) in a violent scientific revolution.

LEIBNIZ, GOTTFRIED WILHELM VON

1646–1716

German philosopher, Leibniz is the third of the three great rationalists, after **Descartes** and **Spinoza.** Like them, his philosophy proceeds from an Aristotelian notion of substance, conceived of as that which is the bearer of property but is itself not a property of anything else. Even so, Leibniz rejected Spinoza's view that there is only one substance, taking the opposite view: that there are an infinity of individual substances, which he named 'monads'.

Philosopher, mathematician and polymath, Leibniz was a high profile figure who spent much of his life as librarian to the Duke of Brunswick in Hanover.

A monad is in one sense similar to the atoms of **Democritus** and yet more akin to the geometrical points of **Pythagoras.** Like atoms, monads are the ultimate indivisible elements of reality of which all material things are constituted. But they are not themselves either extended nor composed of matter. In a completely original thesis Leibniz holds that a monad is a psychological entity, which, when embodied in human beings, he calls 'souls'.

Fundamental to Leibniz's 'monadology' is the notion that a monad is a unified, independent substance. Accordingly, everything that is true of a monad is contained within it and it therefore cannot enter into any causal relation with any other monad (the debt to Spinoza here is clear). Leibniz expressed this point in a logical way, saying that of every true proposition, the predicate is contained within the subject. What this amounts to is the extreme view that every truth is a necessary truth – a conclusion Leibniz does not shy away from but embraces, claiming that everything happens the way it does because it must, and it must because God has chosen to make actual the best of all possible worlds. Things could only have been different if God had chosen to actualize a different possible world.

In his capacity as a mathematician, Leibniz invented a calculating machine for multiplications (shown above), and published his system of infinitessimal calculus in 1684.

This approach makes personal identity a very rigid notion. If God had chosen another world, Julius Caesar could not have not been an emperor of Rome, and you could not have not been a reader of this book. To deny any of these true propositions about these individuals would be to take something essential away from what makes that individual what he or she is.

This view follows naturally from Leibniz's concept of a monad. Commentators have almost universally rejected it, however, not least because it seems to eradicate any possibility of free will. Even so, Leibniz's work here raised a whole new and important debate concerning what the criteria of personal identity are. If not every property of an individual is essential to a person's identity, which, if any, are?

Philosophers have argued that what constitutes personal identity, what makes the Caesar that crossed the Rubicon the same Caesar that entered Rome is 'bodily continuity': the continuous spatio-temporal history of the same physical body from one event to the other. However, this notion is problematic on at least two counts. First, as physiologists well know, the cells that constitute the body are completely renewed every seven years. Since the Caesar seven years after the crossing of the Rubicon is not physically the same Caesar that made the crossing, we stand in need of an account of 'bodily continuity' that does not depend on the physical constitution of the body. This remains problematic. Secondly, both legally and medically, we allow that sometimes an individual is not always one and the same person, if for instance they have suffered some severe psychological trauma. So some element of psychological integrity seems necessary to the concept of personal identity. But finding a suitable criterion of psychological identity has proven as elusive as finding a criterion of personal identity. The issue remains a live one in ethics, metaphysics and psychology.

> *Everything happens the way it does because it must, and it must because God has chosen to make actual the best of all possible worlds*

155

▌ ESSENTIAL READING ▌

The Theodicy (1710)
This book is concerned with a defence of God's goodness and justice in the face of the evil that is found in the world. In it, Leibniz argues that, in spite of the evils it contains, this is 'the best of all possible worlds', a viewpoint ridiculed by **Voltaire** in his novel *Candide*.

The Monadology (1714)
This book outlines Leibniz's view that reality consists of an infinite number of substances, called 'monads', soul-like objects no two of which are exactly alike.

New Essays in Human Understanding (1765)
This work was not published until long after the philosopher's death. Written in the form of a dialogue, this is a detailed critique of **Locke**'s *Essay Concerning Human Understanding*.

LENIN, VLADIMIR ILLYCH

1870–1924

Undoubtedly the most influential exponent of the ideas of **Marx** and **Engels,** Lenin, founder of the Bolshevik party and leader of the October Revolution, led the Soviet government until his retirement due to ill-health in 1922. Trained as a lawyer he turned the theoretical words of Marx and Engels into the practical deeds that led to the formation of the Soviet Republic. His voluminous essays are probably best exemplified by his call-to-arms message in *What is to be Done?*

> ### *What was required…*
> ### *was a determined drive to make*
> ### *the peasantry both class-conscious*
> ### *and revolutionary*

Under the Tsars, Lenin was twice exiled, together with his wife Nadezhda Krupsakaya, for a total of ten years, and these years he spent in Europe, particularly England, Switzerland and France. After observing political events in Europe, Lenin came to the conclusion that the revolution in Russia would have to take a different path. He argued that as the Russian people had no tradition of democracy, the revolution required a 'vanguard': an elite cadre of intellectuals and politically conscious ideologists that would be the leading group of the proletariat.

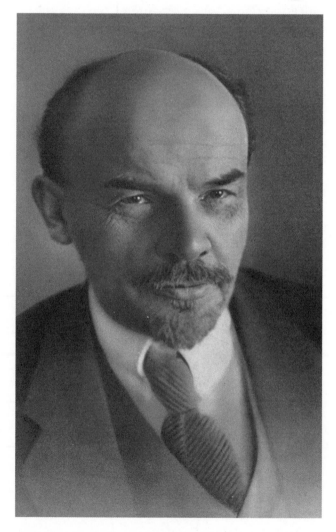

One of the most significant ideas that Lenin contributed to Marxism was that of the need for a revolutionary vanguard to lead the proletariat.

Leader of the Bolshevik Revolution in 1917, Lenin remained in power until 1922, when he suffered a stroke.

However, Lenin felt that, left to the Russian peasantry, the theoretical and organizational problems of running the socialist nation could never be solved. Commentators have suggested that in his European travels, Lenin had become exasperated by the endless controversies and petty arguments within the revolutionary movement and that it was this that persuaded him of the inefficacy of the democratic process. Indeed, in *What is to be Done?*, Lenin opens with an attack on the constant calls for the 'freedom of criticism' by the leftist Marxists. 'Freedom,' Lenin exclaims, 'is a grand word, but under the banner of freedom for industry the most predatory wars were waged, under the banner of freedom of labour, the working people were robbed. The modern use of the term "freedom of criticism" contains the same inherent falsehood.' In the same introduction, he complains, 'the new "critical" trend in socialism is nothing more nor less than a new variety of opportunism…"freedom of criticism" means freedom to introduce bourgeois ideas and bourgeois elements into socialism'. With that pronouncement, it might fairly be argued, the concept of freedom in Soviet politics ended.

Instead, what was required, Lenin saw, was a determined drive to make the peasantry both class-conscious and revolutionary. In his writings, therefore, he pursued an aggressive style in which he proclaimed no one could be politically impartial. The idea that philosophy should be non-partisan was a bourgeois idea professed to keep the proletariat in place. The so-called analytic 'objectivity' espoused by the positivist philosophers like **Mach**, was nothing more than the means by which imperialist forces defended their bourgeois class interests and justified the policies of the ruling class. The means by which Lenin reached this conclusion has, alas, been historically proven to rest

The proletariat, in line with traditional Marxist ideas, must form the basis of absolute rule, but their democratic voice would be expressed by the vanguard, who alone had the vision and ideology to lead the country with competence and skill.

Famously, Trotsky objected to the concentration of power into an elite which, he foresaw, would have the dire consequences that ensued under Stalinism.

on a complete misinterpretation of the scientific discoveries of his day.

Nevertheless, Lenin maintains that philosophy cannot stand apart from the social conflicts in which it is situated. Since society consists in mutually hostile classes, any system of thought, scientific or philosophical, must have arisen out of, and reflect the interests of, those classes. Lenin writes, 'To expect science to be impartial in a wage-slave society is as foolishly naïve as to expect impartiality from manufacturers on the question of whether workers' wages ought not to be increased by decreasing the profits of capital.' The politicizing of philosophy and science would be

The revolution required a 'vanguard': an elite cadre of intellectuals and politically conscious ideologists that would be the leading group of the proletariat

extended to every arena of Russian life. Such was the force and vigour of Lenin's brand of Marxism, based as it was on a dictatorial elite, that it would come to deserve its own name in the history of communism, Marxism-Leninism.

▌ ESSENTIAL READING ▌

What is to be Done? (1902)
In this pamphlet, Lenin calls for the formation of a vanguard party to lead the working class to revolution. Without this party, Lenin argues, the working class would be satisfied with trade unionism. The pamphlet was partly responsible for the split between the Mensheviks and Lenin's party, the Bolsheviks.

State and Revolution (1917)
This book, written just a few months before Lenin's party took power in Russia, discusses the role of the state in capitalist society, describing it as a tool for class oppression. Democracy, he says, is merely a cloak of respectability, but does not alter the ruling class's stranglehold. The only remedy is socialist revolution. He describes the progress of the revolution, the need for a dictatorship of the proletariat, followed by the 'higher stage of communist society' when individual freedom is allowed to be expressed at its fullest.

Lenin pictured with Stalin in 1919 during the 'Red Terror' that followed the Revolution. Stalin, along with Kamenev and Zenoviev, took power of the ruling Communist Party after Lenin's stroke in 1922.

LEVI-STRAUSS, CLAUDE

1908–

Levi-Strauss was elected to the Académie Française in 1973, and is shown here wearing the institution's traditional costume.

Belgian-born anthropologist, Levi-Strauss is famous for his structuralist anthropology which he applied, using the ideas of **Saussure,** to the study of myths. His best-known works are *The Raw and the Cooked* and *The Elementary Structures of Kinship*. Brought up in Paris, Levi-Strauss had an early interest in philosophy, along with **de Beauvoir** and **Sartre**, but

> *Myths are frameworks…*
> *in which human societies*
> *encode certain universal*
> *problems*

in 1935 went to Brazil to study sociology and anthropology. It was as a result of his many encounters with South American tribal cultures that he would develop his structuralist thesis of myths but also, by extension, of the human mind.

Borrowing Saussure's distinction between 'langue' and 'parole' (the common structure of language and the actual use of language by a speaker, respectively), Levi-Strauss took to analysing the variety of myths he came across in different cultures. He realized that the content of the myth, like the 'parole' of linguistics, was unnecessary to the study of the structure of the myth, and that myths across different cultures, though distinct in content, shared a universal structure.

Levi-Strauss explains the genealogy of myth as one of continual evolution and adaptation of a structure whose content is irrelevant. He rejects the view of sociologists and psychologists before him, who thought myths were timeless, meaningful stories whose significance could be traced back to some original story. Rather he maintains that the content of myths only have significance in their transformations from one myth into another. In consequence, Levi-Strauss tells us, the identity of a myth consists in the sum total of its variants through time.

From this viewpoint he goes on to claim that myths are frameworks, or structures, in which human societies encode certain universal problems. He notes that in one South American culture there is a corpus of myths that use culinary themes to symbolize the transformation from nature, the 'raw', to culture, the 'cooked'. Similarly, another corpus of myths uses dress and costume, the hiding of nakedness, to represent the development of society; yet another focuses on women as representing nature, men as representing culture. Levi-Strauss thus identifies a number of oppositions in human mythic structures – raw/cooked, naked/dressed, male/female, all of which encode a universal dualism in human thought, that between nature and culture.

As an example, Levi-Strauss engages in a detailed analysis of the Oedipus myth in which Oedipus unknowingly slays his father and marries his mother to become king. **Freud** made much use of the myth in his psychoanalytic theory. Consistent with his method, Levi-Strauss insists that Freud's reworking

Levi-Strauss detected the similarity of myths across many different cultures, concluding that they dealt with certain universal problems.

of the myth is just another transformation of the story into a modern myth, and thus belongs to the identity of the whole story. According to Levi-Strauss, Freud's reworking of it is just another way of expressing the dualism of nature and culture. Man must suppress his natural desires and conform to rules in order to create a stable society.

Ultimately, what he draws from his analysis is the idea that language encodes certain dualistic elements common to human experience. Levi-Strauss' program is, at root, supposed to be a scientific one that will clear away the inessential details of how different cultures encode problems and leave the fundamental structures and their relationships exposed. He comes to the conclusion that the Western dualisms of subject/object, and mind/matter, are just another version of a myth, like the raw and the cooked, which do not name any essential metaphysical categories, but merely signify an anthropological curiosity. The dualism that they represent is simply that of an individual in contrast with its environment. For Levi-Strauss, what remains once we get down to the level of structure and relations, is merely the actions and words of a physical organism in a physical environment. The transformations of myth come down to nothing more than structural facts about the human body according to how sense-organs transmit data from the environment. What his work does, claims Levi-Strauss, is give us a clear approach to a science of human activity.

‖ ESSENTIAL READING ‖

The Elementary Structures of Kinship (1949)
This work, based on Levi-Strauss' anthropological studies, looks at how people organize their families. By examining relationships within families from a structural point of view, Levi-Strauss was able to demonstrate how relationships within families from very different cultures were based on the same basic kinship structures.

The Raw and the Cooked (1964)
This landmark work of structuralist anthropology looks at a collection of almost 200 myths from tropical South America and uses this as a basis for a new structural approach to the study of mythology. Levi-Strauss argues that myths cannot be understood in isolation but only as part of a 'myth system'. He undertakes a structural analysis of this particular myth system by examining the underlying structure of relationships between the elements of the stories rather than the looking at their content. Although some of Levi-Strauss's connections can seem implausible, his work has become very influential in the study of mythology.

LOCKE, JOHN

1632–1704

In his day, John Locke was an important political figure and author of the liberal exposition *Two Treatises of Government*. An associate of the Earl of Shaftesbury, Locke spent time in exile in Holland, returning to England after the 'Glorious Revolution' of 1688. It is for his views on the nature of human knowledge, however, in his *Essay Concerning Human Understanding* that he is remembered in modern philosophy. Twenty years in the writing, the book was to exert such an influence on the next 100 years of Western thought that its author is considered by many to be the greatest British philosopher of all time. The works of **Berkeley**, **Kant** and **Hume** are all direct successors to Locke's *Essay*.

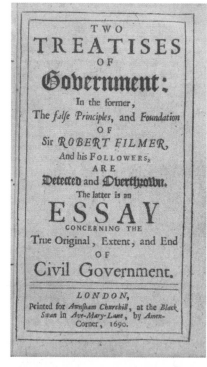

Locke's *Two Treatises of Government*, which criticized hereditary power and other traditional privileges, was first published anonymously in 1690.

influenced by the scientific turn of his day, and a personal friend of two renowned contemporary scientists, Robert Boyle and Isaac **Newton**, Locke's intent was to set the foundations of human knowledge on a sound scientific footing. He had read with great interest **Descartes**' *Meditations*, but rejected the rationalist philosophy that underpinned its conclusions. For Locke, there could be no innate knowledge: rather, everything we know must be derived from experience, through the actions of the physical world on our sense organs. This is the view now known as empiricism, a view still central, in essence if not detail, to the philosophies of **Quine** and other modern thinkers. Locke's detractors, the rationalists (see Descartes, Berkeley, **Leibniz**)

The subject of the *Essay,* as given in the title, is the nature of human understanding, that is, the very way in which the human mind collects, organizes, classifies and ultimately makes judgements based on data received through the senses. Greatly with whom the empiricists battled for ideological supremacy throughout the 17th and 18th centuries, have their modern counterparts in the supporters of Noam **Chomsky** and his philosophy of innate, or generative, grammar.

metaph IV.

Locke was a key pre-Enlightenment figure, his ideas exerting a huge influence over the later philosophers Berkeley and Hume.

Locke states that the mind at birth is like a blank slate, or tabula rasa, waiting to be written on by the world of experience. All human knowledge is derived from ideas presented to the mind by the world of experience. However, these ideas can be classified into two general sorts. There are complex ideas and simple ideas. Simple ideas are the immediate products of sensory stimulation, examples would be 'yellow', 'bitter', 'warm', 'round', 'hard' and so on. Complex ideas are constructions that are made out of simple ideas, and are the product of internal mental operations. These include all our ideas of familiar material objects, such as tables, chairs, cats, dogs and horses. But complex ideas need not represent anything real in the world. This accounts for ideas like that of a unicorn, a complex idea itself made up from conjoining other complex ideas, such as 'horse' and 'horn'.

Among Locke's simple ideas is a distinction between those that are primary qualities of objects and others that are secondary qualities. The distinction divides those qualities thought to be essential and inherent to all objects and those that are apparent only on account of the effect objects have on our senses. Primary qualities are those such as solidity, extension, shape, motion or rest, and number. Secondary qualities are those such as colour, scent and taste. These are secondary because, according to Locke, they do not inhere in objects themselves, but are causally produced only in our minds by the effect of an object's primary qualities upon our senses. Another way of conceiving them is to say primary qualities are objective (really exist) and secondary ones subjective (only exist in the minds of observers). In the popular conundrum of whether a falling tree makes a sound when there is no one to hear it, Locke's view would be that the falling tree creates vibrations in the air, but that there is no 'sound' strictly speaking, since sound is not a 'real' or primary quality. This view, sometimes called 'scientific essentialism', leads to the metaphysical conclusion, plausible to many modern thinkers, that without a perceiving mind, there is no such thing in the world as colour or sound, sweet or sour and so on; but there are really such things as shape, extension and solidity, independently of whether anyone perceives them or not.

Without a perceiving mind, there is no such thing in the world as colour or sound

‖ ESSENTIAL READING ‖

Two Treatises of Government (1690)

These two treatises are important in the history of political ideas. In the first, Locke criticizes hereditary power, absolute monarchy and the divine right of kings. In the second he argues that, while subjects have a duty to obey their rulers, rulers also have duties towards their subjects, and the only legitimate government is one that governs with the consent of those who are governed by it.

An Essay Concerning Human Understanding (1690)

Locke's greatest philosophical work, and the foundation of empiricism, the *Essay* set out 'to inquire into the original, certainty and extent of human knowledge', and to determine how ideas arise in the mind. It includes a discussion of one's knowledge of oneself, the world, and God.

MACH, ERNST
1838–1916

Austrian scientist and philosopher of science, Mach is widely regarded as the most direct influence on the Vienna Circle group of philosophers (see **Schlick** and **Carnap**) and largely responsible for the emergence of logical positivism in the 20th century.

'We know only one source which directly reveals scientific facts – our senses'

Mach railed against metaphysical conjectures that had no basis in sense experience, declaring, 'We know only one source which directly reveals scientific facts – our senses'. Accordingly, all that can be said about reality is whatever is contained in a complete description of sense experience. Anything other than that goes beyond the evidence and therefore beyond justification. The upshot of this, Mach tells us, is that science should be reconstructed as an account of the facts given in sense-experience.

Echoing the thought of William **James**, Mach insists in pragmatic style that, 'According to our conception, natural laws are a product of our psychological need to feel at home with nature; all concepts transcending sensation are to be justified as helping us to understand, control and predict

As well as his work on logical positivism, Mach also studied the properties of wave dynamics, optics and mechanics.

our environment, and different conceptual systems may be used to this end in different cultures and at different times with equal propriety'.

Foreshadowing **Quine**'s philosophy of science, Mach goes on to insist that, given two empirically equivalent conceptual schemes, theory choice is not arbitrary, but should rather be conditioned by considerations of simplicity, consistency and depth. Simplicity is a commonly praised virtue of scientific theories, though there has rarely been given any good philosophical reason to prefer it, other than by invoking the principle of 'Occam's Razor' (see **William of Occam**). Consistency and depth are requirements that insist on a lack of contradiction and the greatest possible explanatory force.

In line with Mach's insistence that scientific laws are merely conceptual tools, it follows that one should not talk of proof in science. To 'prove a theory' implies that one has shown that it must somehow, necessarily, be true but on Mach's conception of science the best a theory can do is order our knowledge so as to help us most effectively 'control and predict' our environment.

An upshot of Mach's philosophy of science, and one he does not fail to notice himself, is that the unobservable 'posits' of our scientific theories, items such as atoms, electrons, fields and waves, cannot be accorded any substantial existence. Indeed, Mach says to accord any material status to such concepts is to invoke 'the sham ideas of the old metaphysics'. The idea is resurgent in Quine, who claims the posits of our physical theory have no greater epistemological footing than 'Homer's gods'. Mach even goes so far in his *The Science of Mechanics* as to work out the content of **Newton**'s mechanics without postulating absolute space and time, force or any other 'transcendent' notions.

Mach's extreme empiricism, however, has implications that seem to engender anti-realism, or idealism. For by relying only on what is given in perceptual experience, Mach is either denying the metaphysical reality of a mind-independent world, or he is denying the possibility that we can ever have any knowledge of such a world, confining it to the same 'noumenal' realm that **Kant** was forced to postulate. Indeed, even in his own time, Mach was criticized by **Lenin** as 'an enemy of materialism.'

‖ ESSENTIAL READING ‖

Contributions to the Analysis of Sensations (1897)
In this groundbreaking philosophical work, Mach advanced the idea that all knowledge is derived from sensation. From this he concluded that no statement can be allowable unless it can be verified by observation. This led him to reject such metaphysical concepts as Newton's absolute time and space, preparing the ground for **Einstein**'s *Theory of Relativity*.

MACHIAVELLI, NICCOLÒ

1467–1527

Florentine-born philosopher of the Italian Renaissance, Machiavelli was a diplomat and dramatist, but is best remembered for his hugely influential and notorious work of political theory, *The Prince*, which has made his name synonymous with political machinations. Providing a detailed analysis of successful, if on occasion immoral, political techniques, Machiavelli's text is still used today by students of both philosophy and politics. In *The Prince*, Machiavelli concentrates on those techniques a successful politician must use if he is to achieve his political ends, without regard to the moral justification of the means thereby employed. Often criticized by detractors for its lack of moral sensibility, it is nevertheless a work of great intellectual integrity and consistency.

In *The Prince*, Machiavelli considers how best a leader can achieve his ends once he has determined that the ends he has identified are worthwhile. Never has the phrase 'the ends justify the means' been more appropriately applied than it is to Machiavellian technique. The book is almost entirely practical, rarely speculating on the rightness or wrongness of the methods adumbrated therein.

Nonetheless, *The Prince* does contain certain theses about which political ends are good. Machiavelli thinks there are three primary political 'goods':

national security, national independence, and a strong constitution. Beyond this, he is almost entirely concerned with practical questions of how to go about securing political success. It is vain to pursue a good political end with inadequate means, for it will surely fail. One must pursue one's convictions with strength and courage if one is to be successful, employing whatever means necessary.

> *One must pursue one's convictions with strength and courage if one is to be successful, employing whatever means necessary*

The heart of Machiavelli's teachings consists in the manipulation of others, including the populace, for power. To this end, although Machiavelli does not teach that virtue is good in itself, it can often serve one's political ends to appear to be virtuous. This is perhaps the doctrine that has caused most outrage against Machiavellian thought. But Machiavelli himself is unconcerned with such weak and even hypocritical sensibility. If, as we have said, one's ends are good in themselves, all that matters is that one brings them about; in order to do this, Machiavelli tells us, one must have more power than one's opponents. Without doubt, *The Prince* is a work meant only for those that have the fibre to take this fact, surely true, however unpleasant, seriously.

Although *The Prince* is unflinching in its teachings, it must be read alongside Machiavelli's longer and more balanced work, the *Discourses*, if his own views are to be fairly understood. In the *Discourses*, he provides more detailed background as to what he thinks makes a good and successful constitution. His political ideal is the republic run by the Princes, leaders of the principalities, but

Machiavelli's advice to leaders in *The Prince* is pragmatic, if sometimes ruthless.

held in check by both the noblemen and ordinary citizens, all of whom share a part in the constitution. As **Russell** rightly says in his commentary on Machiavelli, the *Discourses* might easily be read by an 18th-century liberal without occasioning much surprise or disagreement. Machiavelli has no time for tyrannies, not because people have an inalienable right to freedom, but because tyrannies are less stable, more cruel and more inconstant than governments held in esteem by a reasonably content population. It is the achievement of such a government that is Machiavelli's prime political concern.

‖ ESSENTIAL READING ‖

As well as the two major works listed below, Machiavelli also wrote an extended series of dialogues entitled *The Art of War*.

The Prince (1532)

Completed in 1513 but not published until 1532, this is Machiavelli's best-known work. A textbook on the art of leadership, its amoral stance on how to secure and hold on to political power has given us the term 'Machiavellian'.

The Discourses (1531)

Written about the same time as *The Prince*, *The Discourses* give a rather different or perhaps more complete picture of Machiavelli's political opinions. Nominally a commentary on the works of the Roman historian Livy, they are a defence of republican government, taking ancient Rome as a model.

MALEBRANCHE, NICOLAS

1638–1715

French philosopher, theologian and chief developer of Cartesian thought. Although his principal work, *The Search after Truth,* covers a wide variety of topics, Malebranche is remembered principally for his theory of occasionalism as a solution to **Descartes**' mind-body problem.

In Cartesian thought, the mind ('res cogitans') and the body ('res extensa') are two distinct and utterly different kinds of thing. In fact, in Cartesian ontology there are only three kinds of substance: mind, matter and God. Descartes insisted – as part of his proof of the 'cogito' – that the mind must be utterly distinct from corporeal things. However, this immediately leads to a problem of causal interaction. Clearly we are aware that our minds and bodies interact. When my body is hurt, I feel pain; equally, when I decide to lift my arm, my arm will indeed rise. If Descartes is correct in his assertion that mind and body are distinct, the causal connection between the two is left mysterious. How is it possible that a non-physical thing, the mind, can be the cause of changes in physical things?

Malebranche's occasionalism maintained that all causal power emanates from God.

Malebranche's solution relies on his theological beliefs. According to Malebranche, individual minds are merely limitations of the one universal mind that is God. They have no power to cause anything whatsoever in the physical world. Nor, however, do physical objects have the power to cause movements in other physical objects, since to cause something to happen is to know how to bring that happening about. Accordingly, claimed Malebranche, the only causal power is God.

Whenever we think we are doing something, God is really doing it for us

In order to account for the appearance of causal interaction between minds and bodies, an analogy put forward by one of Malebranche's contemporaries, Geulincx, will be useful. Suppose there are two clocks, running in perfect harmony: when clock A points to the hour, clock B will sound the chime. If you saw only clock A but heard clock B you might be led to believe that clock A caused clock B to sound. So, claimed Malebranche, it is with the mind and body. They are like two clocks wound up by God and kept in synchronicity with each other through divine acts. Whenever I will to move my arm, God causes my arm to move on that occasion. Whenever we think we are doing something, God is really doing it for us.

The doctrine of occasionalism solved the problem of mind-body interaction for Cartesian philosophers (although it is unlikely that Descartes would have accepted it), but proved unpopular with other thinkers. Alternative solutions to the problem, however, have not been forthcoming, and philosophers eventually sought to dissolve the problem by rejecting the

The title page to a 1753 edition of Malebranche's most famous work, *The Search After Truth.*

dualism of mind and body. This, in principle, is **Spinoza**'s solution and is also the impetus behind materialism in the philosophy of mind (that view which claims the mind is really just the brain, or a function of the brain, and consists in nothing other than matter or the arrangement of matter in a certain specified way: see also Gilbert **Ryle**). Faced with the unacceptability of Malebranche's occasionalism, and with **Hume**'s scepticism concerning causation in general, some Cartesians have tried to defer the problem by claiming that since causation is not understood very well in any event, it is not a special problem for Cartesian philosophy, but a problem for philosophy in general. Though this may be true, it is unlikely that any reasonably successful theory of causation would support the Cartesian distinction between two different kinds of substance, mind and matter.

The Search after Truth (1674)

In this defining work, Malebranche outlines his doctrine of occasionalism – the view that God is the true cause of all events, including the actions of our bodies and minds. He also considers all the possible ways in which the human mind might know the nature of things. He concludes it is our soul's connection to God that allows us to see the perfect ideas that are the archetypes of imperfect created beings, and this is what gives us insight into their nature – but only if God wills it.

MARX, KARL

1818–1883

Born in Treves, Germany, Marx lived the latter part of his life in England and is buried at Highgate cemetery in London. His work, along with that of **Engels**, profoundly influenced political events in Russia and Eastern Europe in the 20th century, and he was the darling of both European and American intellectuals up until the 1960s. His most influential works are *The Communist Manifesto* and *Das Kapital.*

Marx's philosophy owes a great deal to **Hegel**, from whom he borrowed the notion of 'dialectic'. Marx, however, rejects Hegel's idealism and his notion of truth unfolding towards the Absolute, in favour of a purely atheistic 'dialectical materialism'.

For Marx, the fundamental condition of humanity is the need to convert the raw material of the natural world into the goods necessary for survival. Consequently, production, or in other words economics, is the primary conditioning factor of life. Taking a historical perspective, Marx records, 'The hand-mill gives a society with the feudal lord; the steam-mill a society with the industrial capitalist'. According to dialectical materialism, there is a three-sided conflict between economic classes. The landowners created by feudalism were opposed by the rise of the middle classes, forcing a 'synthesis', that is, a new economic class, the

Marx's ideas were to have a world-changing effect, through the foundation of revolutionary Communism.

industrial employers of capitalism. However, the new 'thesis' of capitalism generates the antithetical force of the proletariat, or working classes. The synthesis that Marx envisages from this conflict, the inevitable dialectical outcome, is socialism.

His reasons for supposing that socialism is the necessary outcome of the modern economic conflict are not, though such may appear at times to be the case from his passionate revolutionary invective, predicated on ethical judgements about what is best, or right, or just. Rather, Marx insists that socialism is necessarily the most efficient means of securing that which human beings strive for, namely the goods required for survival. Since socialism is the most efficient way to ensure productivity, the progress of 'dialectical materialism' has no need of moral sentiments. Socialism is, according to Marx, a natural outcome of the economic conditions operating on the human being.

It is at this point that the reversal of Hegel's idealism in Marx's materialism can be seen in purely philosophical terms. Whereas Hegel's history of ideas insists that it is the dialectic progress of concepts – developments in human understanding – that fuel social and political change, Marx asserts that it is transformations in economics that give rise to new ways of thinking, to the development of ideas. This reflects Marx's underlying view

In London, Marx and Engels collaborated on *The Communist Manifesto*, published in 1848.

The fundamental condition of humanity is the need to convert the raw material of the natural world into the goods necessary for survival

concerning epistemology and phenomenology. For Marx, the mind does not exist as a passive subject in an external world, as the prevailing empiricist tradition emanating from **Locke** would have it. Along with **Kant**, Marx shares the view that the mind is actively engaged with the objects of knowledge.

But whereas Kant only went so far as to propose that our psychological apparatus imposes certain structures on the flux of experience, Marx held that the subject and object of experience are in a continual process of adaptation. We must order our experience in practical ways, so as to make it useful to our survival. In modern terminology what Marx is proposing is a version of instrumentalism or pragmatism, but at the more basic phenomenological level, as in the existentialist phenomenology of **Heidegger**, rather than at the scientific or epistemological level, as in **Dewey** and **James**.

This Chinese Communist poster shows (left to right) Karl Marx, Vladimir Lenin and Mao Zedong.

▌ ESSENTIAL READING ▌

Paris Manuscripts (1844)
Not intended for publication in its present form, this is Marx's first attempt at the analysis of political economy.

The German Ideology (1846)
This was written jointly by Marx and Friedrich Engels, and published posthumously. It includes a comprehensive and detailed exposition of Marx's materialist philosophy of history.

The Communist Manifesto (1848)
Perhaps Marx and Engel's most famous work, it starts from the premise that 'the history of all hitherto existing societies is the history of class struggle', asserting also that the final struggle would result in the victory of the proletariat and produce a classless society.

A Contribution to the Critique of Political Economy (1859)
In the preface of this book, Marx expounds his materialist philosophy of history and explains how he reached these conclusions.

Das Kapital (3 volumes: 1867, 1884, 1893)
Das Kapital ('Capital') is Marx's masterpiece, once described as 'the Bible of the working class'. A work of political economy, it provides a detailed account of the workings and failings of capitalism. Only the first volume was published in Marx's lifetime; the second and third volumes were edited and published by Engels.

MERLEAU-PONTY, MAURICE

1908–1961

174

French philosopher Maurice Merleau-Ponty is closely associated with the existentialism of Jean-Paul **Sartre**. However, although he, too, believed in the primacy of perception in the analysis of human existence, he disagreed with many of the more radical conclusions of Sartre's existentialism concerning freedom of choice, personal responsibility, 'anguish' and 'despair'. Like Sartre, Merleau-Ponty was a phenomenologist: in other words, he was concerned with the embodied experience (the conscious experience of human beings), without reference to the question of whether what is experienced is objectively real. Merleau-Ponty attempted a new way of explaining embodied experience without resorting to the traditional approaches of modern philosophy, namely empiricism and rationalism, which he regarded as equally flawed and unsatisfactory.

Where empiricism declares that all knowledge is derived from the experience of the senses, rationalism claims that all knowledge is *a priori* – already known to the subject prior to experience – because it has been derived through reason. Neither system is satisfactory for Merleau-Ponty, in part because they fail to resolve Meno's paradox. Meno is a character in one of **Plato**'s dialogues, who poses the following dilemma to Plato: 'How can you look for something when you don't know what it is?

Even if you find the thing, how will you know that what you have found is the thing you didn't know?'

Breaking away from the dualism of empiricism and rationalism, Merleau-Ponty sees the body as existing in a third state, between subject and object

Empiricism is dualistic in nature, in that it separates the subject (consciousnessness) from the object (things outside of consciousness). But, as Meno says, if the objective world is outside human experience, how will we know that we've found what we're looking for once we find it? The idea of the transcendent as something separate from us encourages empiricists to try to perceive the world in a hard-edged and determinate way – as a series of atomistic sense impressions – in order to discern the truth in it. But that is not how we actually experience the world. Our actual experience is rich and multilayered, and always within context. Empiricists must put these atomistic sense impressions into some sort of order to form a meaningful perception. But how do they know that the way they put them together in the mind (the subject) is the way they actually appear in the objective world? The world therefore remains unknowable to them, and Meno's paradox is not resolved.

Rationalism is also dualistic in nature, separating out subject and object. It also sees truth as something determinate and decontextualized, although with rationalism, truth can be determined through the application of reason alone. And in this regard, rationalism also falls foul of Meno's paradox: if knowledge exists a priori, then why bother searching for it? In Merleau-Ponty's view, rationalism is at fault for denying the importance of sensual experience – or perception – in the acquisition of knowledge.

Merleau-Ponty's epistemology gives primacy to perception. Rationalism is at fault for denying this, and empiricism is at fault for its erroneous representation of perception as a series of atomistic sense impressions. Merleau-Ponty prefers to characterize perception as a subject-object dialogue, experienced through the 'lived body'. By the 'lived body', he means that consciousness is not something that exists purely in our minds, but is experienced in and through our bodies. He rejects **Descartes**' claim that the body is simply a machine that is manipulated by the mind. Merleau-Ponty does not deny the

Merleau-Ponty's phenomenology argues that a subject-object dialogue is the foundation of human experience.

physiological reality of the body as a set of separate parts that work together like a machine. But he is saying that the body must be understood as something more than a set of separate parts; it must be understood as a whole, as it is lived. To demonstrate this idea, he gives the example of a phantom limb. If the body was just a machine, it would go on functioning without an amputated limb. Yet amputees often continue to feel a missing limb and still feel the call to use it. The body is therefore something that is lived *through* in relation to possibilities in the world.

Through this idea of the lived body, one can see how experience might be described as a subject-object dialogue. Nothing is experienced independently of one's experience as an embodied being in the world. Any meaning we derive from our experiences is by virtue of our embodied state. It allows us to perceive things as hot or cold, big or small, near or far. Our experience of the spatial is wholly based on our body's location in space. Similarly our experience of time is based on our body's inability to be anywhere but the present. This is what gives us our sense of the past and future as beyond our reach, and of the ever-unfolding nature of experience. Through the subject-object dialogue, we experience the world in a rich, multi-layered way, and each experience arrives in context with everything that surrounds it in space and everything that has preceded it in time.

With his idea of the lived body and the subject-object dialogue, Merleau-Ponty breaks out of the dualism of empiricism and rationalism, which he sees as the fatal weakness of those systems. He sees the body as existing in a third state, between subject and object. And in doing so, he resolves Meno's paradox. How do we know that we have found what we are looking for if we do not yet know what it is? Because the embodied experience gives it meaning. At first, our perceptions are fuzzy and ambiguous, but as we become more bodily engaged with the world, things become more defined and certain.

Running through all of Merleau-Ponty's work is his emphasis on the primacy of perception. In his words, '[the phenomenologist returns] to the world which precedes [scientific description], [the world] of which science always speaks, and in relation to which every scientific characterization is an abstract and derivative sign language, as is geography to the countryside.'

‖ ESSENTIAL READING ‖

Phenomenology of Perception (1945)

In this, his most significant work, Merleau-Ponty rejects the rationalist and empiricist approaches to perception for their overly rigid conception of the relationship between subject and object. He argues that there is an interdependence between subject and object through his idea of the 'lived body'. Our physical state, he says, is more fundamental than our capacity to reason. He does not reject analytical approaches, however, just argues that they are of secondary significance compared to the body's practical experience of the world.

MILL, JOHN STUART

1806–1873

Taught exclusively by his father, James Mill, the young John Stuart was something of a childhood genius, learning Greek at the age of three, and assisting his father in writings on political economics by his early teens. Around the age of twenty he had a breakdown, and began to react against the intellectual influence of both his father and Jeremy **Bentham**. Mill produced his most important work, *A System of Logic,* in mid-life, but is principally remembered now for his short and much later work *Utilitarianism,* published in 1863.

Morality, for Mill, consists in the pursuit of happiness and the reduction of pain.

the absence of pain; by unhappiness, pain, and the privation of pleasure'.

Mill recognized two failings in Bentham's earlier theory. In calculating the relative amounts of pain and pleasure in his 'felicific calculus', Bentham had weighted each unit of good or harm equally. Mill saw that pleasure cannot be reduced to a mere quantitative analysis without taking into account certain qualitative aspects. The pain of losing one's favourite pet is unlikely to be equivalent to the pain of losing a relative, but then on other occasions and for some other people, perhaps it may be; Bentham's calculus made little room for such distinctions. Secondly, Mill insisted that some pleasures were of greater value than others. He famously writes that 'it is better to be a human being dissatisfied than a pig satisfied; better to be a Socrates dissatisfied than a fool satisfied'.

Mill's utilitarianism is a refinement of the views advanced both by his father and Bentham. Like Bentham, Mill maintains that the fundamental guide to moral action should be the maximization of pleasure and the minimization of pain. Mill formulated this as 'the Greatest Happiness Principle', which holds that 'actions are right in proportion as they tend to promote happiness, wrong as they tend to produce the reverse of happiness. By happiness is intended pleasure, and

Accordingly, Mill distinguishes between 'higher' and 'lower' pleasures, to be taken into account in the utilitarian calculation.

'Actions are right in proportion as they tend to promote happiness, wrong as they tend to produce the reverse of happiness'

The utilitarian ethic has a strong intuitive appeal due to its simplicity, but it has nevertheless, particularly in Mill's exposition, come in for wide-ranging and sustained criticism. However, much of the criticism that is directed at Mill in particular (rather than the theory in general) results from taking his utilitarianism out of the context of his overall thought. For example, modern commentators have complained that Mill's ethical principle is too demanding. If every action must tend toward the increase of pleasure and the decrease of pain, it looks as though even our ordinary day-to-day behaviour turns out to be immoral. Surely, if I intend to live sincerely according to Mill's ethic, I should donate all of my disposable income to charity, and think about the wider consequences of my chosen employment. Is everything I do promoting happiness at the expense of unhappiness?

Such universal altruism may be meritorious; it is not, however, a doctrine or consequence of Mill's philosophy. His whole system is one of radical liberalism. He makes it quite clear that we should only be concerned with morality in those aspects of life that require sanctions to deter specific kinds of conduct. Otherwise a person is morally and legally free to pursue their life as they see fit. Critics of Mill have repeatedly overlooked that in the wider context of his philosophy he clearly distinguishes between what is right and what is good. Mill nowhere suggests that we are at all times compelled to act for the good; only that when questions of right and wrong arise, what is right is what is good, and what is good is that which promotes the greatest happiness of all.

▌ ESSENTIAL READING ▌

System of Logic (1843)
In this work, Mill argues that the laws of logic and mathematics are empirical in nature, being generalizations from experience rather than known a priori. The book also contains a consideration of induction and deduction, and of free will.

On Liberty (1859)
Here, Mill defends the rights of individuals and minorities against governments, even democratically elected governments, arguing that 'the only purpose for which power can be rightfully exercised over any member of a civilized community, against his will, is to prevent harm to others'.

Utilitarianism (1861)
In this exposition of utilitarian moral theory, Mill sets out some significant improvements to Bentham's earlier version of utilitarianism, arguing that pleasures can differ not only quantitively but also qualitatively.

MONTAIGNE, MICHEL DE

1533–92

Michel de Montaigne was born into a wealthy French family. His humanist father provided him with an unusual childhood and education, which included, among other things, three years in the sole charge of a peasant family, the exclusive use of Latin, and almost constant exposure to music. He attended a prestigious boarding school near Bordeaux, studied law in Toulouse, and began an eleven-year career at the regional and national courts. On his father's death in 1568 he returned to the family chateau, and devoted the remaining decades of his life to thinking and writing.

The reflections which Montaigne recorded in his three books of essays were – unusually for his time – rarely concerned with man's relationship to God. Montaigne was more interested in secular issues, in how he and other humans related to each other and the world. He brought immense erudition and a ceaselessly enquiring mind to a wide range of themes and subjects.

The new beliefs of the scientific revolution had not only undermined old beliefs, but also brought the very idea of knowing into question. If the old truths were no longer true, who was to say that the new ones would prove any more durable? In such a light, Montaigne realized, certainty was impossible to come by. Reason, it seemed, was not a universal standard, and a general scepticism seemed appropriate. In his essay *Apology for Raymond Sebond* he first used his famous motto – 'what do I know?'

He cites the famous case of Martin Guerre as an example. The real Guerre went off to war, and two years later another man returned in his place. The impostor had knowledge that only Guerre could have, and even Guerre's wife was fooled. If she could not be certain of her own husband, Montaigne argued, then what could humans be certain of?

> ## *Montaigne was engaged in a sort of dialogue with himself, which he commended to other individuals and cultures*

In *Apology for Raymond Sebond* Montaigne's scepticism is charged with negativity. Bereft of any hope of certainty, the sceptic is cast adrift in a sea of relativism. In many of his other essays the scepticism is given a much more positive aspect, becomes, in fact, a liberation from a mental world of false certainties. Despite his scepticism, Montaigne remained a practising Catholic. He saw no contradiction in this. On the contrary, he claimed that the belief in secular certainty – a lack of scepticism, in other words – made it harder to accept religious truths, which could only be justified through faith.

Montaigne applied his scepticism to both new truths and old. New scientific theories should be seen as contributions in an endless process of discovery, not as new mental shackles. Knowledge, he believed, was just as likely to stifle enquiry as promote it. The important thing was to keep talking, keep experiencing, and keep living. Intellectual enquiry should involve each individual in continually balancing opinions, in testing his or her own judgement. Philosophy, by his definition, was less a science than a way of life.

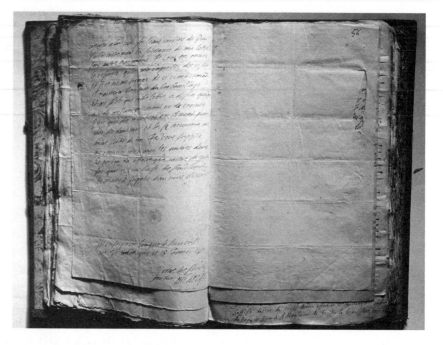

Montaigne's writings include a journal of his travels in Italy and a collection of letters, some of which are preserved at the Royal Palace in Monaco.

By denying certainties, scepticism is implicitly relativistic, and Montaigne certainly accepted the full implications of such relativism. There were no good reasons, he decided, for believing that humans were superior to other species. They were different, but there was no universal standard by which one could judged superior to another.

The same could be said of cultures. In his essay *On Custom,* he claims that 'the laws of conscience, which we say are born of nature, are born of custom. Each man, holding in inward veneration the opinions and behaviour approved and accepted around him…' Different cultures have different customs. In another essay, *On Cannibalism,* he attacked the notion that European culture was any

closer to God, truth or goodness than supposedly less developed cultures. The South American 'savages', he pointed out, only ate their dead. Europeans did the same in a less direct manner – at that time, European pharmacies made considerable use of human blood and body parts – and routinely applied torture to living bodies.

Montaigne only carried his cultural relativism so far. All customs were not equally acceptable, and individuals were not equally in thrall to the culture they inhabited. Here again, judgement was everything. Individuals could reflect on and evaluate the customs they lived by, and if necessary challenge them. Montaigne claimed that no universal standard was necessary, that individuals could look at different ways of doing things and then use their judgement as to which works best for those involved. However, he accepted that the idea

This statue of Montaigne at the Sorbonne in Paris commemorates him as a genial, learned sceptic and a key Renaissance philosopher.

of universal standards like 'reason' and 'nature' – standards which only God could truly define – might help humans in the exercise of their judgement. Montaigne's writings were not always consistent, which he would probably have regarded as a virtue. He was engaged in a sort of dialogue with himself, which he commended to other individuals and cultures.

Montaigne's influence has been widespread. His scepticism inspired many later thinkers, most notably **Pascal** and **Descartes**. The latter was also heavily influenced by Montaigne's notion of philosophical enquiry, which stressed self-education over school, and placed great value on the garnering of experience through travel. Shakespeare's *The Tempest* owed a great deal to the essay *On Cannibals*. More recently, Montaigne was considered the pioneer of cultural relativism by the anthropologist Claude **Levi-Strauss**, and his belief in the essential equality of species has contemporary echoes in the animal rights movement. His insistence that philosophy should move beyond self-referential jargon and immerse itself in normal life has inspired recent philosophers like **Rorty**. Montaigne's eloquent writing and evident love of enquiry caused Friedrich **Nietzsche** to comment: 'That such a man wrote has truly augmented the joy of living on earth.'

∥ ESSENTIAL READING ∥

Essays (1580, 1588 and 1595)

This publication contains all of Montaigne's writings. Montaigne wrote three 'books' of essays, and three recognized editions of his work were published before and shortly after his death. The first two 'books' were published in a single volume in 1580, and all three – the first two much reviewed – in a second volume in 1588. Recently published collections have often been less than complete – many, for example, omitting Montaigne's foremost exposition of scepticism, 'Apology for Raymond Sebond'.

MOORE, GEORGE EDWARD
1873–1958

British philosopher and contemporary of **Russell** and **Wittgenstein**, Moore used the analysis of language as his starting point in a so-called 'common-sense' philosophy. Moore's early work rejected both idealism and its chief rival empiricism, in favour of a realism which attempts to justify our ordinary claims to knowledge against the sceptical and outlandish views of philosophers. Moore's linguistic method also underlies his work in ethics, most notably propounded in his *Principia Ethica* of 1903. His other important works include *Ethics, Some Main Problems of Philosophy* and *Philosophical Papers*.

In Moore's view, we are entitled to our ordinary conceptions of how things are. Questions of meaning and truth hardly arise in ordinary language, inasmuch as we know how to use and understand the things we say. The only important questions are what Moore calls 'analysis of meanings', by which he intends to refer to a deeper level of reflection on the connections between concepts and their definitions. Such knowledge is not needed for everyday use, but is an essential method of philosophical analysis. Particularly, Moore finds, when dealing with the more outlandish of philosophical claims, which may turn out not to mean very much at all once analysed properly. This view was to have a striking influence on the development of Wittgenstein's later thought,

and indeed the work of Wittgenstein's now published as *On Certainty* can be seen as a direct response and development of Moore's 'common-sense' approach.

The question of whether something is good is always an 'open' question

According to Moore, any concept can be analyzed primarily in one of two ways. It can either be dissected into constituent parts, in other words into more elementary concepts, or it can be defined negatively by its relations to and distinctions from other concepts (this second idea is similar to that of the structuralists: see **Saussure**).

Moore goes on to use this method of analysis in his discussion of 'what is good?', a question he takes to be the central problem of ethics. In Moore's view 'good' is a concept that cannot be defined or analysed into constituent parts. It is analogous to the concept of 'yellow'. Moore says that 'good' is 'a simple notion, just as "yellow" is a simple notion; that, just as you cannot, by any manner of means, explain to anyone who does not already know it, what yellow is, so you cannot explain what good is'. Even though all things that are good might be pleasurable, Moore goes on to argue that although one can say of some natural property, like pleasure for instance, that it is good, this assertion can always meaningfully be followed by the question, why is it good? Moore famously claims that the question of whether something is good is always an 'open' question. To suppose otherwise is to commit what Moore called 'the naturalistic fallacy', the tendency of empiricist philosophers to confuse an idea of what is natural with what is good.

In *Principia Ethica,* Moore's view was that 'good' denotes some simple non-natural, (i.e. abstract in the Platonic sense) property of which we are intuitively aware. He rejects both **Kant**'s view that ethics is concerned with reason, and the utilitarian view (see **Mill**) that some natural property can be identified with 'the good', in favour of an ethics predicated on value judgements which are as distinct and mind-independent as any ordinary matter of fact. Value can never be defined in non-evaluative terms, hence the naturalistic fallacy. But in his later writings Moore abandoned the Platonic conception of value in favour of one in which value-judgements are really expressions of approval or emotion, a view later developed in detail in the 'prescriptivist' theory of R.M. Hare.

Moore is remembered for his defence of common sense against implausible sceptical arguments.

Moore's work in the philosophical analysis of meaning also pre-empted the ideas of J.L. **Austin**. 'Moore's paradox', as Wittgenstein called it, asserts that though it looks like a nonsense, there are contexts where the assertion, 'It is raining, but I don't believe it' makes sense. Moore's explanation of what appears to be a contradiction when we assert that a proposition is true but claim not to believe it draws a distinction between what is asserted and what is implied. To claim that it is raining makes an assertion which is either true or

At least some of our beliefs about the world are absolutely true, for example 'my body existed yesterday'

false. Someone making this assertion implies that they believe it. When they go on to assert 'but I don't believe it', they contradict not the original assertion but the original implication. Nevertheless, Moore realized, it is the contradiction between the assertion and the implication that gives the expression the appearance of nonsense. Such fine distinctions in meaning have only become apparent due to the centrality of linguistic analysis, of which Moore is an early exponent, to much recent philosophy and have helped solve some long-standing philosophical puzzles.

Moore's paradox focussed on the question of contradictory meaning in language, pre-empting Austin's work on linguistic analysis.

‖ ESSENTIAL READING ‖

Principia Ethica (1903)
In this major work of his early career, Moore criticizes the study of ethics for its assumption that goodness can be defined in terms of, say, pleasure or desire. Moore states that goodness is indefinable and therefore ethics cannot have a basis in natural science or even metaphysics.

A Defence of Common Sense (1925)
In this influential essay, Moore attacks the philosophy of scepticism by arguing that at least some of our beliefs about the world are absolutely true. His basis for this assertion is that these beliefs are common sense. One example of this is: 'My body existed yesterday.' He argues that any sceptical arguments against such an assertion were bound to be less plausible than the reasons we have to believe in it.

MOORE, GEORGE EDWARD

MORE, THOMAS
1478–1535

Sir Thomas More, friend and supporter of **Erasmus**, led a dangerous but incorruptible political life which would earn him the death penalty from the same King who once knighted him, Henry VIII. Unimpressed by Henry's solicitations, More's determined adherence to Catholic orthodoxy prevented him from recognizing either Henry's divorce from Catherine of Aragon or his subsequent self-appointment as head of the English Church in order to marry Anne Boleyn. Fortunately for the history of Western thought, More managed to complete his most important philosophical work, *Utopia*, in good time, 1518 in fact, before Henry took his head in 1535.

In More's *Utopia*, a traveller brings back tales of an island in the South Seas where everything is organized in the best possible way. The book takes the form of a dialogue, in which the traveller, Raphael Hythloday, divulges the wise ways of Utopia as he found them in the five years he spent there. More's vision of Utopia is a kind of Christian communism, in which there is no personal property, internal commerce or personal ambition. Each member of society works six hours a day regardless of their job. This, says More, is entirely satisfactory in terms of providing enough labour. For other societies only require the poor to work long and exhausting days because of the existence of the idle rich.

This portrait by Hans Holbein the Younger shows More in the robes of Lord Chancellor, a post he held from 1529 to 1532.

The Utopia provides for its citizens by means of a system of farms, each consisting of at least forty workers. There are intellectuals and governors in More's visionary society, but these are chosen by merit and only remain in their jobs so long as they prove satisfactory. There is also an elected Prince who acts as head of state, but can be removed in case of tyranny. Interestingly, More does not rule out slavery in his ideal society. So-called 'bondsmen' are given the distasteful jobs that More does not want his happy citizens to partake in, such as slaughtering the livestock and serving up communal dinners. The bondsmen are people serving penal sentences for the breaking of any of the Utopian laws, such as virginity before marriage and chastity during wedlock. Bondsmen are also drawn from other societies from among those who have been condemned to death.

Whilst More's Utopia possesses some admirable liberal qualities it is also, alas, aesthetically oppressive in the same way as Maoist and Cambodian regimes have been in the real world. More expects all his citizens to wear the same plain, undifferentiated dress. Architecturally it is oppressively dull. Each of the fifty-four towns are built according to an identical plan. The streets are all twenty feet across and every home is exactly alike.

Utopia is a kind of Christian communism, in which there is no personal property, internal commerce or personal ambition

The residents swap homes on a regular basis according to the law to discourage the idea of private ownership, although since all the houses are alike this seems somewhat unnecessary.

Like *The Republic* of **Plato**, it is doubtful that More's utopian vision could provide the basis for a realistic model of any society, let alone the transformation of an existing one. Nevertheless, the value of Utopia lies in the articulation of certain social and socialistic ideals in an age very far removed from such philanthropic concerns. Bertrand **Russell** probably sums up the problem with More's vision best when he says, 'life in More's Utopia, as in most others, would be intolerably dull. Diversity is essential to happiness, and in Utopia there is hardly any'.

▌ ESSENTIAL READING ▌

Utopia (1518)

In his famous work, More describes the political and social organization of the imaginary island of Utopia. (The word derives from the Greek *eu-topos*, meaning 'good place'.) In Utopia there is no private property, and religious toleration is practised – except for atheism. In More's opinion, if a man did not believe in God, then he could not logically be trusted to acknowledge any authority outside of himself. More may have chosen to set his vision of an ideal state on an imaginary island because it allowed him to write more freely about politically contentious subjects. His own personal views about the society he describes are not clear and have been the subject of much debate. The book inspired a whole genre of Renaissance literature, in which different authors described their ideal societies.

NEWTON, ISAAC

1642–1727

A mathematician and physicist, Newton produced work – philosophical to a degree – which served mainly as an impetus for many of the philosophers of his and succeeding generations, including **Locke** and **Kant**, both of whom owed much to him. Newton's principal work, the *Philosophiae Naturalis Principia Mathematica* contains his theory

> ### *Every planet in the solar system at all times accelerates towards the sun*

of gravity and laws of motion. His later work, the *Opticks,* is primarily concerned with optical physics but also contains speculations on mechanics, religion and morals. He was to be involved in a series of disagreements with **Leibniz**, initially over which of them was the first to invent the calculus,

Newton's discoveries in the fields of physics, astronomy and mathematics were to have a world-changing effect.

Newton's experiments with the refraction of light led to the discoveries set out in *Opticks*.

understanding in a way consistent with Newtonian mechanics. As a result, he argued for a causal theory of perception and for a distinction between primary and secondary qualities of objects.

Kant, in similar fashion, recognized that everything in the phenomenal world had to conform to Newton's principles, but that this order was for the most part imposed by the psychological apparatus of the mind. Kant's philosophy gave support to Newton in the quarrel with Leibniz over whether space and time should be conceived of as absolute or merely as relations between objects. The debate seemed to have been won hands down by the Newtonians until the advent of **Einstein**'s relativistic physics (see also **Democritus**). Claiming that his method was empirical and inductive, rather than rationalist and deductive, Newton was also fond of criticizing **Descartes**.

and later over the issue of the status of space and time (see below).

The insight behind Newton's physics was that the universe runs according to law-governed mechanical principles. This idea was to have a profound influence on John Locke, whose philosophy may be seen as the philosophical working out of Newton's physical principles. Locke was determined to make sense of human

It is thanks to Newton that empiricism began to enjoy a period of dominance over rationalist philosophy. However, Newton owed much to Descartes' thought, and it is likely that his own speculations could not have begun but for the work already undertaken by his rationalist predecessor.

Undoubtedly Newton's greatest achievement was his theory of gravity, from which he was able to explain the motions of all the planets, including the moon. Newton proved that every planet in the solar system at all times accelerates towards the sun. The acceleration of a body towards the sun is at a rate inversely proportional to the square of its distance from it. This led to Newton's law of universal gravity: 'every body attracts every other with a force directly proportional to the product of their masses and inversely proportional to the square of the distance between them'. The law of universal gravity allowed Newton to predict all of the planetary motions,

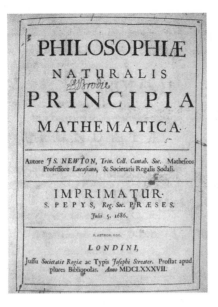

The title page of Newton's *Principia*, first published in 1687, in which he sets out the laws of gravity and those of motion.

the tides, the movements of the moon and of the comets. It was a striking achievement that would not be superseded until Einstein, although even with the advent of Einsteinian relativity, Newton's mechanics still holds good – and indeed is still used on account of its simplicity for predicting the movement of so-called 'medium-sized' objects – that is, anything that is neither bigger than the solar system nor smaller than the eye can see. Newton's work, both scientific and philosophical, is a profound and remarkable achievement in the history of human thought.

‖ ESSENTIAL READING ‖

Philosophiae Naturalis Principia Mathematica (1687)

The title of Newton's masterpiece is translated as *The Mathematical Principles of Natural Philosophy*, but it is more commonly known as the *Principia*. In this work, Newton describes the three laws of motion and the law of gravity. These laws enabled him to explain the motion of the planets, moons and comets of the solar system and the earth's tides. The *Principia* combines the ideas of **Copernicus**, **Galileo** and Kepler into a single theory and explains the laws of the universe in mathematical terms.

Opticks (1704)

In this, his second major work of physical science, Newton examined the properties of light and colour. It is mainly a record of his experiments on the dispersion of light into its component colours and what he deduced from this. The great achievement of this work was to show that colour was a mathematically definable property.

NIETZSCHE, FRIEDRICH

1844–1900

One of the most profound, enigmatic and ultimately controversial philosophers in the whole of the Western canon, Nietzsche has been variously appropriated, vilified, venerated or simply misunderstood. Through the relationship of his sister, Elisabeth, with the National Socialists in Germany, Nietzsche's philosophy has wrongly gained the reputation of supporting Nazism, though his concept of the *Übermensch* or 'superman', is in fact closer to **Aristotle**'s man of virtue than the glorified Aryan hero. Elisabeth's edited and altered collection of Nietzsche's writings, published shortly after his death as *The Will to Power*, has done much to mar the reception of Nietzsche's thought in the 20th century. As a result, despite comprehensive reassessment in academic circles, it may be another hundred years before Nietzsche's philosophy is widely appreciated for the genius that it is. **Freud** said of Nietzsche that 'he had a more penetrating knowledge of himself than any other man who ever lived or was ever likely to live'.

Son of a Protestant minister, Nietzsche gained a professorship at the University of Basel at the remarkable age of only twenty-four. After ten years, ill health forced him to retire into a solitary and vagrant lifestyle travelling across Europe, whence he devoted himself to writing and recuperation. He eventually achieved worldwide fame during the last ten years or so of his life. Of this he was probably unaware, since, in 1889, Nietzsche suffered a final and irreversible breakdown and remained insane until his death.

> *The strong are those who are more complete as human beings, who have learnt...to channel the will to power into a creative force*

Nietzsche's writings are varied and cover diverse topics, from ethics and religion to metaphysics and epistemology. He is most renowned, however, for his concept of 'the will to power'. Influenced by **Schopenhauer** to a certain extent, albeit without so much metaphysical baggage, Nietzsche saw the fundamental driving force of the individual as expressed in the need to dominate and control the external forces operating upon him. As such, Nietzsche's individual requires what the existentialists would later give him, the power to be master of his own destiny (see in particular, **Sartre**).

The frustration of this urge, Nietzsche saw, is responsible for the existence of various moral systems and religious institutions, all of which attempt to bind and subdue the will. Perhaps because of his father's influence, Nietzsche was particularly hostile to Christianity, which he famously calls a 'slave morality'. In it he saw the resentment of the weak towards the strong. Those who failed to have the courage to master their own passions, who lacked, ultimately, inner strength of character, sought revenge on those stronger than themselves, not in this life, but in a fictional 'other' world, where some other power, namely God, would wreak vengeance on their behalf.

Unlike Schopenhauer, Nietzsche did not see the will to power as something to be resisted, but pursued and affirmed. It is, Nietzsche insists, the exuberance of spring, the affirmation of life, the saying of 'Yes!' However, as has already been suggested, Nietzsche did not advocate the dominance of the strong over the weak, nor suggest that mastery of the will to power belonged to some special elite by virtue of birth. Rather he described, historically, how the domination of the strong results in, and is necessary to, what we would now call the 'evolutionary progress' of the human being. But strength, as Nietzsche

Nietzsche as a student at the University of Liepzig in 1867, two years before he accepted a professorship at Basel at the age of 24.

understands it, is not constituted in physical, but rather psychical, force. The strong are those who are more complete as human beings, who have learnt to sublimate and control their passions, to channel the will to power into a creative force.

Neither, contrary to popular misunderstanding, did Nietzsche endorse the 'master morality' –

The original manuscript of Nietzsche's fictional work, *Thus Spake Zarathustra.*

moral systems peculiar to the aristocracy – although it is true he thought it more life affirming than 'slave morality', as typified in Christianity. Rather, Nietzsche held that the strong had a duty towards the less fortunate: 'The man of virtue, too, helps the unfortunate, but not, or almost not, out of pity, but prompted by an urge which is begotten by the excess of power'.

‖ ESSENTIAL READING ‖

The Birth of Tragedy (1872)

The full title of this book is *The Birth of Tragedy from the Spirit of Music*. Nietzsche contrasts the Apollonian arts (sculpture, painting and epic poetry) with the wilder Dionysian arts (music and tragedy), blames Socrates for the death of Greek tragedy, and tries to show a connection between Greek tragedy and Wagner's operas.

Human, All Too Human (1878)

This work is written in the form of aphorisms and short aphoristic paragraphs covering a wide range of topics, among which the notion of power.

Thus Spake Zarathustra (1883–85)

This book tells the story of Zarathustra, a prophet who speaks of the death of God and prophesies the coming of the 'Superman'. Zarathustra also teaches Nietzsche's doctrines of 'eternal recurrence' and the 'will to power'.

Beyond Good and Evil (1886)

Here, Nietzsche's aim is to change people's opinions on morality, about what is good and what is evil. It contrasts 'slave morality' and 'master morality', and includes an exposition of the 'will to power'.

The Genealogy of Morals (1887)

This is Nietzsche's most complex book, and a sequel to *Beyond Good and Evil*. In it, Nietzsche discusses suffering and how people cope with it. It contains a critique of Christian morality and an account of the 'slave revolt' in morality. The third section of the book discusses asceticism.

NOZICK, ROBERT

1938–2002

Nozick's most influential work, *Anarchy, State and Utopia* (1974), has been widely seen as a libertarian response to John **Rawls**' *A Theory of Justice* (1971). Both these American philosophers argued their cases from an anti-utilitarian perspective, preferring the Kantian emphasis on individual rights. But whereas Rawls used his theories to justify a form of social democracy, Nozick used his to make a case for a full-blooded libertarianism.

A welfare state is institutionalized theft, and progressive taxation a form of forced labour

Nozick took **Kant**'s dictum – 'Act so that you treat humanity, whether in your own person or in that of another, always as an end and never as a means only' – and interpreted it in a particular way. All individuals, Nozick said, were 'self-owners'. As a consequence of this, all individual rights were property rights, whether over that individual's body, mind, abilities or justly-acquired goods. And no communality or collectivity, no state, could override those rights.

According to Nozick, a welfare state was institutionalized theft, and progressive taxation a form of forced labour. Both violated the rights of the individual by wrongly assuming a collective right – whether democratically sanctioned or not – to requisition an individual's time, labour or money. Nozick favoured a minimalist 'nightwatchman' state, which protected its citizens from violence and enforced laws governing the acquisition and transfer of property. Other traditional functions of the state – like education, health care and welfare – should be left to private business and charitable organizations.

In the absence of political direction, socio-economic development was driven by the invisible hand of the free market. Measures to regulate this – like rent controls or a statutory minimum wage – were also violations of individual rights. The idea of distributive justice was irrelevant, because society had nothing to distribute – only individuals had. Nozick preferred 'entitlement justice', whereby an individual was entitled to anything justly acquired. The 'justness' was decided by a complex set of rules governing acquisition, transfer and the rectification of unjust acquisitions and transfers.

In *Anarchy, State and Utopia,* Nozick used a hypothetical situation involving the famous basketball player Wilt Chamberlain to demonstrate his concept of 'entitlement justice'. Let us start, he said, with a non-entitlement conception of distribute justice – an egalitarian one in which everyone has the same amount of money. Now suppose that Wilt Chamberlain agrees to play in return for each spectator leaving him 25 cents at the gate. Say a million people watch him over the course of the season, giving him $250,000 and making him a lot richer than his fellow citizens. Is this new distribution of wealth just? The answer, according to Nozick, has to be yes. Since there is no injustice in the egalitarian starting-point, since those who paid the 25 cents did so voluntarily, and since those who did not still have theirs, no one can have any reason for complaint. As no injustice has occurred, the new distribution must be as just as the old one.

Nozick's political philosophy found great favour with right-wing governments of the 1980s – like those of the United States, Great Britain and Chile – which favoured reductions in welfare spending and greater deregulation of economic activity. Margaret Thatcher's famous statement that there was 'no such thing as society' encapsulated what many saw as his essential point. But other implications of Nozick's focus on individual rights were less welcome to those on the political right. He insisted that the criminalization of prostitution, suicide and drug-taking were all

Nozick was primarily a political philosopher, arguing for the defence of individual rights against state interventionism.

violations of the individual's right to do whatever he or she wished with his or her body. If individual rights like these were not protected, Nozick argued, then other property rights were impossible to justify. More whimsically, he argued that the European acquisition of America failed his test of entitlement justice, and that the land should be returned to the Native Americans.

Unlike Rawls, who spent the rest of his career refining his early work, Nozick devoted only four or five years to political philosophy. *Anarchy, State and Utopia* had made him famous, but he claimed that he had no desire to spend the rest of his life writing 'Son of Anarchy, State and Utopia'. He did want to back up his theory of rights with a theory of human nature, but failed to do so. His final contribution to political philosophy was to moderate his earlier ideas. He was, he said, 'no longer as hardcore a libertarian as I had been before.'

His work in other fields has generally been considered interesting, but lacking the originality and lasting importance of his political philosophy.

Philosophical Explanations (1981) presented his main contribution to epistemology. Traditional theories of knowledge, in holding that proof of the knower's claim to knowledge must come from inside, created logical difficulties for themselves. Nozick sought to overcome these with his 'externalist theory of knowledge', which claimed that knowing could be inferred if shown to 'track the truth'.

In the same book he tackled problems of identity theory, like that posed by **Locke**'s example of the cobbler who wakes up with a prince's memories instead of his own. Which is he? According to Nozick's 'closest continuer' theory he was the one who most closely continued the man who went to sleep. If that man took his identity from his body, he remained the cobbler. If he defined himself by his memory, he was the prince.

❙ ESSENTIAL READING ❙

Anarchy, State, and Utopia (1974)

This is Nozick's most influential work. Often considered a rebuttal of Rawls' *A Theory of Justice,* it also dismisses utilitarianism, but favours instead a minimal state and the overriding importance of individual rights to all forms of personal property, including the individual's abilities and physical body.

Philosophical Explanations (1981)

Concerned with a wide variety of philosophical issues, and most notably Nozick's contribution to epistemology – his 'externalist' notion of 'tracking the truth' – and identity theory – his 'closest continuer' notion.

The Examined Life (1989) and the papers collected as Socratic Puzzles (1997)

Together, these tackle a wide range of philosophical topics, from love to animal rights, Austrian economics to the meaning of life.

The Nature of Rationality (1993) offers a new theory of rational choice.

Invariances (2001) examines a new theory of objective reality.

PAINE, THOMAS

1737–1809

English-born political philosopher, Paine not only invented the term 'United States of America', he inspired the revolutions both there and in France. He was forced to flee England when he tried to do the same thing there. Awareness of his importance in the formation of the American constitution and the American 'way of life' is pivotal to understanding the entity that is modern day America.

Having emigrated to the New World in the early 1770s, Paine became editor of the *Pennsylvania Magazine* and published one of the first essays calling for the abolition of slavery. With the beginning of the American Revolution, Paine made himself famous by publishing his book *Common Sense*. In it, he argues against the notion of a ruling class, insisting that government and society must be kept distinct. Independence for the American colonies, Paine argued, was both morally and practically justified. He continued to write and publish pamphlets throughout the War of Independence in support of the revolution.

After the success of the war, Paine went first to France and then to England. In response to Burke's *Reflections on the Revolution in France*, Paine wrote and published *The Rights of Man*, his seminal treatise on democracy and republicanism. According to Paine, all men are born with equal rights. The necessity of social living can, however, bring about situations where we impinge on the rights of others. Moreover, we may not always have the means to protect our rights from others who do not respect them. Consequently, it is necessary to develop the state and a constitution in which individual rights are encoded as civil rights, enforced by the state on behalf of the individual. The only morally acceptable constitution is that of the democratic republic in which citizens are granted the further right to vote in order to choose their own leaders. It is just this right, to choose one's leaders, that the hereditary monarchies of France and England deny to their people, providing justification enough to abandon them as immoral constitutions.

The British Government, in response, charged Paine with treason, causing him to flee back to France. With Paine gone, the government quashed the British revolution before it had a chance to gain momentum. In France, Paine was at first welcomed and given a seat in the National Convention. However he was later imprisoned and only just escaped execution.

Paine developed his ideas on civil rights and justice in his *Agrarian Justice*. He argues that a state is predicated on the basis that it makes its citizens better off than they otherwise would be without its constitution. But, he finds, many of the poorest people in the civilized societies of Europe are in a worse state than the so-called 'uncivilized' native American Indians. The inequity has much to do with land and property ownership, a privilege Paine suggests should be taxed since the generation of wealth that makes it possible requires the support of society. The proceeds of land and property taxes should be invested in a welfare system, access to which is a right of every citizen.

In 1802 Paine returned to America, but it was not to be a happy homecoming. In *The Age of Reason,* Paine had argued against both atheism and Christianity in favour of a deism which rejects any appeal to divine revelation. Rather, the belief in God is claimed to be intrinsically reasonable, a logical conclusion to the question of why anything exists at all. Paine rejects

The only morally acceptable constitution is that of the democratic republic

both organized religion and the Bible's portrayal of a vindictive, vengeful God. Unfortunately for Paine, America was deeply Christian and frowned upon his religious writings, despite his previous service to her. Though he remained in the United States for the rest of his life, he died in obscurity.

Paine's work is characterized by a rare integrity that rails against political oppression, organized religion and poverty. Despite the massive influence of his early writings he remains a philosopher who, curiously, is rarely mentioned.

197

Paine emigrated to America in 1774, where he met Benjamin Franklin and became a key campaigner for American independence.

▌ ESSENTIAL READING ▌

Common Sense (1776)
Written during the American Revolution, this pamphlet argues that monarchy is wrong in both principle and practice, and sets out both moral and practical grounds for American independence from Britain.

The Rights of Man (1792)
Writing in reply to Edmund Burke's critical *Reflections on the French Revolution*, Paine argues that the only legitimate form of government is that of a democratic republic. Among other things, he supports national independence, people's rights and revolutionary war.

The Age of Reason (1794)
Here, Paine sets out the case for deism. He argues against the Christian concept of a vengeful God and against the idea of the Bible as the Word of God.

Agrarian Justice (1797)
In this pamphlet, Paine advocates an inheritance tax on land which would be used to fund grants to everyone at the age of 21 and annual pensions for everyone over the age of 50 and for those unable to work, not as a matter of charity but of justice, to compensate people for the loss of their share of the land which is God's gift to everyone.

PARMENIDES OF ELEA

c. 510–?440BC

Little is known of Parmenides' life and background, and fragments of a poem entitled *On Nature* are all that survive of his work. Nevertheless, it contains one of the first examples of reasoned argument in which, perhaps as a reaction to **Heraclitus**, Parmenides attempts to prove that change is impossible and that reality is singular, undivided and homogenous.

In the first part of his poem, 'The Way of Truth', which was revealed to him, he claims, in meeting with a goddess, Parmenides distinguishes between an inquiry into what is and an inquiry into what is not. The latter, he says, is impossible. 'One cannot know that which is not – that is impossible – nor utter it; for it is the same thing that can be thought, that is'. The essence of this somewhat cryptic argument is that in order to think of something which is not – let us say, 'a unicorn' for example – one must be thinking of something: there must be some idea present to the mind, presumably the idea of a unicorn. But to think of a unicorn means that the unicorn (or the idea of a unicorn) exists in the mind, and therefore it cannot be truly said that unicorns completely fail to exist. The argument turns principally on two

Parmenides' reflections on the nature of perception and reality mark him out as one of the most significant Presocratic thinkers.

complex issues. First, exactly what is meant by 'exists' here? What is the difference between existing in the world and existing in the mind? This begins a controversy that will reappear throughout much of the history of philosophy in many different contexts, but most notoriously in **Anselm**'s ontological argument, some 1,500 years later. Second, what are the connections between thoughts, words, and things? If that debate started with Parmenides, it has taxed almost every major thinker ever since, up to and including the seminal works of the 20th century by philosophers such as Bertrand **Russell**, Ludwig **Wittgenstein** and **Quine**.

Since Parmenides thought that to think of something is to give it some semblance of existence, then one cannot think of anything that is truly 'not'. It follows that one can only think of that which is. Now comes the second part of Parmenides' deductive reasoning, the first known example of a formal deduction in the history of Western thought. For to think of anything that is implies the existence of something that is not. If something is green, it is not red, if something is a man, it is not a dog, a house is not a cart, and so on. But since by his previous argument Parmenides has shown that negative existential claims are impossible, it seems one cannot make positive existential discriminations either. To distinguish X from Y, is to say that X is not Y, precisely that which Parmenides claims is impossible. Therefore, one cannot logically discriminate between different things in the world. One can only say, Parmenides concludes, that everything is and hence, the true nature of reality – that which is – must be that of an undivided, homogenous, single entity.

By similar argument Parmenides attempts to show that change is also impossible. If one can think of something that will exist in the future, then it must exist in one's mind now. If one can remember something or someone that has passed away, then they must be present to your mind at the time you are thinking of them. Therefore, Parmenides concludes, coming into being and passing away are illusory, change is illusory: everything is one, undivided, changeless and eternal.

It is clear to the modern reader that Parmenides' reasoning is unsound, but it would not be until the rise of modern philosophical logic in the late 19th and early 20th centuries that negative existential claims would be clearly understood. However, apart from the historical importance of the first known attempt at logical deduction, later to be perfected in the work of **Aristotle**, Parmenides is significant for highlighting the intricacies and logical complications inherent in the notions of existence and the relationship between language, thought and reality.

The true nature of reality…must be that of an undivided, homogenous, single entity

▍ ESSENTIAL READING ▍

On Nature

This poem is Parmenides's only known work. The original is believed to have been 3,000 lines in length, but just 150 lines remain today. The original was apparently divided into three parts: a *Proem,* or introduction (which has survived); a section called 'The Way of the Truth', or *Alethia* (some of this has survived); and a section called 'The Way of Appearance/Belief', or *Doxa* (most of which no longer exists). The poem is about a man who goes on a journey to a goddess to receive a revelation about the nature of reality. The *Proem* describes his journey. The *Alethia* and *Doxa* sections make up the goddess's spoken revelation.

PASCAL, BLAISE

1623–62

Blaise Pascal was a man of many talents. In his short life he made significant contributions to the fields of philosophy, mathematics, physics and theology. His philosophical ideas were mainly concerned with scientific methodology and religion.

His ideas about scientific methodology arose directly from his work as a scientist. In his book *Experiments on a Vacuum,* based on four years of experimental research, Pascal cast doubt on the widely held Aristotelian view that nature abhors a vacuum. In response to a critic of his book, Pascal set down what he considered to be the principles of scientific methodology, namely that appeals to authoritative texts, such as the works of **Aristotle**, should have no place in scientific reasoning. In Pascal's view, science is a progressive enterprise, with new generations of scientists building on the knowledge handed down to them by their predecessors.

However, Pascal did not entirely rule out a role for authority in the quest for knowledge, for when it comes to theology, different rules come into play. In fact, according to Pascal, authority is the *only* measure of truth in theological matters; when we want to know about a realm that is beyond the reach of reason, then we have little choice but to rely on the authority of sacred texts. This might seem strange from someone so committed to reason and

evidence in the pursuit of scientific knowledge. However, Pascal, certainly in the latter part of his life, was a deeply religious man.

In his theological views, Pascal clearly showed the influence of **Augustine**. He was committed to the Augustinian idea that the fall of man had left human beings spiritually corrupt. It is only by the grace of God that people – and by no means all people – can be redeemed; in his view, God's grace is such that those people he had blessed will always choose to follow his path. However, as a good Augustinian, Pascal was also committed to the idea of predestination; that is, the idea that salvation is preordained. Therefore, there is nothing specifically that the individual can do to attain salvation; either God will make his presence felt in the heart of a particular individual, or he won't.

This belief makes it slightly paradoxical that Pascal spent the final years of his life putting together the beginnings of an apologia for Christianity, known as *Pensées.* It is in this work that he includes his famous wager. The argument is as follows: either God exists or he does not. If God does not exist, then we lose very little by believing that he does. If he does exist, then we stand to gain an awful lot by believing that he does, and to lose an awful lot by thinking that he doesn't. Therefore, it is sensible to wager that he does exist, and to behave appropriately. As Pascal put it, 'I should be much more afraid of being mistaken and then finding out that Christianity is true than of being mistaken in believing it to be true.'

The wager then is not an argument for the existence of God, but rather an argument for the rationality of belief in God. It was aimed not so much at people who were convinced that God did not exist, but at the waverers. It does, however, sit uneasily with his Augustinian view of predestination. If a person's future is predestined, why try to persuade that person to believe in God? Pascal responded that God might choose to do his work through other people, so it was his duty to attempt to bring people to faith. However, whilst this might explain Pascal's motives, it isn't clear that Pascal's wager can function as a motive to action. If all is predestined, why do anything? Why not just sit back and wait for God to act? Despite this difficulty, the wager has remained an influential argument, and is seen as an early example of decision-theory.

Although best known for the formulation of his 'wager', Pascal also invented the first operational calculating machine.

'I should be much more afraid of being mistaken and then finding out that Christianity is true than of being mistaken in believing it to be true.'

∥ ESSENTIAL READING ∥

Experiments on a Vacuum (1647)
This work, detailing Pascal's experiments with liquids and air pressure, gave reasons why it was indeed a vacuum above a column of liquid in a barometer tube, contradicting traditional views that a vacuum cannot exist.

Provincial Letters (1657)
A series of eighteen letters, which amount to a scathing attack on the views of the Jesuits. In essence, they are accused of expediency in their theological and moral outlook, willing to sacrifice doctrinal accuracy for the purposes of political gain.

Thoughts (or Pensées) (1670)
An apologia for Christianity. Unfinished at Pascal's death, this work comprises a series of short essays and aphorism. It is best known for featuring Pascal's famous wager ('Pascal's Wager'), an argument for the rationality of a belief in God.

PEIRCE, CHARLES SANDERS

1839–1914

American scientist whose interest in philosophy began as a hobby, Peirce is responsible for one of the most recent influential movements in philosophy, pragmatism or, as he later renamed it to distinguish his views from **James** and others, pragmaticism.

According to Peirce, the guiding principle of his 'pragmaticist' philosophy is 'if one can define accurately all the conceivable experimental phenomena which the affirmation or denial of a concept could imply, one will have a complete definition of the concept'. This view, then, is principally concerned with establishing the meaning of concepts and beliefs, a philosophical emphasis that would come to dominate in the 'linguistic turn' of the 20th century.

One immediate effect of Peirce's pragmaticism is to distinguish metaphysical propositions that are,

Peirce spent most of his career working for the U.S. Coast and Geodesic Survey, and his philosophical work went largely unrecognized during his lifetime.

literally, nonsense from the genuinely meaningful propositions of 'scientific metaphysics'. The former are those propositions which have no sense on account of not representing any idea that has observable, sensible effects that can be accorded any practical significance. Scientific metaphysics, Peirce maintains, is an observational discipline concerning the first and most very basic elements of experience, often just those elements that are so fundamental they are difficult to discern. Thus scientific metaphysics and science are not part of one continuous discipline – as many of Peirce's philosophical descendents would later claim – but maintain the traditional

> *Peirce sees knowledge as a means of stabilizing our habitual behaviour in response to doubt*

hierarchical order of foundational and succeeding disciplines, respectively.

Peirce's foundational, scientific metaphysics accordingly begins with phenomenology, the way things are presented to us in experience. He is particularly concerned with the difference between belief and doubt. He rejects **Descartes**' 'paper doubt' – doubts considered merely as an intellectual exercise – and so sidesteps the whole issue of epistemological scepticism. Rather, says Peirce, real doubt ensues when recalcitrant experience – not reflection – causes us to waver in our beliefs. A belief, as Peirce understands it, is not some intellectual disposition to assent to a proposition, but a behavioural habit manifest in action. Accordingly, when real doubt ensues it disrupts our usual behavioural patterns. Cartesian doubt, on the other hand, can make no difference to the way we act. Always scientific and pragmatic in his work, Peirce suggests that knowledge, which he defines as the resolution of disrupted habits by the revision of belief, is a 'homeostatic' process. Homeostasis is a concept borrowed from physiology, in which the body employs reaction systems to return to normal functioning in response to environmental upsets. Similarly, Peirce sees knowledge as a means of stabilizing our habitual behaviour in response to doubt.

Unusual in Peirce's pragmatic philosophy is the continued insistence that truth is neither a matter of coherence in our belief systems nor success in action. Peirce never denies that truth in some way corresponds with reality, and that there must be general, independent laws of nature. Though commentators have found this to create a tension in Peirce's work, it is uncompromisingly honest. For Peirce recognizes that the assumption on which all pragmatic theories are based – that prediction is possible – logically requires regularities in experience. Moreover, the only scientific hypothesis that can make sense of the appearance of such regularities is one that takes reality to consist of phenomena governed by laws.

▌ ESSENTIAL READING ▌

Peirce wrote many articles for academic journals, but did not publish any work that set out his philosophy. Useful sources for Peirce's philosophy are *The Essential Peirce* (2 volumes: 1992, 1998) and *The Cambridge Companion to Peirce* (2004).

PHILO OF ALEXANDRIA

c.20BC–?

Philo of Alexandria, sometimes known as Philo Judaeus or Philo Alexandrinus, was something of an odd fish in classical thought. A Jew both by birth and upbringing, he is principally remembered for his philosophical commentaries on the scriptures. His family, of a sacerdotal line, was one of the most powerful of the populous Jewish colony of Alexandria. His brother Alexander Lysimachus was steward to Anthony's second daughter, and married one of his sons to the daughter of Herod Agrippa, whom he had put under financial obligations. Philo received a Jewish education, studying the laws and national traditions, but he also followed the Greek plan of studies (grammar with reading of the poets, geometry, rhetoric, dialectics) which he regarded as a preparation for philosophy. His works show that he had a first hand knowledge of the stoical theories then prevailing, and his thought is heavily influenced by **Plato** and the Stoics, and his great knowledge of Greco-Roman culture and philosophy was always put to service in the defence of Judaism. Particularly concerned with interpreting the book of Moses, Philo's thought was nevertheless never really popular with his Jewish contemporaries and it appears his thought was largely preserved for posterity by early Christian thinkers.

Nonetheless, Philo's reading of the Old Testament, and in particular the Book of Moses, takes a definite Platonic turn, and specifically the Plato of the *Timaeus* rather than the later, more considered works. For Philo, man is created by God, first as a

The two parts of the soul, the rational and the irrational, are bound together by the spirit

form in the mind – or logos – of God, and next as a corporeal being possessed of an incorporeal soul. So constituted, man is 'a border-dweller, situated on the borderline between the divine and the non-divine'. Philo claims that the corporeal body belongs to the world, the mind to the divine. Following Plato's tripartite account of the soul, Philo maintains that the two parts of the soul, the rational and the irrational, are bound together by the spirit.

The resemblance with Greek philosophy does not end there, however. Combining Plato's ideas in the *Republic* with a dash of **Aristotle**, Philo holds that the telos or goal of man is to become like a god, to reach out to the divine in contemplation and so return as far as possible to the divine source. Moreover, Philo is also heavily influenced by the Stoics, and in particular is keen to emulate their use of allegory to provide a philosophical exegesis of the scriptures. The scriptures should not be read literally, says Philo, but as containing hidden truths, waiting to be found by those with the patience and will to discover them.

All this leads to the question of how far, or whether at all, Philo is an original thinker. We have included him here not just to represent an unusual class of philosopher – an orthodox Jew with a bent for Greek intellectualism, but also because Philo aims to do more than just synthesize Greek and Jewish wisdom. His ambition is wholly Judaic. By showing that what is valuable in Greek thought is already present in Judaism he

Philo tried to show how universal truths were embedded in the Scriptures, long before the advent of ancient Greek philosophy.

offers a defence and justification for the received wisdom of his culture. Surprisingly, he was popular amongst and exerted a great influence upon many early Christian scholars that followed him, in particular Origen (second century AD). But the danger for Philo, as more than one commentator has noted, is that the influence Greek philosophy exerts on him is so strong that he does not appear to realize that his own religious foundations are in danger of being swept away. No one would claim Philo's thought has been completely overwhelmed by its Greek influence, but it is surely compromised by it.

Philo came from a powerful Jewish family in Alexandria.

║ ESSENTIAL READING ║

Most of Philo's surviving works were preserved by early Christian theologians. Many of these are philsophical essays dealing with the main themes of biblical thought and describing his own views. These included the following:

On Abraham

This was one of a number of biographies of biblical figures, who Philo believed demonstrated by their virtuous behaviour universal types of morality.

Every Good Man is Free

One of a series of works classified as philosophical treatises. This one had a sequel, now lost, called *Every Evil Man is a Slave*. In this work, Philo argues that good men, since they are not enslaved by avarice, ambition and lust, are free.

Hypothetica

One of a series of historical-apologetic writings. This one is a rationalistic version of Exodus, giving an account of Moses and a summary of Mosaic law, contrasting its severity with the laxity of gentile laws.

PLATO

c.427–347BC

Student of **Socrates** and founder of the Academy, the first reported institution of higher education – no philosopher has had a greater or wider-ranging influence in the history of philosophy than Plato. Alfred North **Whitehead** once said, with much justification, that the safest characterization of Western philosophy is that of a series of footnotes to Plato. There is no topic of philosophical concern for which one cannot find some view in the corpus of his work.

Accordingly it can be difficult to characterize such a vast and comprehensive canon of thought. However, much of Plato's work revolves around his conception of a realm of ideal forms. The world of experience is illusory, Plato tells us, since only that which is unchanging and eternal is real, an idea he borrowed from **Parmenides.** There must, then, be a realm of eternal unchanging forms that are the blueprints of the ephemeral phenomena we encounter through sense experience. According to Plato, though there are many individual horses, cats and dogs, they are all made in the image of the one universal form of 'the horse', 'the cat', 'the dog' and so on. Likewise, just as there are many men, all men are made in the image of the universal 'form of

Plato's influence on the history of philosophy is incalculable, particularly through his appeal to Christian theology.

Educated by Socrates, Plato went on to found his own Academy in Athens, said to be the first institution of higher learning.

man'. The influence of this idea on later Christian thought, in which man is made in the image of God, is only one of many ways in which Plato had a direct influence on Christian theology.

Plato's *Theory of Forms,* however, was not restricted to material objects. He also thought there were ideal forms of universal or abstract concepts, such as beauty, justice, truth and mathematical concepts such as number and class. Indeed, it is in mathematics that Plato's influence is still felt strongly today, both **Frege** and **Gödel** endorsing Platonism in this respect.

The *Theory of Forms* also underlies Plato's most contentious and best known work, *The Republic.* In a quest to understand the nature and value of justice, Plato offers a vision of a utopian society led by an elite class of guardians who are trained from birth for the task of ruling. The rest of society is divided into soldiers and the common people. In the republic, the ideal citizen is one who understands how best they can use their talents to the benefit of the whole of society, and bends unerringly to that task. There is little thought of personal freedom or individual rights in Plato's republic, for everything is tightly controlled by the guardians for the good of

> *'The safest characterization of Western philosophy is that of a series of footnotes to Plato.'*
> ### A. N. Whitehead

the state as a whole. This has led some, notably Bertrand **Russell**, to accuse Plato of endorsing an elitist and totalitarian regime under the guise of communist or socialist principles. Whether Russell and others who level this criticism are right or not is itself a subject of great debate. But it is important to understand Plato's reasons for organizing society in this way. *The Republic* is an attempt, in line with his theory of forms, to discover the ideal form of society. Plato thinks there must be one ideal way to organize society, of which all actual societies are mere imperfect copies, since they do not promote the good of all. Such a society, Plato believes, would be stronger than its neighbours and unconquerable by its enemies, a thought very much in Greek minds given the frequent warring between Athens, Sparta and the other Hellenistic city-states. But more importantly, such a society would be just to all its citizens, giving to and taking from each their due, with each citizen working for the benefit of the whole. Whether Plato's republic is an ideal, or even viable society, has had scholars divided ever since.

▌ ESSENTIAL READING ▌

Republic
The *Republic* is Plato's masterpiece. In it, he discusses the ideal state, the nature of justice, and harmony between social classes, and he condemns democracy, which he sees as a source of bad government. Other topics covered are education, the status of women, art, and the immortality of the soul.

Meno
This is a dialogue between Socrates and Meno regarding virtue and knowledge and whether virtue can be taught.

Parmenides
This book purports to record a discussion between Parmenides, **Zeno** and Socrates, and contains a critique of Plato's Theory of Forms. It is of particular interest because Socrates appears to lose the argument.

Theaetetus
This book is concerned with the nature of knowledge.

Symposium
The *Symposium* consists of a series of speeches on the nature of love made by participants at a drinking-party. It has been described as one of the most beautiful things ever written.

PLOTINUS
205–270

Born in Egypt and educated almost entirely in the Greek tradition, Plotinus eventually settled in Rome after an expedition to the Orient with the Emperor Gordian was abandoned when Gordian was assassinated by the Roman army. The times of Plotinus were the beginning of a troubled era that would soon spell the end of the old Roman Empire, and its division into Eastern and Western Empires. Indeed, Plotinus is regarded as the last great thinker of the Roman age.

Plotinus' fame lies in his reworking and development of the philosophy of **Plato**, work that would give rise to what later became known as 'Neoplatonism', although his philosophy is also influenced by **Aristotle** and the Roman Stoics.

His many works were collected and edited by his student Porphyry under the title *Enneads*. The title derives from the Greek word for 'nine', reflecting the fact that there are nine chapters or treatises to each of the six books in the collection.

Plotinus' philosophy combines the mystical with the practical, and was to have a great influence on Christian theology. His philosophy is aimed at helping the student to return, in union or communion, to the One or ultimate Being by means of contemplation. As in Christian theology, Plotinus

It is up to us to choose between being concerned with the lower level concerns of the body, or to look inward and contemplate the higher realities of the Intellect

believed in a tripartite of divinities, these being the One, the Intellect and the Soul. However, unlike the Christian trinity, these are not on an equal footing but are rather successive 'stages' or emanations of contemplative being.

The One, which Plotinus – following Plato – sometimes referred to as 'the Good', is beyond description. Language can only point to the One, and even the many names of the One are not its true names. Rather, it is the ineffable, mystical source of reality. After the One comes the Intellect or 'Nous', which corresponds to intuitive knowledge. The Intellect is also difficult to describe in language, but Plotinus offers us various analogies. The Intellect is like the light of the sun, it illuminates the One, and is the means by which the One contemplates itself.

The Intellect is the source and ground of the archetypes, or Platonic Forms (see Plato), of material things. Thought and the objects of thought are united in the Intellect, there is no division between subject and object, perceiver and perceived. The next level of reality is Soul, which corresponds to rational or discursive thinking. There is a higher and lower division, between the higher and inward-facing Soul, looking towards the divine by means of the Intellect, and the lower and outward-facing Soul. Plotinus calls this lower part Nature. It is this, lower, outer-facing Nature, that is responsible for the material world. As human beings, both levels of the Soul are present in us, and it is up to us to choose between being concerned with the lower level concerns of the body, or to look inward and contemplate the higher realities of the Intellect.

The key to understanding Plotinus' cosmogony lies in understanding that the three levels of reality, the One, the Intellect and the Soul, are logical progressions, or levels of contemplation, of a singular eternal reality, rather than temporal successions of coming-into-being. Time is only created by the inadequate ability of Nature to contemplate the divine. According to Plotinus, it comes about in the lower order of material existence because the Soul, unlike the Intellect, is unable to contemplate the Forms immediately, but instead must contemplate them as fragmented objects perceived in moments of succession.

‖ ESSENTIAL READING ‖

Enneads (c. 264)

This work comprises the collected treatises of Plotinus, compiled by the philosopher towards the end of his life. The treatises are filled with refutations and corrections of the positions of various schools of philosophy, including Peripatetics, Stoics, Epicureans, Gnostics and Astrologers. Plotinus was guided by Plato in his philosophical views, but this work proves that he was an original thinker in his own right. The work was edited by Plotinus's student, Porphyry, who divided it into six books of nine treatises each.

210

POPPER, KARL

1902–1994

Viennese philosopher of science, Popper's principal writings such as *Conjectures and Refutations* and *The Open Society and its Enemies,* have been a major influence on 20th-century thought. Popper's brand of scientific method, 'falsificationism' gave rise to a whole new area of debate in the philosophy of science, and even claimed to have solved **Hume**'s 'problem of induction'.

> *The mark of a scientific theory is whether it makes predictions which could in principle serve to falsify it*

According to Popper, the mark of a scientific theory is whether it makes predictions which could in principle serve to falsify it. The more predictions a theory makes, 'the better it is'. This falsificationism is part of Popper's response to what he calls the 'myth of induction'. Induction, as characterized by Hume, is the method of arriving at theories, laws or generalizations by observing regularities in experience. But Popper agrees with Hume, that any generalization goes beyond the possible evidence for it. No number of observed cases of some A having property B licences the conclusion that all A's have that property. One simply never observes all A's to justify this conclusion.

Popper's answer to this problem is based on the claim that this characterization first erroneously assumes that scientific generalizations are conclusions; and secondly, fails to describe accurately the process by which scientists go about forming hypotheses. Rather than generalizations being conclusions inferred from evidence, they have the logical status, Popper insists, of conjectures. They are tentative hypotheses on trial, as it were, 'in the court of experience'. Hume's problem of induction disappears because generalizations are not supported or justified by observation. On the contrary, generalizations are logically prior, being first conjectured and then either refuted by experience, (for instance when some A is observed that lacks property B), or survive to await further observations of A's. Experience can never verify a theory as true, only falsify it. Generalizations are first conjectured, then held up to the scrutiny of experience for refutation.

Critics have complained that Popper's own theory implicitly employs inductive reasoning. Popper's view is that a single counter-instance to an

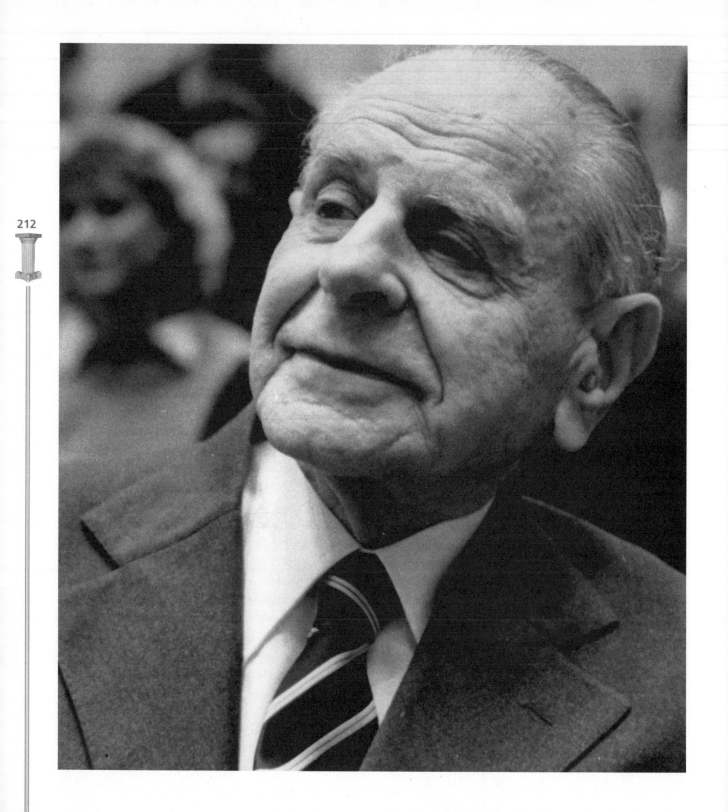

POPPER, KARL

hypothesis is enough to falsify it. But this seems to assume that induction is reliable, otherwise a theory falsified this time around might yet turn out to be true in the future. Of course, Popper is right to claim that universal generalizations, such as 'All A's are B' are shown false on the occasion of a single A that is not B; but he applies his falsification principle to scientific theories as a whole, not just universal statements. Moreover, an instance that falsifies 'All A's are B's' also confirms the theory 'Some A's are B's'. The logic of falsification and verification cannot be separated, as Popper had thought.

Closely tied to Popper's conception of science as generating theories capable of falsification is his attack on the dialectics of **Marx** and **Hegel**. Such 'theories' seem immune from empirical falsification, since any experience can be accounted for by some suitable interpretation of the doctrine. It is particularly outrageous, Popper finds, that Marxism explicitly claims to be a 'science'. For similar reasons Popper is equally scathing of both **Plato** and **Freud**, as enemies of the 'open society'.

Ultimately, Popper's influence has been crucial in furthering many debates in the philosophy of science, and helped give rise to the work of Lakatos, **Kuhn** and **Feyerabend**.

213

‖ ESSENTIAL READING ‖

The Logic of Scientific Discovery (1934)

Considered by many as one of the most important philosophical works of the 20th century, this book sets out Popper's theory of 'falsificationism'. It also discusses such topics as theories, testing, probability, corroboration, and quantum theory.

The Open Society and Its Enemies (1945)

Popper's 'open society' is one which allows its citizens to put forward a wide range of differing proposals, followed by criticism, followed by the making of any necessary changes to benefit society. He offers critiques of the totalitarian societies advocated by **Plato** and Marx, which preclude such openness by claiming knowledge that they cannot have and obliging others to submit to it.

Conjectures and Refutations (1963)

In this book, Popper applies falsificationism to both the philosophy of science and political philosophy.

PYTHAGORAS OF SAMOS

c.570–480BC

Probably born around the mid-6th century BC, although no exact date is known as to when Pythagoras lived. Despite his name being familiar to every schoolchild for Pythagoras' Theorem, which states that the square of the hypotenuse of a right-angled triangle is equal to the sum of the squares of the remaining two sides, it is likely that this was already known both to the Babylonians – where Pythagoras is thought to have travelled in his youth – and the Egyptians.

Pythagoras was a somewhat shadowy figure and like **Socrates** after him wrote nothing himself, preferring to leave his students to document his thoughts. Reputed to be a mystic as well as a thinker, the school he founded would nowadays be thought of as a religious cult that taught many unusual and strange doctrines including, notoriously, the veneration for – and abstinence from the eating of – beans. Pythagoras also preached reincarnation and the transmigration of souls and is largely responsible for the modern belief in numerology, later popularized by Nostradamus.

According to Pythagoras, the ultimate nature of reality is number. This idea developed out of his theory of music, in which he proved that the intervals between musical tones could be expressed as ratios between the first four integers (the numbers one to four). Since part of Pythagoras' religious teaching consisted in the claim that music has a special power over the soul, infused as it is into the very fabric of the universe, the belief that number is the ultimate nature of reality quickly followed.

The ultimate nature of reality is number

The Pythagoreans went on to venerate certain numerical patterns, especially the so-called 'tetractys of the decad'. The tetractys is a diagram that represents the first four numbers in a triangle of ten dots:

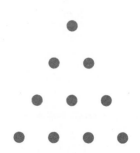

Both the triangle and the number 10 – the decad – became objects of worship for the Pythagoreans. In Pythagorean thought, the number 10 is the perfect

Pythagoras lived in a religious community in Italy, committed to a disciplined existence and the observance of certain taboos.

number because it is made up of the sum of the first four integers, as shown in the tetractys. The integers themselves were thought to represent fundamental ideas – the number one representing the point, two the line, three the surface and four the solid. Further, it was thought that there were ten heavenly bodies – five planets, the sun, the moon, the earth and a mysterious and invisible 'counter-earth' (probably invented to make the celestial number up to ten) all revolving around a central fire.

After Pythagoras' death, his school splintered into two camps. One maintained his religious and mystical teachings, while the other concentrated on his mathematical and scientific insights. The latter continued to believe the nature of the universe must be essentially arithmetical. Units of number, points, were somehow thought to possess spatial dimensions and be the ultimate constituents of objects. An idea later criticized by both **Parmenides** and **Zeno**. The Pythagorean cosmogony also encountered grave problems due to one of Pythagoras' own discoveries. For Pythagoras had shown how the ratio of the diagonal through a square to its sides could not be expressed as a whole number. The problem of 'the incommensurability of the diagonal' led to the discovery – or invention,

Raphael's *School of Athens* shows Pythagoras among the great philosophers of the ancient world.

depending on your philosophical point of view – of irrational numbers. Though a major problem for the Pythagorean cosmogony, irrational numbers have proven a major and lasting development in mathematical thinking.

▌ ESSENTIAL READING ▌

No writings of Pythagoras survive, although a few works masqueraded as his in ancient times, some of which remain extant. Pythagoras's followers usually prefaced any quotations from their master with the phrase *autos ephe* ('he himself said'), emphasizing that his teachings were passed on by word of mouth.

216

QUINE, WILLARD VAN ORMAN

1908–2000

Born in Akron, Ohio, Quine was, before his death on Christmas Day 2000, widely regarded as America's greatest living philosopher. His early work was influential in mathematical logic, but he came to prominence through an article published in 1951 entitled *Two Dogmas of Empiricism*. Now regarded as a 20th-century classic and de rigueur reading for philosophy students everywhere, the article attacked the prevailing assumptions of empiricist metaphysics, then widely held and chiefly promoted by his great friend and mentor, Rudolph **Carnap**. In over twenty books and many more articles, Quine went on to develop and expound a systematic philosophical program the depth and breadth of which had not been seen since the days of the great metaphysicians of the 18th and 19th centuries.

Science is ‘the final arbiter of truth’

Key to Quine's thought is the view that science is, as he put it ‘the final arbiter of truth’. Only science can tell us about the world, and one of the things it tells us is that our knowledge of the world is constrained by and limited to sensory stimulations. Quine is the arch-empiricist, rejecting **Kant**'s attempted synthesis of empiricism and rationalism to found metaphysics both in *Two Dogmas* and throughout his later works,

encapsulated principally in the abstruse *Word and Object* (1960) and the more reader-friendly *The Pursuit of Truth* (1990).

In *Two Dogmas,* Quine attacks two unempirical assumptions of the positivist program. First, the idea originating from Kant that there are two different kinds of propositions, analytic ones – known to be true in virtue of their meaning alone (for example, ‘all bachelors are unmarried’) and synthetic ones – propositions known to be true or false according to how things stand in the world (that it is raining, for example, or that George Bush is the President of the USA). Second, Quine rejects the positivist assumption that the meaning of a proposition can be reduced to talk about sensory stimulations. Quine convincingly shows that no proposition can be true independent of experience, but also that the meaning of a proposition cannot be ascertained in isolation from the ‘web of beliefs’ of which it forms a part. This web of belief is itself conditioned by sensory experience. However, experience cannot be divorced from the theory of the world used to describe it. Theory and experience go hand in hand, and what there is, what exists, says Quine, is what our best theory of the world says there is. The upshot is that science is essentially a pragmatic exercise concerned with predicting future sensory experience.

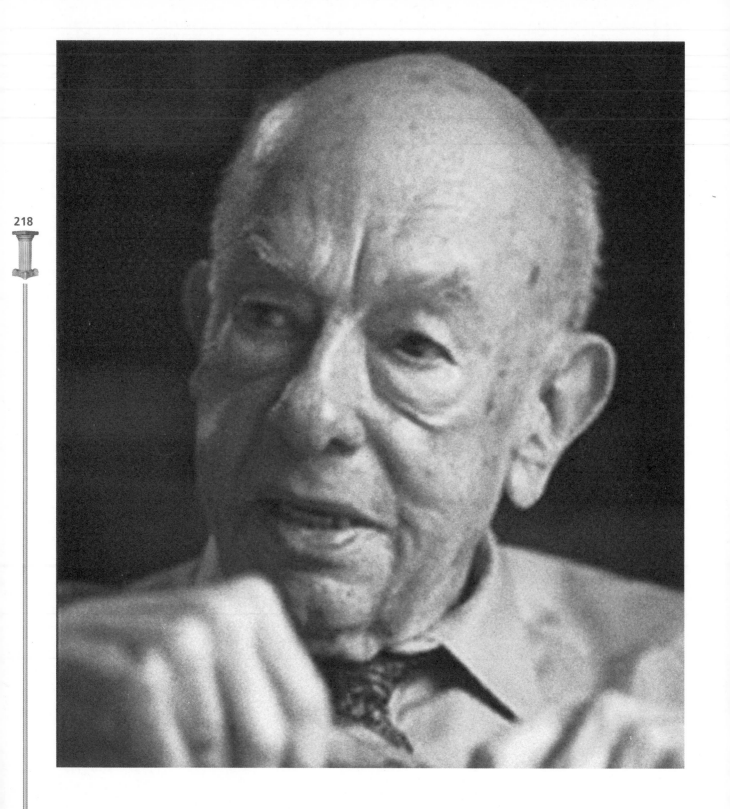

QUINE, WILLARD VAN ORMAN

After working in naval intelligence during the Second World War, Quine resumed his philosophical career at Harvard.

In *Word and Object*, Quine expands on earlier themes developing his conception of philosophy and epistemology as scientific theory building, conditioned but not determined by sensory experience. He develops his critique of the concept of meaning begun with the attack on analyticity in *Two Dogmas,* with a devastating thought-experiment designed to undermine the notion of synonymy or sameness of meaning. Quine envisages a scenario of radical translation in which a field linguist, faced with a completely unknown native language, has to import his own conceptual scheme as an hypothesis in order to make sense of the natives' behaviour, since behaviour alone woefully underdetermines the possible meanings of the natives' utterances. If importing a conceptual scheme is required for translation, it follows that meaning is relative to the translator and the idea of sameness of meaning across different translation manuals evaporates.

Quine's philosophy does not shy away from the conclusion that ontology, the study of what there is, is relative to background theory. Indeed, Quine boldly claims that physical objects are 'posits' of our current best theory, whose existence we could conceivably deny given suitable revisions in light of recalcitrant experience. Thus, Quine says 'For my part I do, qua lay physicist, believe in physical objects and not in Homer's gods; and I consider it a scientific error to believe otherwise. But in point of epistemological footing, the physical objects and the gods differ only in degree and not in kind. Both sorts of entities enter our conceptions only as cultural posits.'

▌ ESSENTIAL READING ▌

Two Dogmas of Empiricism (1951)

In this celebrated paper, Quine attacks two key parts of the philosophy of logical positivism: analyticity (the distinction between analytic truths and synthetic truths) and reductionism (the theory that a statement is given meaning by its empirical verification).

Word and Object (1960)

This study of the philosophy of language demonstrates how linguistic analysis may be used as a method of resolving philosophical problems. Quine explains how uncertainty about the reality of concrete or abstract objects may be resolved by defining the relation between words and objects.

The Pursuit of Truth (1990)

In this work, Quine updates, summarizes and clarifies his thinking on the philosophical issues that have preoccupied him over the course of his career.

RAWLS, JOHN
1921–2002

American philosopher John Rawls was one of the most important political philosophers of the 20th century. In a series of works that began with the seminal *A Theory of Justice* (1971), he grappled with the classic questions of restrictions on liberty, the obligations of the citizen, and distributive justice (the fairness or otherwise of the distribution of wealth and power). Rawls' solution, refined and expanded over the ensuing thirty years, was his 'Justice as Fairness' theory, which rejected the utilitarian model in favour of an updating of the traditional social contract, and attempted the difficult trick of both protecting individual rights and promoting distributive justice.

Rawls' *Theory of Justice* was a seminal work in political philosophy that sparked an ongoing debate about social structures.

The starting-point for Rawls' social contract was his 'original position'. This hypothetical construct imagined people deciding what will be just in their society from behind a 'veil of ignorance'. As he says in *A Theory of Justice:* 'No one knows his place in society, his class position or status, nor does anyone know his fortune in the distribution of natural assets and abilities, his intelligence, strength, and the like.'

Given that people will have no idea how they will fare in competition with their fellow-citizens, Rawls claimed that they were bound to adopt a minimax strategy of avoiding the worst, and to come up with a set of principles that are fair for everyone. These were 'the principles that rational and free persons concerned to further their own interests would accept in an initial position of equality as defining the fundamentals of the terms of their association.'

According to Rawls, there were two such Principles of Justice. The First (Liberty) Principle stated that 'each person is to have an equal right to the most extensive scheme of equal basic liberties compatible with a similar scheme of liberty for others.' For Rawls these basic liberties included not only freedom of speech, assembly, thought and conscience, but also the right to hold personal property. They did not include the classic 'freedoms from', like freedom from unemployment, exploitation or fear.

The Second (Justice) Principle came in two parts. Firstly, levels of social and economic inequality must be such that everyone has 'fair equality of opportunity' when it comes to winning jobs and positions of power. This means more than equal opportunity to offer a certain level of merit – each individual must also have equal opportunity to acquire that the level of merit. Equalities of opportunity meant little without equality of educational provision.

'No one knows his place in society... nor does anyone know his fortune in the distribution of natural assets and abilities...'

Secondly, the levels of social and economic inequality must be of the greatest benefit to the least-advantaged members of society. According to this second part of the Justice Principle – often known as the Difference Principle – inequality is only acceptable if it raises the absolute level of the worst-off. Rawls' egalitarianism is bolstered by his insistence that no one should expect greater rewards simply because they were born with greater gifts.

Rawls recognized that his two Principles of Justice could work against each other in practice, and

sought to solve this problem by making the Liberty Principle more or less absolute. When a society was forced to choose, the protection of freedoms (The Liberty Principle) should take precedence over the promotion of distributive justice (The Justice Principle). He allowed that this priority could be reversed in situations of low economic development, but his failure to define or specify this 'low level' left basic questions unanswered.

He insisted that theories built from abstract principles needed testing against common sense. Philosophical reflection on the guiding principles of his own 'Justice as Fairness' theory would adjustment them to a non-theoretical reality, bringing them into what he called 'reflective equilibrium'.

Political Liberalism (1993) further refined Rawls' ideas. Its primary thrust was to differentiate between liberalism as a philosophy of life and liberalism as a purely political creed. The former was concerned with moral and religious precepts, and these, Rawls believed, were bound to emphasize political divisions. The latter, by contrast, dealt in less controversial notions like reciprocity and mutual respect. If the latter was given precedence, then people of differing moral and religious persuasions could focus on the 'public reason' that united them, rather than the beliefs that divided them. What Rawls called an 'overlapping consensus' could be created. This, though not a particularly original idea, had clear relevance to the growing debate about multi-culturalism.

In *Justice as Fairness, A Restatement* (2001), Rawls offered an overview of his ideas. He also reviewed the suitability of various political systems when it came to implementing his guiding principles. He listed five systems – laissez-faire capitalism, state socialism with a command economy, welfare-state capitalism, property-owning democracy, and market socialism. In *A Theory of Justice* he had thought the last three offered fertile ground, but by 2001 only the last two were considered acceptable. The increasingly right-wing welfare-state capitalism of the 1980s and 1990s no longer included 'arrangements designed to satisfy the two principles of justice.' In considering his own country, Rawls drew attention to the American campaigning system and healthcare system, both of which rewarded wealth and penalized poverty.

After the publication of *A Theory of Justice*, several philosophers tried to apply Rawls' principles to the international politics, and Rawls himself finally followed suit with *The Law of Peoples* (1999). Much to the disappointment of his more liberal followers, Rawls' ideas proved more conservative than expected. Though stressing the defence of human rights, he refused to accept the necessity of a minimal level of democracy. 'Decent hierarchical' regimes, which featured corporate styles of participation and/or monopoly power of a single religious group, were considered acceptable proved they did not violate basic human rights.

Rawls refused an international application of the 'Difference Principle', claiming that countries, unlike individuals, had no right to expect compensation for a lack of natural resources. He did not accept Charles Beitz's argument that global inequality, like domestic inequality in his own original theory, could only be justified when it served the interests of the poorest.

‖ ESSENTIAL READING ‖

A Theory of Justice (1971)

This contains Rawls' most influential contribution to political philosophy, his Justice as Fairness theory. In this work Rawls sets out his hypothetical 'original position', and derives his two principles of distributive justice, the liberty and difference principles.

Political Liberalism (1993)

An update and defence of Rawls' Justice as Fairness theory. It also introduces the supportive concepts of 'public reason' and 'overlapping consensus'.

The Law of Peoples (1999)

This work explores the possible application of the Justice as Fairness theory to the international arena. Rawls apparent refusal to give the most disadvantaged the same theoretical precedence on the international stage disappointed many of his supporters.

Justice as Fairness: A Restatement (2001)

An edited summary of Rawls' later work, shows a declining faith in the welfare capitalist system's ability to deliver acceptable distributive justice.

REID, THOMAS

1710–1796

Scottish philosopher who, like **Kant**, was inspired by the writings of his fellow Scot, David **Hume**. Reid produced two principal works, namely his *Inquiry into the Human Mind* and the later *Essays on the Intellectual Powers of Man.*

Reid felt that Hume's sceptical conclusions were inevitable but also unacceptable. Consequently, and logically, the only move left open to him was to object to the assumptions upon which Hume's philosophy was based. Principally, this amounted to rejecting the assumption, common to **Descartes**, **Locke** and **Berkeley** as well as Hume, that ideas in the mind are intermediaries between the subject and the world. Rather, Reid espoused a form of direct perception in an attempt to deny Hume's conclusions and bring philosophy back to common-sense.

Reid countered Hume's sceptical empiricism with a theory of direct perception and an emphasis on common sense.

Although he made original contributions in this regard, Reid's importance in philosophy has gone down not so much for his own work but for his masterful criticisms of Locke and Berkeley. In particular, his criticism of Locke's criterion of personal identity helped to highlight this debate in philosophy (also see **Leibniz**).

Locke had maintained that a sufficient criterion of personal identity was psychological connectedness. What this amounts to is the idea that an individual is the same person over time just so long as they maintain a psychological connection, principally memory, from one time to another. Reid objected to this with his famous 'Brave Officer' argument, which can be no more succinctly put than in Reid's own words:

The transitivity of identity is the principle that if A = B, and B = C, then A = C

'Suppose a brave officer to have been flogged when a boy at school for robbing an orchard, to have taken a standard from the enemy in his first campaign, and to have been made a general in advanced life; suppose, also, which must be admitted to be possible, that, when he took the standard, he was conscious of his having been flogged at school, and that, when made a general, he was conscious of his taking the standard, but had absolutely lost the consciousness of his flogging.'

Now Reid proceeds to argue that on Locke's criterion of personal identity, the general is the same person as the brave officer, and the brave officer is the same person as the boy, but since there is no psychological connection between the general and the boy, it turns out the general and the boy are not the same person. The force of the argument is not just that we intuitively think the boy and the general are the same person. A defender of Locke might maintain that in a very real sense the general is a vastly different person from the child. Rather the strength of the 'Brave Officer' argument lies in showing that Locke's position results in a contradiction, entailing, as Reid puts it, that 'the general is, and at the same time is not, the same person with him who was flogged at school'. This result comes about because of a logical principle known as the transitivity of identity. In short, the transitivity of identity is the principle that if A = B, and B = C, then A = C. Reid's 'Brave Officer' argument shows that Locke's criterion of personal identity contradicts this rule. As a result the contradiction makes a nonsense of Locke's criterion as either a necessary or sufficient condition of identity. Accordingly, Locke's criterion must be rejected.

▌ ESSENTIAL READING ▌

Inquiry into the Human Mind (1764)
Reid's *Inquiry* looks at the philosophical problem of the relationship between the mind and the real world. He refutes the scepticism of Hume, Berkeley and Locke that perception is a product of the senses, proposing instead that there must be a direct awareness by the mind of the material world. He shows this by looking at each sense in turn and showing its inadequacy in providing us with the full picture of the world as we know it through perception.

Essays on the Intellectual Powers of Man (1785)
In this work, made up of his lectures from the previous twenty years, Reid sets out to refute Hume's scepticism and establish in its place a philosophy of common sense. It contains discussions on the senses, the theory of perception, personal identity, memory, morality and beauty.

RORTY, RICHARD

1931–

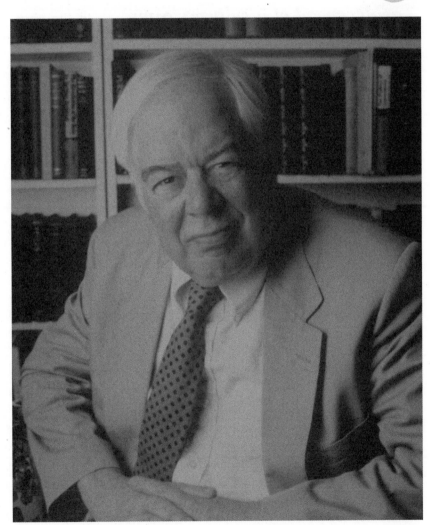

The American philosopher Richard Rorty's *The Linguistic Turn* (1967), though a work of analytic philosophy, concentrated on the inherent difficulties of that tradition, and doubts about the nature and worth of philosophical enquiry would remain central to his work over succeeding decades. His next, and most important work, *Philosophy and the Mirror of Nature* (1979), was a full-blooded critique of analytic philosophy, and, by implication, an assault on the importance of traditional philosophy in modern culture.

Rorty began by rejecting the Cartesian mind-body split. He held that this scientification of philosophy, which had provoked several centuries' worth of debate between rationalists and empiricists, idealists and materialists, was based on a false premise. The idea that the mind was a 'theatre of representations', forever dealing with a reality

Rorty's scepticism targets the tradition of philosophy itself, raising doubts about its findings, usefulness and ultimate purpose.

outside itself, was faulty. So too was the later attempt to replace mind in the equation with language. The long philosophical search for foundational values, true nature or a priori truths, though sometimes mentally stimulating, would never yield the hoped-for results, would never 'produce noncontroversial

Those beliefs which help in the achievement of a culture's aims are those which can be justified

results concerning matters of ultimate concern.' The Cartesian project had substituted science for God, and, not surprisingly, had gone nowhere. Its only achievement, according to Rorty, was the raising of philosophers to an eminence they scarcely deserved.

In place of the intellectually bankrupt representationalism and foundationalism, Rorty offered 'epistemological behaviourism'. We know what our society lets us know. What we accept has nothing to do with how well a statement mirrors the world – it has everything to do with how well it fits in what we have already come to believe. Answers as to why we believe what we believe will be found in psychology, sociology or biology, not philosophy.

So what is philosophy good for? A lot less than most philosophers would care to believe, according to Rorty. By elevating the mind above and beyond physical reality, and taking that mind as their own intellectual territory, analytic philosophers had, in effect, placed themselves above and beyond other intellectual disciplines. They had made themselves the arbitrators of what was real and meaningful, had placed themselves outside history. But if, as Rorty

claimed, there were no foundations to be uncovered, no *a priori* truths to be discovered, then philosophers were just 'redescribers' and 'conversationalists'.

Thinkers through the ages – Copernicans, Marxists and modern scientists in one of Rorty's examples – came up with sentences which redescribed reality, sentences like 'the earth goes round the sun', 'all history is the history of class struggles' and 'matter can be changed into energy'. These redescriptions were initially seen as false, then accepted as hypotheses, and finally 'became accepted, at least within certain communities of inquiry, as *obviously* true.'

Philosophy's value was pragmatic, and Rorty has often recognized his debt to the pragmatic philosopher **Dewey**. His own version of pragmatism has changed over the years, from the classic view that truth was what current cultural practise justified to a complete rejection of the concept's usefulness. Since there are no ultimate truths, truth cannot be a meaningful goal of inquiry. Philosophers should aim instead for the practical matter of 'honest justification'. Those beliefs which 'work', which help in the achievement of a culture's aims, are those which can be justified.

Rorty's anti-foundationalism has also informed his political philosophy. He desired a political culture which maximized creativity and freedom, and which protected people from cruelty or extreme want, but not because these wishes reflected absolute values. His beliefs, like anyone else's, reflected the time and place he lived in. Rorty agreed with **Rawls** that notions like the latter's 'reflective equilibrium' and 'overlapping consensus' were, pragmatically, the furthest anti-foundationalist political philosophers could go. What social hope there was lay in imagination and redescription, in people 'describing a future in terms which the past did not use.'

Rorty's attacks on the importance of philosophy, and his oft-repeated notion that society would do better to take its moral vocabulary from novelists than from his fellow-philosophers, has not endeared him to the profession. His views have been consistently challenged, and in recent years he has often been accused of no longer doing philosophy, of being, in effect, an anti-philosopher. Rorty and his supporters have claimed in response that the version of philosophy which his critics perpetuate has now outlived whatever usefulness it had.

While Raphael's 1510 masterpiece *The School of Athens* represented the ancient Greek school as the pinnacle of human civilization, Rorty called the wisdom of philosophical inquiry into question.

‖ ESSENTIAL READING ‖

The Linguistic Turn (1967)

In seeking to define the difficulties facing analytical philosophy, *The Linguistic Turn* sets out the doubts about the nature and place of philosophical enquiry which Rorty refines in later works.

Philosophy and the Mirror of Nature (1979)

This is Rorty's most important work. It dismisses Cartesian representationalism, the notion that the mind (or language) reflects some objective reality outside itself. The lack of a foundational 'holy grail' makes philosophy and philosophers less important than has been previously assumed, especially by the latter. Philosophy is only important for pragmatic reasons, for how useful it is in helping a culture achieve its aims.

Contingency, Irony, and Solidarity (1989)

Begins where *Philosophy and the Mirror of Nature* leaves off, and explores, among other things, the implications of replacing abstract ideas with pragmatism as the binding blocks of political community.

ROUSSEAU, JEAN-JACQUES

1712–1778

Rousseau was born in Geneva, the son of a watchmaker. Rousseau's mother died in childbirth and his father showed little interest in him: the young Rousseau was left in Geneva when his father was exiled to Lyons. At the age of fourteen Rousseau left Geneva and after several adventures, ended up in Turin. Several more years of wandering from place to place passed until he was taken into the private care of a certain Madame de Warens. Under her care he took to reading and study and spent some eight years there until obtaining a job as

> ## 'Men in a state of nature do not know good and evil, but only their independence'

secretary to the French Ambassador in Venice. He did not write his first independent work until he was nearly forty years old, but soon became famous on its publication. He became the leading French philosopher of the Enlightenment, responsible for inaugurating the Romantic movement in continental philosophy. Despite his success as a writer, Rousseau fell out with almost everyone who knew him, including the Catholics and Mme de Warens, who had by this time become his mistress. He fell out too with the Protestants and the Government of France after publishing *The Social Contract*. He ended his days alone in poverty and despair having fled from country to country. After quarrelling with his one-time friend David **Hume** in England, he finally expired in Paris, most probably committing suicide. Apart from his collaboration on Diderot's *Encyclopaedia*, Rousseau's best works are his *Confessions, Emile,* and *The Social Contract*.

The Social Contract is Rousseau's magnum opus, in which he provides a blueprint for the ideal society, in contrast to the contemporary social, political and educational climate which he had criticized in his earlier work, particularly *Emile* and *The Origin of Inequality*. In these works, Rousseau had argued that injustice was a result of institutions which suppress the natural will and ability of men. In the later book, Rousseau introduces his famous concept of 'the noble savage', declaring that 'Men in a state of nature do not know good and evil, but only their independence', and this along with 'the peacefulness of their passions, and their ignorance of vice, prevents them from doing ill'.

Man was born free, and he is everywhere in chains'. With this famous opening line, Rousseau begins *The Social Contract*. Frequently misinterpreted as a blueprint for totalitarianism, Rousseau's work stressed the connection between liberty and law,

Rousseau believed that 'civilized' society had a corrupting influence on man, who could only really be free in his natural, 'uncivilized' state.

is for the greater good of the state, thus eroding any notion of individual rights. Indeed, Rousseau insists explicitly that any notion of individual rights must be forsaken.

The general will, Rousseau tells us, is the will of all those directed to their own common interests and must be understood as distinct from 'the will of all', which is merely the aggregate of individual selfish wills. 'Each of us puts his person and all his power in common under the supreme direction of the general will, and, in our corporate capacity, we receive each member as an indivisible part of the whole'. The general will, however, appears to generate a force that is greater than the sum of its parts. There is a suggestion in Rousseau's writings that the general will takes on the aspect of a personal will, over and above the members of the society that give it power. The populace have a duty to obey, leading to the interpretation of Rousseau as condoning totalitarianism. What is often missing in this interpretation, is, firstly, Rousseau's insistence that the direct democracy he advocates is only really practicable in small city-states, and indeed Rousseau takes as his model and ideal the city-states of Ancient Greece that were known at times to practise just this sort of democracy. Secondly, and this is the significance of the small

freedom and justice. The ruler, emphasizes Rousseau, is the agent of the people not the master, and yet his doctrine of an abstract general will appears to license the tyranny of the majority over minorities. For although Rousseau esteems the democratic process, he combines it with a duty of all those who participate in society to obey that which city-state, insofar as the sovereign can impose legislation upon the members of the state in the name of the general will, the sovereign is no more than the community itself in its legislative and collective capacity. In other words, as Rousseau sees it, there can be no disharmony between the interests of the sovereign and the interests of the people, since by definition, the former is constituted from the latter.

However, one should not overlook the fact that there are serious tensions in Rousseau's concept of

'Man was born free, and he is everywhere in chains'

a social contract. Rousseau is not so much the idealist that he does not realize there will be times when an individual's will runs counter to the general will. In such cases there is no compromise: the individual shall be forced to comply, or in Rousseau's pithy but rather chilling words, 'This means nothing less than that he will be forced to be free'.

‖ ESSENTIAL READING ‖

Discourse on the Sciences and Art (1750)
In this work, the winning entry in an essay competition on the question 'Have the arts and sciences conferred benefits on mankind?', Rousseau argues that civilization has corrupted people's natural virtue and morality, and that everything that distinguishes civilized people from ignorant savages is evil.

Discourse on the Origin of Inequality (1755)
This essay is an important critique of the ideas of philosophers such as **Locke**. Rousseau holds that human beings are naturally good, and only made bad by the institutions of civilization. He argues that society and social inequality arise from people having private property.

The Social Contract (1762)
Generally considered to be Rousseau's greatest work, *The Social Contract* advocates democracy and denies the divine right of kings. It argues that when people live in social groups, their freedom to follow their own interests must be limited by submission to the general will of the social group to which they belong.

Emile (1762)
Describing the education of Emile, a rich man's son, by a tutor, this novel is a treatise on education on 'natural' principles, aimed at freeing children from the corruptions of modern society and making them good citizens.

The Confessions (1782)
This is Rousseau's autobiography, notable for its honesty.

RUSSELL, BERTRAND

1872–1970

Britain's most famous modern philosopher, whose magisterial *History of Western Philosophy* is still a classic of its kind. Russell first became famous for his attempt, only partially successful, to show how mathematics was grounded in logic. Despite eventually abandoning that project, he was famous within philosophy for his work in logical analysis and, in later life, in society for his humanist social philosophy. Interestingly, Russell saw no essential connection between these two strands of his thought, claiming of his latter views, 'On these questions I did not write in my capacity as a philosopher; I wrote as a human being who suffered from the state of the world, wished to find some way of improving it, and was anxious to speak in plain terms to others who had similar feelings'. Critics might complain that this, rather than his formal work in logical analysis, is surely the task of philosophy, but it is not a view Russell would share.

The scope of Russell's work spans all the traditional areas of philosophy and incorporates many of the new ideas generated in the first half of the 20th century. His thought continued to change and develop throughout his life. However, it is generally held that his most important contributions came in the first decade or so of the new century.

Russell was a radical liberal and a committed campaigner for nuclear disarmament. In 1950, he was awarded the Nobel Prize for literature.

Concerned with the semantic problems of meaning and reference, Russell solved a long-standing philosophical conundrum with his famous 'theory of definite descriptions'. The conundrum is generated out of considering whether to call a sentence true or false when it fails to refer. For example, consider:

The present King of France is bald.

Since there is no such person as 'the present King of France', do sentences of this kind count as false, or meaningless? Either view creates problems. To say it is meaningless defies the very simple fact that one can understand what the sentence is trying to assert. But to say it is false, seems to entail that the contradiction of (1), namely

The present King of France is not bald,

is true. But (2) is no more true than (1). So how do we settle the analysis of sentences that fail to refer in this way? Russell's answer was ingenious. He proposed that such sentences are really descriptions which consist of a conjunction of separate claims. Namely, first, that there is some person who is the King of France, second, that there is only one person who is the King of France, and thirdly that any person that is the King of France is bald. Now these propositions can be formally decided. For they amount to a conjunction in which the first proposition is false (that there is a King of France). Logically, any statement that is a conjunction of propositions is false if any one of the conjuncts is false. Accordingly, the conjunction turns out false regardless of whether the other conjuncts are treated as true or false.

The theory of definite descriptions, in showing how it is possible to speak meaningfully of things that do not exist, has become a standard tool of logical analysis. It is essential to all those whose work in the philosophy of language is predicated on theories of meaning which seek to essentially connect the meaning of words with items in the world. For if that is the underlying basis of meaning, assertions about non-existents are surely problematic without Russell's analysis.

Russell solved a long-standing philosophical conundrum with his famous 'theory of definite descriptions'

‖ ESSENTIAL READING ‖

Principia Mathematica (3 volumes: 1910, 1912, 1913)
A seminal work in the field of mathematical logic, written jointly with **Whitehead**, this book defends 'logicism', the goal of which is 'to show that all pure mathematics follows from purely logical premises and uses only concepts definable in logical terms'. The book also contains the theory of 'types', which Russell and Whitehead used to deal with certain logical or mathematical paradoxes.

The Problems of Philosophy (1912)
Still one of the best and most readable introductions to philosophy, this book includes chapters on knowledge, induction, idealism, matter, universals, and truth and falsehood.

A History of Western Philosophy (1945)
This is a very readable book on the development of European and American philosophy from **Thales** to **Dewey**.

Logic and Knowledge (1956)
This is a collection of Russell's essays written between 1901 and 1950, and includes descriptions of his theory of 'logical atomism'.

RYLE, GILBERT

1900–1976

Oxford philosopher who followed **Wittgenstein** in asserting the importance of linguistic analysis, Ryle believed for a time that the task of philosophy was to resolve metaphysical problems by showing how the concepts employed in their formulation were misunderstood. Principally, such problems involve the confusion of logically distinct categories, an idea that led to his discussion of a 'category-mistake'.

In his best known work *The Concept of Mind*, Ryle is concerned with the difficulties raised by Cartesian dualism. Dualism maintains that the body and mind are separate substances, one material, the other immaterial respectively. Accordingly, mental properties can only be ascribed to the latter and physical properties the former substance. This gives rise to a number of problems, including the nature of causal interaction between mind and body, and personal identity and the individuation of 'minds', to name just two.

This apparent split of a distinct but immaterial mind inhabiting a material body, Ryle calls the myth of 'the ghost in the machine' and, he insists, rests on a 'category-mistake'. Category-mistakes do not just arise in philosophical discourse, but can appear in quite ordinary contexts. For example, imagine a student guiding his parents around his university. He shows them the Library, the Faculty building, the Students' Union, the sports facilities and so on until they have toured the whole campus. Now suppose the parents say, 'yes, they are fine buildings, but when are we going to see the University?' Clearly the parents have misunderstood the concept of 'a University'. Ryle says their mistake is in thinking that ' "the University" stood for an extra member of the class of which these other units are members' rather than a term which describes 'the way in which all that [they have] already seen is organized.'

Cartesian dualism, the myth of 'the ghost in the machine', rests on a 'category-mistake'

Ryle believed, then, that the concept of the mind as a distinct but non-physical entity with distinct non-physical properties was just such a 'category-mistake'. In this case, the mistake arises from assuming that either the mind or mental properties can be understood in non-physical terms. As Ryle expertly puts it, the concept of mind as non-physical is always defined in negative physical terms, non-spatial, non-observable, neither in motion nor at rest. Indeed dualists, Ryle mockingly notes, define the mind as 'not bits of clockwork ... just bits of nonclockwork'.

Ryle goes on to investigate exactly how mental properties are explained in ordinary language in order to adumbrate his own theory of mind. He finds that mental properties are ascribed not according to the possession of some mysterious, unobservable private process – indeed, how could they be? – but with reference to dispositions to behave in certain ways. To say of someone that they are angry is not to describe their inner mental state, but to describe a disposition to behave in a certain way, to shout, throw things around, to brood or fume, accordingly. This idea was massively influential upon two distinct but related schools of 20th-century thought, the 'logical behaviourists' (see **Carnap**) and the Oxford 'ordinary language philosophers' (see **Austin**).

Ultimately, Ryle revised his notion of 'category-mistake' in light of criticisms that the notion of a 'category' could not be precisely formulated. Both **Aristotle** and **Kant** had made systematic attempts to define logical categories, but neither met with complete success.

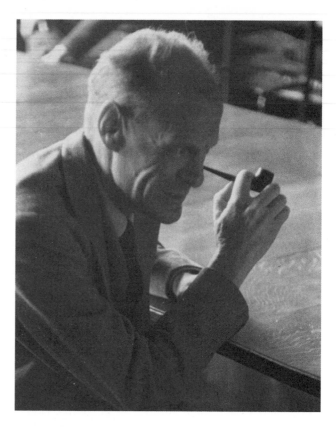

Ryle attending a meeting between the Aristotelian Society and the Mind Association in 1952.

‖ ESSENTIAL READING ‖

The Concept of Mind (1949)

In this influential work, Ryle claims that there is a fundamental error, a 'category mistake', at the heart of Cartesian dualism. He says it is wrong to talk of mind and body as though they are both same type of thing. The book famously coins the phrase 'the ghost in the machine' to ridicule **Descartes'** idea of the mind existing within the body. Descartes, he says, describes the mind, which is in one category, using language appropriate for another category – the body. Ryle argues that every concept belongs in a certain category and one of the purposes of philosophy is to sort out the errors and place concepts in their proper categories.

SARTRE, JEAN-PAUL

1905–1980

French philosopher and principal spokesman for the existentialist movement in post-war France. Sartre's most important work, *Being and Nothingness,* owes a great debt to many who had gone before him, principally, **Kierkegaard** and **Heidegger**. Nonetheless, Sartre's philosophy possesses a clarity and force that captured the spirit of his times in a far more powerful way than that of either his predecessors or his existentialist contemporaries, such as **Camus**, **Merleau-Ponty** and **de Beauvoir**.

The central theme of all existentialist philosophies is the claim that 'existence precedes essence'. By this Sartre intends to convey the view that man first exists without purpose or definition, finds himself in the world and only then, as a reaction to experience, defines the meaning of his life.

It is the flip-side of an argument presented by **Aristotle** in his *Ethics,* that man is created to fulfil some purpose or goal, and that fulfilment of a life consists in striving towards that goal. By contrast, Sartre argues that since there is no God or designer to give man a purpose, it is up to the individual to choose the life they think best.

However, Sartre's subtle argument does not rely on his atheism to prove the existential premise. For even a belief in God is, according to Sartre, a personal choice – it is a life and purpose chosen. The belief in a deity can never be forced upon a person. Even if one were to have the miraculous visions of Abraham, it is still up to the individual to interpret those visions: the voice of the divine or lunatic hallucinations? Only the individual, not God, can make that interpretation.

Indeed, it is a wider tenet of Sartre's philosophy that man is never compelled; he is faced with a choice at every turn. Even if a man is imprisoned or a gun held to his head, argues Sartre, it is his choice whether to comply or defy – the consequences do not exempt one from making that choice.

This radical freedom, Sartre realizes, has weighty consequences. We are responsible for everything we do. One cannot, in Sartrean existentialism, make excuses or defer responsibility to either a divine being or human nature: to do so would constitute a self-deception, or 'bad-faith'. This leads to three, related burdens on the individual. Firstly, 'anguish', arising from the awareness of the weight of responsibility we each hold. Everything we do affects not only ourselves, but by our choices and actions we set examples for the rest of mankind. Such responsibility is a consequence, Sartre insists, of the fact that we define our own meaning of life, which is reflected in our actions. When we make a choice, it is not merely a personal preference, but a statement to the world that this is how life should be led. The second burden is 'abandonment'. The existentialist finds it 'extremely embarrassing' that God does not exist. For it follows that we are thus left alone without help or guidance in moral matters. Literally, we must make it up as we go along. Thirdly, there is 'despair'. By this Sartre means that we must act without hope, foregoing the instinct to trust that things will turn out for the best. There is no providence. We must each rely only on that which we can affect by our own will and action.

The consequences of Sartre's existentialism are clearly burdensome but unavoidable. We are 'condemned to be free'. But this should not give cause for any kind of pessimism, as his detractors often accused his philosophy of engendering. Existentialism exhibits 'a sternness of optimism', Sartre tells us. Its optimistic message is that 'the destiny of man is placed within himself.'

An active political campaigner and prominent cultural figure, Sartre was the acknowledged leader of the French intellectual elite for many years.

Man is 'condemned to be free'

▌ ESSENTIAL READING ▐

The Transcendence of the Ego (1936)
Sartre presents here a phenomenological description of the ego, which he regards as something not given by consciousness but rather created by it.

Nausea (1938)
This novel is written in the form of a diary which describes the writer's feelings of 'nausea', a feeling of disgust caused by awareness of the world of matter, including our own bodies.

Sketch for a Theory of Emotions (1939)
Here, Sartre expounds and criticizes some theories of emotion, and then provides his own phenomenological account of emotion. Emotions, according to Sartre, do not simply arise; we actively construct them in order to transform our experience of the world.

Being and Nothingness (1943)
This is Sartre's major work. In it he describes three modes of being and also the concept of non-being, and describes some of the key elements of existentialism such as 'anguish' and 'bad faith'.

Existentialism and Humanism (1948)
This is a short brochure in which Sartre defends existentialism against various criticisms that have been levelled at it.

Critique of Dialectical Reason (1960)
This book can be seen as a Marxist version of existentialism in which the freedom envisaged in Sartre's earlier philosophy is now constrained by social, political and historical circumstances.

SAUSSURE, FERDINAND DE

1857–1913

Swiss philologist whose work has had a monumental impact, first on linguistics and second – through the advent of the 'linguistic turn' – on philosophy. Saussure published little of wide interest during his lifetime, but in the last years of his life taught general linguistics at the University in Geneva. It is said that Saussure destroyed his notes after each lecture and thus, upon his death, left little work to indicate his ideas. Fortunately, his lectures were so extraordinary that his students collected and collated their notes over the three years he taught the course, and published them in 1916, as *Cours de linguistique générale* (A Course in General Linguistics), often simply referred to as the *Cours*.

In the *Cours,* Saussure rejects the task of linguistics as having anything to do with either grammar, philology or etymology. Rather, he defines the proper object of linguistic study as the system of signs employed by human beings, the relationships of which can be studied in the abstract, or as he says 'synchronically' rather than 'diachronically', in other words, without reference to any particular historical implementation of that language. The proper object of linguistic study, says Saussure, is not the linguistic output of any given individual but the shared knowledge of a community of language users. Saussure tells us 'You can conjure up a very precise idea of this product – and thus set the language, so to speak, materially in front of you – by focusing on what is potentially in the brains of a set of individuals (belonging to one and the same community) even when they are asleep; we can say that in each of these heads is the whole product that we call the language'. He goes on 'The language, in turn, is quite independent of the individual; it cannot be a creation of the individual, it is essentially social; it presupposes the collectivity.'

Saussure defines language as a system of signs which can be studied in the abstract

Saussure conceives of language as 'a system of signs', but this necessarily calls for a definition of 'sign'. Saussure gives it as the collation of a word with a concept. When a sign is employed in speech it has a two fold effect. There is the physical sound pattern – the signifier – generated by vocalization and received by the brain or mind – and there is the concept or idea – the signified – that the sign stands for. Both are 'deposited in the mind' as effects of one and the same speech event. The signifier and the signified are inseparably linked; they are like 'the front and back of a single sheet of paper'. Key

Saussure's conception of language as a system of signs was to spark the 20th-century structuralist movement.

to this conception is the claim that the signifier and the signified are wholly distinct from the spoken word. The first is the cause of the other two, which are psychological events.

The relation between the abstract sound pattern and the concept signified is, Saussure insists, wholly arbitrary. But the relationship between sound patterns in any given language can be abstracted and schematized. Saussure called such a schematization 'langue' – the socially shared system of signs employed by people to effect speech. 'Langue' is distinguished from 'parole': the intentional production of a speech act. Saussure compares the difference between langue and parole as like that between the score for a piece of music and the particular performances of it.

That said, Saussure also thought that one could analyse language merely by paying attention to the internal relationships between signs, by analysing 'langue'. A sign's role in 'langue' is defined not by considering its content or positive contribution, but merely by its differences to other signs in the system. Thus, for example, the vowel sounds in the signifiers 'Mary', 'marry' and 'merry' can only be identified by contrasting them with each other. Similarly, the ideas expressed by the signified 'male' must be opposed to 'female': one cannot predicate both of the same subject simultaneously, and so on.

This idea of negative inter-definition in a closed network gave rise to the 'structuralist' movement. Broadly speaking, the structuralist movement, following Saussure, sought to undertake studies in various social sciences by concentrating on the deep structures underlying social practices. Typical examples of such structures are grammar or syntax, (rather than vocabulary use), rules of narrative rather than linguistic style, and in general anything that studies sign systems and their rules rather than particular expressions of the system in use.

Later in the 20th century there would come the 'poststructuralist' reaction, with philosophers such as **Foucault** and **Derrida**. Foucault would reject the Saussurean assumption that one can define all the possible relationships of an element, arguing that one can only look at the permutations that have historically arisen in language use. Accordingly, the structuralist project to define abstract linguistic structures has not yet been successfully carried out.

▌ ESSENTIAL READING ▌

A Course in General Linguistics (1916)

Saussure's seminal work was published posthumously by former students Charles Bally and Albert Sechehaye, based on notes taken during Saussure's lectures at the University of Geneva. The Course proved highly influential, mainly because of Saussure's innovative approach to linguistics, breaking language down into elements, including the linguistic sign, the signifier and the signified. In 1996, a manuscript by Saussure was discovered in his house in Geneva. The text, published as *Writings in General Linguistics*, offers important clarifications on the *Course*.

SCHELLING, FREDERICK WILHELM

1775–1854

German philosopher who took up the challenge of bridging the gap between subjectivity and objectivity engendered by **Descartes**, and not satisfactorily answered by either **Spinoza** or **Kant**. Schelling tried to resolve the problem of Cartesian dualism, with the conscious self on one side and the external world on the other, in a number of his works, the most important of which is his early, yet monumental *System of Transcendental Idealism*.

Following Kant, Schelling makes a distinction between 'transcendental philosophy', concerned with the most fundamental elements of cognition and experience, and natural philosophy, the science of what we ordinarily take to be the external world. Schelling invites us to consider that they presuppose each other. If one begins with natural philosophy one must give an account of the phenomenon of the conscious self as it arises in nature. If one begins with the phenomenology of consciousness one must give an account of the origin of material objects as they arise in conscious experience. Thus, as **Hegel** comments on Schelling, 'these two separate processes are as a whole very clearly expressed: the process which leads from nature to the subject, and that leading from the ego to the object'.

Schelling outlines his enterprise as the reconciliation of the subjective with the objective.

Schelling argued that the Absolute, or the reconciliation of subjective and objective, could only be expressed through art.

These are really one and the same. A proper transcendental philosophy should show how the two are united into one, part of the same all-embracing truth, aspects of the Absolute.

Schelling describes the way in which the scientific investigation of the natural world leads to the inevitable conclusion of the existence of a subject, and thereby the recognition of intelligence in the natural order. In this respect he follows the Aristotelian conception of a teleological or purpose driven natural world. But Schelling's vision is much more encompassing than **Aristotle**'s and only really comes to light when he discusses how one starts from the subjective and works towards the objective.

According to Schelling, transcendental philosophy must begin with the subjective awareness of self, in other words, self-consciousness. The system of transcendental idealism is 'the mechanism of the origination of the objective world from the inward principle of spiritual activity'. In self-consciousness, the self is both subject and object. The ego is infinite, unbounded possibility. But insofar as it posits itself as an object of study, it must become finite to itself. In trying to make sense of this paradox, Schelling says the limiting and the ideal are really reflections of one another. The subject and the object in self-consciousness are one and the same thing. They are identical. Schelling now sees the spiritual activity of self-consciousness as identical with the Absolute, or God. Tellingly, Hegel, one of the most abstruse philosophers of all time, says of Schelling's work at this point, 'All this is a tangled mass of abstractions'.

The position Schelling arrives at after such tangled abstractions is not that far removed from that of Spinoza. For Schelling, the Absolute or 'World-Soul' is expressed through the dual aspects of nature and mind. Everything that exists is part of the One. The Universe or cosmos is a complete entity unfolding in time, and it is Absolute, by which Schelling means nothingness is not part of its nature. However, Schelling goes further than Spinoza, for he argues that the conscious self is itself the consciousness of the Universe, the 'World-Soul', as it unfolds and expresses itself through time. Through man, then, the Absolute becomes conscious of itself.

The idea, though criticized in parts by Hegel and other post-Kantian philosophers, was enormously popular at the time. It elevated the individual artist into someone expressing not only his own ideas but the ideas of the Absolute, of God himself. Ultimately, however, even Schelling's supporters had to admit his attempt at showing how the subjective and objective are reconciled was a failure. His ideas remain important philosophically, however, for the influence they exerted on the various works of **Schopenhauer**, **Nietzsche**, **Heidegger** and **Whitehead**.

241

Schelling outlines his enterprise as the reconciliation of the subjective with the objective

‖ ESSENTIAL READING ‖

System of Transcendental Idealism (1800)

In this work, Schelling attempts to reconcile the objective (nature) with the subjective (ego, or spirit), for only in their agreement, he argues, does true knowledge arise. Nature, he claims, has its own objective reality, independent of the ego. Nature and spirit are two poles, positive and negative, of the reality of the Absolute. Nature contains spirit, endowing it with life and making it possible for individual egos to arise. Nature makes itself apparent to ego through sensation. But only through art, says Schelling, can we represent the Absolute.

SCHILLER, JOHANN CHRISTOPH

1759–1805

German philosopher inspired by **Kant**, Schiller produced work of great importance in the philosophy of art, or aesthetics. Aesthetics is that branch of philosophy concerned with our experiences in relation to music, poetry and the visual arts. Profound aesthetic experiences can induce contemplative and emotional reactions, which we tend to describe using such terms as 'beautiful', 'inspiring', 'moving', 'exquisite' and the like. Philosophers are interested in aesthetic experience and judgement partly for sake of the subject itself, but also for the connected issues it raises in ethics, epistemology, the philosophy of mind and metaphysics. Schiller's best thoughts on this subject are contained in his essay *Of the Sublime*.

Schiller's philosophy of art begins in his psychology and philosophy of mind. Schiller distinguishes two kinds of basic, natural impulses. First there is the impulse of self-preservation, which impels us to maintain our circumstances, to continue our existence, what Schiller calls 'the preservation-drive'. Second, there is what Schiller calls 'the conception-drive'. This conception-drive is the urge to change our circumstances, to be efficient and give expression to our existence. These two different drives are the twin impulses of preservation and progression. The preservation-drive, Schiller asserts, is allied with the sensations or feelings of the body, whilst the conception-drive is allied, naturally, with perception, thinking and representation.

Schiller uses this dichotomy to give an interesting psychological account of fear, and subsequently of aesthetic experience. Fear, he tells us, is a natural defence mechanism to alert the preservation-drive to kick into action when natural conditions become adverse to our survival. Schiller says, 'If

A poet of the Romantic movement as well as a philosopher, Schiller was most influential in the domain of aesthetics.

This illustration shows Schiller as a student in 1779, receiving a prize from the Duke of Weimar. Goethe is among those attending the event.

the danger is of the kind to which resistance is futile, then must fear ensue. Thus an object, whose existence conflicts with the requirements for ours, is, if we do not feel that our power measures up to it, an object of fear'. Yet, he goes on to say, fear only affects us as sensuous beings, and cannot hold sway over our will.

Schiller uses this idea to give his account of aesthetic experience, or as he calls it 'the sublime'. The

> *'Great is he,*
> *who conquers the frightful.*
> *Sublime is he,*
> *who, while succumbing to it,*
> *fears it not'*

sublime is generated when the force of nature is so vast that it dwarfs the possibility of resistance from the preservation-drive. In our 'sensuous being' this gives rise to the mortal fear of pain, but in our conception-drive the awareness of the independence of the will results in a kind of delight. Thus, Schiller says, even as we succumb as beings of Nature, 'we as beings of Reason, as beings not belonging to Nature, feel absolutely independent'. To experience the sublime, 'it is thus absolutely required, that we see ourselves fully isolated from every physical means of resistance, and seek succour in our non-physical self. Such a subject matter must therefore be frightful to our sensuousness.' The necessity of fear to the sublime is shown up by experience. Just insofar as man tames nature, building dams to stop floods, or a yoke to tame the natural power of the horse, to that degree does nature become less sublime. Equally, when at times nature overwhelms and, as Schiller puts it, 'shames the artifice of man' – the horse breaks free of the yoke, the river overwhelms the dam – so nature becomes sublime again.

Schiller goes on to argue that just as wherever there is mortal fear there is the sublime, so is it true that wherever we experience the sublime, fear is generated in the preservation-drive? Our aesthetic reactions to works of art as opposed to the power of nature lie in the fact that they do not threaten our physical security, but rather our moral security. Great works of art call into question the established, conservative and preserved notions that constitute our moral security. The conception-drive is startled by, but does not fear, the danger. Thus Schiller's notion of aesthetic experience is perhaps best summed up in his own epigram: 'Great is he, who conquers the frightful. Sublime is he, who, while succumbing to it, fears it not'.

‖ ESSENTIAL READING ‖

Letters on the Aesthetic Education of Man (1794–5)

In a series of 27 famous letters, Schiller enquires into the source of art and beauty and their relationship to human freedom. He asserts that beauty is an aesthetic unity of thought and feeling, of reason and intuition. The attainment of this unity enables human nature to be realized and fulfilled. Only when our sensual and rational drives are integrated can true freedom be experienced.

Of the Sublime (1801)

In this intriguing essay, Schiller, who was himself a dramatist and poet of great renown, provides a valuable insight into the process by which we are moved by works of art.

SCHLICK, MORITZ

1882–1936

Founder of the celebrated positivist movement the 'Vienna Circle', Schlick's work was heavily influenced by the young **Wittgenstein**'s *Tractatus Logico-Philosophicus (Treatise of Philosophical Logic)*. As a result, Schlick's primary interest was in language and meaning and led him to develop the 'verificationist' theory of meaning.

A statement is meaningful if it is either true by definition or is in principle verifiable by experience

According to Schlick, a statement is meaningful if it is either true by definition (such as 'All bachelors are unmarried men') or is in principle verifiable by experience. Thus, for Schlick, the statements of science are meaningful only in so far as there is some method, in principle, by which they can be verified. The 'in principle' caveat is necessary to allow that false statements are just as meaningful as true ones. False statements are statements which could have been true but, as a matter of fact, turn out not to be. Meaningless statements, on the other hand, are those for which no experience could ever in principle lead to a confirmation. Typical examples of such statements, Schlick adamantly insists, are littered throughout the history of metaphysical philosophy. 'The soul survives after death', 'God is all-knowing and benevolent', 'Everything is One' and such like are neither true nor false but simply meaningless, according to Schlick.

The verification principle was to have enormous impact during the mid-20th century. Since only the statements of science and those true by definition are meaningful, some account had to be given of the propositions of ethics, aesthetics and other non-propositional statements. For Schlick, such utterances have no literal meaning, but merely express an attitude or exclamation on behalf of the speaker. The influence of this idea can be seen on the emergence of a number 'emotivist' theories in both ethics and aesthetics during this period (see, for example, G.E. **Moore**). As for mathematics and logic, their propositions fall into the same bracket as those true by definition. They are, according to Schlick, literally tautologies.

This presents a major problem for the verificationist account of meaning. For although it was not the first time that philosophers had claimed mathematical propositions to be merely true by definition, to equate them with tautology seems rash to say the least. By definition a tautology merely repeats or implies something already stated. Yet mathematics is as much a discipline of discovery as science is. One only need look at its development from **Pythagoras** to the modern maths of Cantor, Hilbert, Chaos Theory and Mandelbrot's Fractal Generations to appreciate this. Moreover, since discoveries in pure mathematics often underlie and inform predictions made by physical theories, particularly since the advent of **Einstein**'s theory of relativity and Schrödinger's quantum mechanics, the dividing line between propositions of pure mathematics and pure physics is fuzzy at best.

A similar criticism was made, albeit from a different angle, by **Quine** in his famous paper, *Two Dogmas of Empiricism,* in which he argues that there can be no dividing line between 'analytic' and 'synthetic' (i.e., empirical) statements.

Problems for the verificationist principle became apparent before Quine and modern mathematics, however. The principle criticism of verificationism is that it seems to fall foul of its own criteria for meaningfulness. The claim that a statement is only meaningful insofar as there is a means for its verification is itself neither analytic, nor empirically testable. The principle therefore appears to rule itself as meaningless. This rather embarrassing conclusion led Schlick and others to try and rescue verificationism by weakening or modifying the principle, but none of their attempts proved very convincing. In the end, and particularly in light of Quine's work, the principle was eventually abandoned as a formal criterion of meaning.

Schlick and the other philosophers of the Vienna Circle, however, had highlighted an important methodological principle through their reflections on verification. Prior to their work, philosophers had been somewhat lax at settling the precise meaning of a proposition before raising questions of its truth and falsity. Their work helped to further the growing emphasis on language and the need for a theory of meaning prior to the settling of further philosophical issues.

In 1936, Schlick was assassinated at the University of Vienna by a former student.

∥ ESSENTIAL READING ∥

General Theory of Knowledge (1918)
First published in 1918, and then revised in 1925, this carefully reasoned treatise explores the mind-body problem of philosophy, and offers a new epistemology acknowledging a reality beyond the senses. He refutes **Kant**'s arguments for synthetic a priori knowledge. The book sets out many of the ideas that would later be identified with the Vienna Circle.

Problems of Ethics (1931)
In this book, written over a period of four years, Schlick looked at ethics (meaning the study of human desires and their consequences for human action), expounding the view, in opposition to Kant, that punishment should not be about retribution or retaliation for previous acts. What justifies punishment, according to Schlick, is its consequences in preventing similar actions in future.

SCHOPENHAUER, ARTHUR

1788–1860

A pessimistic post-Kantian philosopher, Schopenhauer's best work, *The World as Will and Representation,* is a remarkably erudite exploration of some key Kantian themes combined with a helping of Eastern philosophy. Schopenhauer helped popularize the abstruse work of **Kant** to the general public and brought the philosophical ideas contained in the *Vedas* and *Upanishads* into Western culture for the first time.

Having taken a violent dislike to Hegel, his colleague at the University of Berlin, Schopenhauer retired to private life in 1831.

Like **Hegel**, to whom he took a vain dislike whilst they both taught at the University of Berlin, Schopenhauer takes as his starting point the unknowability of things-in-themselves, the very reality that stands behind the phenomenal world in Kantian metaphysics. Unlike Hegel, Schopenhauer accepts Kant's point that the reality behind the world of appearances – the noumenal world – is unknowable to the subjective self. However, there is a back-door into the world of things-in-themselves, or as Schopenhauer puts it in typical picturesque style, 'a way from within stands open to us to that real inner nature of things to which we cannot penetrate from without. It is, so to speak, a subterranean passage, a secret alliance, which, as if by treachery, places us all at once in the fortress that could not be taken from outside'.

This 'subterranean passage' is found by realizing that 'we ourselves are also among those entities we require to know, that we ourselves are the thing-in-itself'; a view Schopenhauer claims is implicit in Kant's work but one the great metaphysician overlooked.

Schopenhauer's idea is roughly this. The subjective 'I' is only revealed to us in the world of phenomena, so it cannot be this that constitutes our real essence (that which is a 'thing-in-itself'). Our real essence is will. The will is the thing-in-itself which, while exhibited in the world of appearances as striving – the will to live – is nevertheless revealed to my subjective self immediately and non-conceptually. Schopenhauer never really explains in what this immediate awareness consists, only that the will is not something that belongs to the individual, but is a universal striving force manifest, trapped, in the

Schopenhauer was much influenced by the teachings of the ancient Hindu scriptures the *Vedas* and the *Upanishads*.

individual being by its insatiable desire to reveal itself in the world of appearances.

Unlike **Nietzsche** who would later take up and venerate this idea of will, Schopenhauer does not see the will as something to be glorified, but something to be resisted. We are all at the mercy of the will, it infects everything we think and do, it is the true essence of the universe but also the cause of all our suffering, since we are slaves to its demands.

Schopenhauer does believe, however, that there is a way in which we can overcome the will, through contemplation of the arts and in particular, of music. In music and the arts we can contemplate the universal will apart from our own individual strivings. In contemplation, we can attain a measure of objectivity and relinquish the constant demands and striving of the will for transient goals.

Schopenhauer is also keen to point out that the will can be overcome by the intellectual realization that

We can overcome the striving of the will for transient goals through contemplation of the arts and in particular, of music

our mortal selves are mere slaves, tools of the universal will and that death, consequently, is not to be feared. The universal will is eternal, and our individual lives are not to be valued since it is the will's desire to exist in the world of appearances that gives rise to our individual existence and, consequently, our suffering. This view leads naturally to a justification of suicide, but Schopenhauer tries to circumvent this by claiming that suicide is an act of will and constitutes a surrender of the intellect rather than the victory that can be attained through contemplation.

An original manuscript of *The World as Will and Representation*, with extensive marginal notes by Schopenhauer.

‖ ESSENTIAL READING ‖

On the Fourfold Root of the Principle of Sufficient Reason *(1813)*

Originally Schopenhauer's doctoral thesis, this book challenges the assumption that the universe is completely understandable and that what is real is necessarily rational.

The World as Will and Representation *(1819)*

This is Schopenhauer's major philosophical work. He argues that if one looks deeply into oneself one can discover not only one's own inner nature but also that of the whole universe. The underlying reality of the world is one vast 'will', a non-rational aimless urge which is the source of suffering.

SEARLE, JOHN

1932–

John Searle, who was born in Denver, Colorado, began his career in the 1960s as a philosopher of language. This led him in the late 1970s into the study of the mind and consciousness, and he became one of the pioneers in the field of cognitive science.

Today, Searle is most widely known as a major opponent of the view, held by such thinkers as Daniel **Dennett** and Ray Kurzweil, that the mind is similar to a computer program and that computers are, in fact, conscious. To counter this view, which Searle dubbed 'strong AI' (AI stands for artificial intelligence), Searle developed a famous thought experiment, called the Chinese Room argument. The argument goes as follows: imagine you find yourself in a room containing an enormous rule book, which allows you to look up Chinese sentences and tells you how to reply to them in Chinese. Through a hole in the wall, you are handed a piece of paper with a question written on it in Chinese. Using the rule book, you look up the answer to this question, which you write on another piece of paper, in Chinese, and pass through another hole. To the people outside the room you appear to have a thorough understanding of the Chinese language, whereas in fact you could perform the required task without understanding a word of it.

Searle argues that the Chinese room is an analogy for so-called artificial intelligence. The rule book is the equivalent of a computer program, which manipulates symbols according to a set of rules, and produces answers. By doing so it can give the appearance of being intelligent, though it is nothing of the sort. A computer model of the mind is not actually conscious, argues Searle, just as a

The basic ingredient that distinguishes human minds from computers is intentionality

computer model of the digestive system cannot actually eat pizza. A computer model of falling in love or reading a novel or getting drunk does not actually experience these things, but simply produces a simulation of these processes. The basic ingredient that distinguishes human minds from computers, according to Searle, is intentionality. Computers are defined syntactically, in terms of formal symbol manipulation, and that, he argues, is insufficient to imply consciousness.

So if consciousness is not something that can be experienced by a computer, what is it exactly, and how does it emerge? In his theories about the mind and consciousness, Searle rejects

Cartesian dualism – that the mind is something non-physical and separate from the body. He also rejects the reductionism of thinkers such as Dennett, who believe that consciousness can be reduced to a series of physical processes in the brain, similar to a software program.

Instead, Searle takes a position which he calls biological naturalism. According to this view, consciousness is an emergent phenomenon of the brain. To explain what he means by this, he cites as an analogy the liquidity, or wetness, of water as being an emergent phenomenon brought about by the behaviour of the molecules that it is composed of. You cannot pinpoint a particular molecule and say 'this one is wet' – the wetness is a feature of the whole system of molecules. In the same way, one cannot point to a neuron and say 'this one is conscious'. Consciousness emerges as a result of the whole system. Events at the micro-level – perhaps at the level of individual neurons – causes a phenomenon, which we call consciousness, at the macro-level.

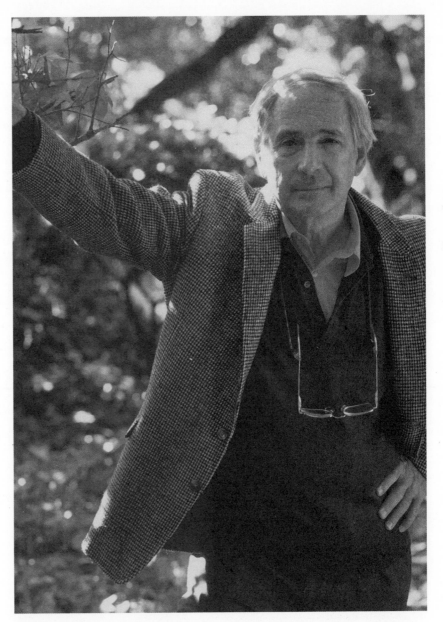

Searle's work embraces the moral and ethical problems thrown up by modern technology, in particular by artificial intelligence.

Some have seen biological naturalism as a form of dualism since micro-level properties can be objectively studied by, for example, a brain surgeon, but the brain surgeon cannot in the same way access macro-level properties such as pain, desire or joy. Searle rejects this suggestion. He stresses that consciousness *is* a type of physical property; it is not something separate like a kind of juice that is squirted out by the neurons, it is the state that the system is in – part of that system and inseparable from it. How it works – how micro-level behaviour creates consciousness at the macro level – is a question for the neuroscientists. But as a problem for philosophy, Searle regards it as solved.

Another major strand of Searle's philosophy is his study of intentionality, that is, the attachment of meaning to an object, such as a belief about it, possession of it or contempt towards it. In *Collective Intentions and Actions*, Searle seeks to show how intentionality can operate on the collective level. He contends that collective intentional behaviour exists and is not the same as the sum of individual intentional behaviour. But, he emphasizes, there is no such thing as group mind or group consciousness; society consists of nothing but individuals. In this there are clear parallels with his

theories of mind and his rejection of dualism and reductionism as explanations of consciousness.

In *The Construction of Social Reality* (1996), Searle applies his theory of intentionality to society, looking at the way certain aspects of our world are created as a result of the combined intentionality of those who make use of them. We assign functions to physical objects – turning matter into chairs, money, swimming pools and countries, for example – by our common intention to treat objects in that way, and by our willingness to conform to rules for the treatment of those objects.

According to Searle, the fundamental difference between the human mind and artificial intelligence is that the latter lacks 'intentionality'.

║ ESSENTIAL READING ║

Speech Acts: An Essay in the Philosophy of Language (1969)
In this important early work, Searle analyses language as a rule-governed form of behaviour, using this as a context for the discussion of different types of speech act, such as statements, questions, promises and orders.

Minds, Brains and Programs (1980)
In this seminal paper, Searle set out his objections to the mind-as-computer argument, introducing his famous Chinese Room thought experiment and coining the expression Strong AI.

Intentionality: An Essay in the Philosophy of Mind (1983)
In this book, Searle emphasizes his disagreement with the reductionists, who claim that consciousness can be reduced to a simple physical process involving parts of the brain – something that could be simulated by a computer. The key difference, he says, is that conciousness incorporates intentionality.

SENECA, LUCIUS ANNAEUS

4BC–AD65

Son of Seneca the Elder, the younger Lucius was born in Cordoba, Spain. He was educated in philosophy from an early age in Rome, where he would flirt with death at the hands of three emperors during his lifetime. Caligula would have had him killed but was dissuaded on the – inaccurate – grounds that Seneca was anyway destined to live a short life. Claudius exiled him and finally, after falsely being accused of plotting against Nero, whom he had tutored as a small boy, Seneca took his own life in AD65. Nevertheless, he had a successful career as a lawyer and amassed a personal fortune. He wrote many works, which can be categorized into broadly three main kinds. First, there are his essays on Stoic philosophy, then the sermonizing *Epistles*, and finally his plays, often depicting graphic violence. His many plays include *The Trojan Women*, *Oedipus, Medea, The Mad Hercules*, *The Phoenician Women, Phaedra*, *Agamemnon* and *Thyestes*.

Seneca lived a high profile and hazardous life among the notoriously fickle Roman emperors, finally falling victim to the emperor Nero.

Seneca was a Stoic philosopher but with a somewhat pragmatic bent. Unlike the other Stoics who often aspired to lofty goals few if any could ever reach, Seneca moderated his philosophy with a more practical approach. As with the other Stoics, the heart of his philosophy was the belief in a simple life devoted to virtue and reason. However, his extant works, particularly the 124 essays of his *Epistles*, but also to a degree his essays, contain the same tone, being often persuasive entreaties rather than expositions of technical philosophy. He is constantly trying to administer advice to his reader rather than impart philosophical wisdom. It is said that **Boethius** was consoled by reading Seneca whilst in prison. One particular passage by Seneca to his grieving mother is illustrative of his sermonizing style: 'You never polluted yourself with make-up, and you never wore a dress that covered about as much on as it did off. Your only ornament, the kind of beauty that time does not tarnish, is the great honour of modesty. So you cannot use your sex to justify your sorrow when with your virtue you have transcended it. Keep as far away from women's tears as from their faults'.

This type of sermonizing is typical of Seneca's work and becomes more frequent as he matures. His Stoicism is tinged with a kind of pseudo-religious flavour but importantly reflects a concern with ethical and moral principles at the expense of metaphysics. Seneca's stoicism is less a theoretical philosophy than a guide to living. Like the Epicureans, the Stoics thought that a proper understanding of the world would transform our daily lives. Unlike the Epicureans, the Stoics did not pursue a hedonistic lifestyle. Rather, Seneca insists that the only good is virtue. Doing the right thing is of paramount importance and one should show an attitude of indifference to all else. Each and every one of us, professes Seneca, has a god within him guiding us along the path set for us by Providence. We can attain happiness only by acting in accord with our own true nature, as revealed by our inner guide, and by being content with one's lot in life. Altruism and simple living are essential to Seneca's idea of correct living.

This painting by Rubens portrays the dramatic moment of Seneca's forced suicide, after being accused of plotting by the emperor Nero.

The importance Seneca places on doing the right thing in his philosophy appears to be sincere, given the manner of his death as reported by the Roman historian, Tacitus. Upon hearing Nero's sentence, Seneca slashed his arms and legs and gave an erudite speech to his wife and a gathered audience.

254

His wife Paulina, in despair, attempted to take her own life at the same time, to which Seneca said, 'I have shown you ways of smoothing life; you prefer the glory of dying. I will not grudge you such a noble example.' However, the Emperor's soldiers prevented Paulina from carrying out the deed by tying her up. Despite his wounds, Seneca lingered on. Tacitus reports that Seneca 'begged Statius Annaeus...to produce a poison with which he had some time before provided himself, the same drug which extinguished the life of those who were condemned by a public sentence of the people of Athens [i.e. the hemlock of **Socrates**]. It was

The heart of his philosophy was the belief in a simple life devoted to virtue and reason

brought to him and he drank it in vain, chilled as he was throughout his limbs, and his frame closed against the efficacy of the poison...He was then carried into a bath, with the steam of which he was suffocated, and he was burnt without funeral rites. So he had directed in his will, when even in the height of his wealth and power he was thinking of his life's close.'

255

▌ ESSENTIAL READING ▌

De Ira (On Anger)
A study of the consequences and control of anger.

De Clementia (On Mercy)
A letter addressed to Nero arguing that mercy is the great sovereign quality of an emperor.

De Tranquillitate Animi; De Constantia Sapientis; De Vita Beata; De Otio (On Tranqillity; On Steadfastness; The Happy Life; On Leisure)
Seneca's studies on the life and qualities of a wise Stoic.

De Beneficiis (On Gift Giving)
Examining the benefits of both giver and receiver in an exchange.

De Brevitate Vitae (On the Brevity of Life)
Seneca argues that the human lifespan is long enough only if time is used properly, which it seldom is.

Epistulae Morales (Epistles)
This collection of 124 essays, written in the form of letters to someone called Lucilius (who may or may not exist), are full of advice about how to become a better Stoic. Titles include 'On noise', 'The Influence of the Masses' and 'How to Deal with one's Slaves.' The collection is regarded as Seneca's most important philosophical work.

SIDGWICK, HENRY

(1838–1900)

Henry Sidgwick's entire career was spent at Cambridge University. After graduating in classics and mathematics, he was in 1859 appointed to an Assistant Tutorship in classics, but during the 1860s his interests turned increasingly to philosophy, a subject which he began to teach in 1867. In 1883, he was appointed to the Knightbridge Professorship of Moral Philosophy, a post he held until his death. He was also a founder of the Society for Psychical Research, and its first president.

Sidgwick's reputation was established by his first major work, *The Methods of Ethics,* considered by many as one of the classics of moral philosophy. Although often seen as defending utilitarianism, the ethical theory advanced by Jeremy **Bentham** and John Stuart **Mill** and to which Sidgwick was also largely committed, the *Methods* has a much broader purpose, which is to set out the 'methods of ethics' implicit in everyday moral reasoning and to consider whether it is possible to find a rational, principled basis for deciding how one ought to act. For Sidgwick, a 'method of ethics' is 'any rational procedure by which we determine what individual human beings 'ought' – or what it is 'right' for them – to do, or to seek to realize by voluntary action'. While people, when deciding what they ought to do, follow different principles, and often a mixture of principles, the 'methods' can be summed up in three basic approaches: egoism, utilitarianism and intuitionism.

Egoism, or egoistic hedonism, bases the morality of an action on the amount of happiness it produces in the person performing the action: 'the rational agent regards quantity of consequent pleasure and pain to himself as alone important in choosing between alternatives of action; and seeks always the greatest attainable surplus of pleasure over pain'.

Utilitarianism, or universalistic hedonism, considers an action good according to its effect on the general happiness of all: 'the conduct which … is objectively right, is that which will produce the greatest amount of happiness on the whole … taking into account all whose happiness is affected by the conduct'.

Intuitionism ignores the concept of happiness altogether, and holds that we are simply required to conform to 'certain rules or dictates of Duty'; indeed, it assumes that we have the ability to see clearly what actions are right and reasonable in themselves, independent of their consequences: 'The moral judgments that men habitually pass on one another in ordinary discourse imply … that duty is usually not a difficult thing for an ordinary man to know, though various seductive impulses may make it difficult for him to do it'.

The third book of the *Methods of Ethics* examines the relationship between intuitionism and the 'morality of common sense', the ethics which guides people's everyday behaviour. Sidgwick shows that common-sense morality is to some extent 'unconsciously utilitarian', while utilitarianism itself rests on intuitive moral principles, and he demonstrates that intuitionism and utilitarianism can be reconciled and integrated into a single ethical system: 'The common antithesis between intuitionism and utilitarianism must be entirely discarded; since such abstract moral principles as we can admit to be really self-evident are not only not incompatible with a utilitarian system', but even seem to be required to furnish a rational basis for such a system'.

There remains, however, the question of egoism, the ethical doctrine that roots correctness of behaviour in personal happiness. This too seems to reflect reason and common sense, but cannot be reconciled with utilitarianism. Utilitarianism requires a person to sacrifice their own happiness,

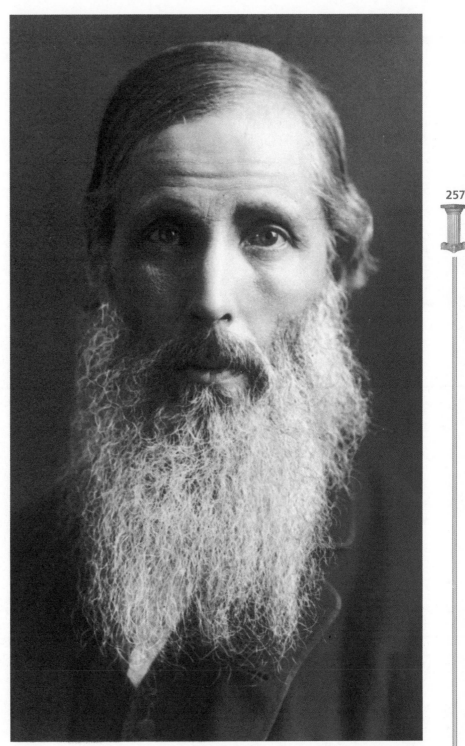

257

Sidgwick was a staunch supporter of education for women, founding the first college for female education at Cambridge with his wife, Eleanor Balfour.

even their own life, if the sum total of universal happiness is thereby increased – and not only their own, but also that of their family and friends. But if that is what utilitarianism demands, common sense and what has been called the 'traditional wisdom of mankind' say otherwise: 'There are very few persons …who…feel for the pleasure and pains of mankind generally, a degree of sympathy at all commensurate with their concern for wife or children, or lover, or intimate friend'.

Sidgwick is faced, then, with two conflicting principles, utilitarianism and egoism, irreconcilable but both based on common sense and valid reasoning. When reason in the form of a utilitarian concept of duty acting out of a concern for universal happiness makes harsh demands on us, reason that affirms the legitimacy and wisdom of enlightened self-interest may rightly decline these demands. Unable to find any demonstrable basis for asserting the superiority of one position over

'The deepest bent of my nature was towards the life of thought… exercised on the central problems of human life'

the other, and so overcoming this 'dualism of practical reason', Sidgwick admits that the conflict remains insoluble without bringing in God and some notion of divine rewards and punishments, which he is unwilling to do. The first edition of the *Methods* closes with the despairing admission that 'the Cosmos of Duty is…reduced to a Chaos; and the prolonged effort of the human intellect to frame a perfect ideal of rational conduct is seen to have been foredoomed to inevitable failure'. Later editions, however, end on a slightly less pessimistic note.

‖ ESSENTIAL READING ‖

The Methods of Ethics (1874)

Although ending on an apparently unsatisfactory note, this book has been described by C.D. Broad as 'the best treatise on moral theory that has ever been written' and by John **Rawls** as 'the first truly academic work in moral theory'.

The Principles of Political Economy (1883)

This book deals with both economic analysis and the role of state intervention in economic life.

The Elements of Politics (1891)

The aim of this book, as Sidgwick himself put it, is 'not to supply an entirely new method of obtaining reasoned answers to political questions; but rather …to introduce greater clearness and consistency to the kind of thought and reasoning with which we are all more or less familiar'.

SINGER, PETER

(1946–)

Peter Singer is possibly one of the best-known and most influential, and certainly one of the most controversial, modern philosophers. A co-founder of the International Association of Bioethics, he established the Centre for Human Bioethics at Monash University, Australia, and is currently Professor of Bioethics at Princeton University.

Singer is best known for his work in applied ethics, in particular with regard to animal rights, the ethics of abortion, infanticide and euthanasia, and the just distribution of global wealth. His ethical position is that of 'preference utilitarianism'. While classical utilitarianism, the ethical theory associated with **Bentham**, **Mill** and **Sidgwick**, measures the morality of an action by its consequences with regard to 'the greatest happiness of the greatest number', preference utilitarianism defines the moral rightness of an action by the extent to which it satisfies desires or preferences. In any situation, equal consideration must be given to the interests of all concerned, and that action is deemed right which satisfies most and frustrates fewest interests and desires.

Singer first came to prominence with the publication of *Animal Liberation,* and he has continued to write on animal rights. He argues that the way in which animals are treated by human beings is morally indefensible, as it places human beings' interests above those of animals, regardless of the pain and suffering this causes to the animals concerned, as, for example, in the use of animals in medical research and in factory farming. Singer argues that if in any given situation the interests of human beings should be given equal consideration, there is no rational or moral reason for not extending such consideration to animals as well. Animals are sentient beings and can suffer and feel

'The only moral absolute is that we should do what will have the best consequences for all those affected by our actions'

pain just as humans do, and there are no valid grounds for condemning pain and suffering caused to members of one species while condoning that caused to members of another. Singer uses the analogy of racism and sexism: while the racist violates the principle of equality by giving greater weight to the interests of members of his own race than to those of another race, and the sexist does so by favouring the interests of his own sex, 'the speciesist allows the interests of his own species to override the greater interests of members of other species'. The argument that non-human animals lack human intelligence is irrelevant: 'If possessing a higher degree of intelligence does not entitle one human to use another for his own ends, how can it entitle humans to exploit nonhumans?' Humans therefore have no more right to make a dog or an ape suffer than a person with brain-damage or severe learning difficulties. Singer has campaigned for basic 'human' rights, such as the right to life, liberty and freedom from torture, to be granted to the great apes. Nevertheless, he does admit the possibility of cases in which harming or killing animals may be justified, as in some forms of animal experimentation, given that human beings are a more complex life form.

If Singer first came to prominence with his work on animal rights, he has certainly gained most notoriety with his work on the ethics of abortion, infanticide and euthanasia, in which he has followed his utilitarian principles to conclusions which challenge the traditional view of the sanctity and value of all human life. For Singer, life is not *inherently* worthwhile: when consideration is given to the quality of the life being lived or that would be lived, based on an individual's self-awareness and their capacity to experience pleasure and self-fulfilment and to avoid suffering, it becomes clear that some lives might be better not lived at all. On these grounds, Singer would support voluntary euthanasia and assisted suicide, where an individual chooses not to go on living, and also in some cases non-voluntary euthanasia, where an individual is incapable of understanding and making a choice between life and death, either because, through accident, illness or old age, they have lost the capacity to do so, or because, through lack of mental development, they have never attained it. On similar grounds of potential quality of life and

Singer has tackled many of the ethical dilemmas posed by globalization, medicine and modern technology.

likely future suffering, Singer would permit the abortion of foetuses known before birth to be severely abnormal, and, more controversially, the killing of handicapped infants up to the age of 28 days, there being, from an ethical point of view, no distinction between a foetus and a newborn baby. Both abortion and infanticide are not only justifiable if in the best interests of the baby, but also if in the interests of the parents or family as a whole.

Singer's acceptance of abortion and infanticide derives from his conception of 'personhood'. For

Singer, a 'person' is a conscious being who is self-aware and has the capacity to feel and reason and to imagine a future, and neither a foetus nor a newborn baby has this awareness or capacity. Killing a foetus or newborn baby is, therefore, morally different from the killing of an autonomous, self-aware, rational person. Many of Singer's critics cannot understand how he can advocate that higher apes should be accorded the status of persons while at the same time denying this status to human foetuses and newborn infants and others, but his position is nevertheless a logical outcome of his definition of a person.

A third important area of Singer's work is in the ethics of wealth distribution. Beginning with the assumption that 'suffering and death from lack of food, shelter, and medical care are bad', Singer argues that if it is in our power to prevent such suffering and death, without causing anything equally bad to happen, then we ought to do it. The analogy he uses is that of seeing a child drowning in a pond: in such circumstances, one would surely immediately wade into the pond to rescue the child, even though this would entail getting one's clothes muddy and perhaps ruining a pair of shoes: getting one's clothes muddy or ruining one's shoes, although not good, would be insignificantly bad compared to the death of the child if he or she was not rescued. Once the principle is accepted that one should alleviate suffering even at some lesser personal cost or inconvenience, it is clear that the distance between oneself and the sufferer is of no relevance, especially in the modern world. If one is in a position to alleviate suffering, even on the other side of the globe, one should do so: just as the possibility of ruining a good pair of shoes while rescuing the child from the pond is not a good reason for allowing the child to drown, so 'if for the cost of a pair of shoes we can contribute to a health program in a developing country that stands a good chance of saving the life of a child, we ought to do so'.

▌ ESSENTIAL READING ▌

Animal Liberation (New York 1975, 2nd ed. 1990)
The Bible of the animal liberation movement, it is this book that led to animal rights being taken seriously as a moral issue.

Practical Ethics (Cambridge 1979, 2nd ed. 1993)
In this book, Singer addresses issues such as abortion, euthanasia and infanticide; equality; the obligations of the wealthy to the poor; the refugee question; human interaction with animals and ecological systems; and obedience to the law.

How Are We to Live? Ethics in an Age of Self-Interest (Melbourne 1993)
To quote from the book, 'there is a desperate need to do something *now* about the conditions in which beings live and die. …We must reinstate the idea of living an ethical life as a realistic and viable alternative to the present dominance of materialist self-interest.'

SKINNER, BURRHUS FREDERIC

1904–1990

Psychologist, philosopher and arch-proponent of 'radical behaviourism', Skinner attempts to explain human behaviour without recourse to any psychological or mental properties, an attempt that has been the cause of one of the greatest controversies in 20th century psychology and philosophy of mind. Familiar to students of psychology and sociology, Skinner has been described as 'the most honoured and the most maligned, the most widely recognized and the most misrepresented, the most cited and the most misunderstood' of all contemporary psychologists. His most famous works are *Verbal Behaviour* and *Beyond Freedom and Dignity*.

The roots of behaviourism lie in a rejection of **Descartes**' dualism of a non-physical mind lodged in a physical body. With the advent of materialism in the 18th and 19th centuries, Cartesian dualism became untenable. Ever since Descartes' work had been published, critics had found troublesome first the idea that these two metaphysically different entities could ever interact and second, what evidence could we ever have of what goes on in the mental realm beyond our own case, or even that others have a psychological existence? The early 20th century saw a simple and powerful answer to the Cartesian problem. Behaviourists, following Pavlov and Watson, began to realize that the mental realm was unnecessary to the explanation of human behaviour. If psychology is conceived of as the science of predicting and explaining human behaviour, the whole project could be undertaken by paying heed only to patterns of physical responses to physical stimuli. Inner processes were not the psychologist's domain: biologists and neurophysiologists could deal with those.

All human behaviour can be explained in terms of environmental stimuli or 'operant conditions'

The program began with enormous success. Attributions of psychological phenomena such as 'John is in pain' could be analysed not as attributing some inner experience to John's mental life, but as a claim that John is wincing, groaning or in some other way exhibiting 'pain-behaviour'. The obvious problem that John might be in pain but not observably so, could be explained away by claiming some other overriding stimulus was preventing the ordinary expression of pain-behaviour.

Skinner's contribution to the behaviourist doctrine lies in his consistent employment of behaviourist methodology in spite of continuing criticism which ought, it seems, to have made behaviourism obsolete a long time ago. Skinner, however, continued to develop behaviourism along ever more austere lines. He maintained that all human behaviour can be explained in terms of 'operant conditions'. Operant conditions are simply environmental stimuli that have reinforcing or adverse effects on the individual's future behaviour in the presence of those stimuli. The upshot of this is that for Skinner, there are no criminals, no heroes or cowards, geniuses or fools, there are merely – when one takes a proper account of science – individuals whose behaviour is determined by the environment. He says, 'The hypothesis that man is not free is essential to the application of scientific method to the study of human behaviour. The free inner man who is held responsible for the behaviour of the external biological organism is only the pre-scientific substitute for the kinds of causes which are discovered in the course of a scientific analysis.'

Skinner's 'radical behaviourism' maintained that human behaviour is merely the result of environmental stimuli, thus eliminating the possibility of free will.

In *Beyond Freedom and Dignity,* Skinner tries to work out the social implications of his radical behaviourism. Criminals and sociopaths are people whose behaviour deviates from some preference or generalization imposed by society. Labelling such people as wrongdoers is a reflection of our ignorance of the factors which caused their behaviour. This view is highlighted by the fact that we clearly do not hold people responsible in cases where we understand the causes of their behaviour (drug dependency, for instance). The idea might be given credence from the evolutionary perspective that humans are physically continuous with animals and Skinner, having spent a lot of time controlling the behaviour of rats in his laboratory, sees no reason why animal behaviour cannot be explained in terms of purely operant conditions.

There have been many valid objections to behaviourism, not least the fact that it ignores the causal role of our own psychological experience. Skinner's later work is ambivalent towards these inner experiences. Sometimes he denies their existence as a Cartesian myth, at other times he allows that they may exist but are irrelevant to a proper scientific understanding of human behaviour.

In this psychological experiment, Skinner rewarded those pigeons who were able to match a coloured light with a coloured panel.

❘❘ ESSENTIAL READING ❘❘

Walden Two (1948)

In this novel, Skinner describes a fictional utopia based on his own philosophical views. In Walden Two, children are raised communally and taught self-control techniques to handle the negative emotions and promote positive approaches. The result is a community where there is no competition, social strife or conflict.

Verbal Behavior (1957)

Here, Skinner develops a behaviourist approach to language. Speech, he asserts, is simply a form of behaviour, subject to the same methods of control as can be applied to other forms of behaviour. Each act of speech is a consequence of the speaker's current environment and behavioural and sensory history. Skinner's theories in verbal behaviour have been used with some success in the treatment of autistic children.

Beyond Freedom and Dignity (1971)

This book-length essay argues that people's fixed belief in free will and the moral autonomy of the individual (which Skinner calls 'dignity') is damaging the prospect of creating a happier society through the use of scientific techniques for modifying behaviour.

SKINNER, BURRHUS FREDERIC

SMITH, ADAM
1723–1790

Scottish philosopher of morals, politics and economics, Smith was a contemporary of **Hume** and is very close to him in outlook and philosophic temperament. His lectures on ethics and logic were published under the title *Theory of the Moral Sentiments* but he is most famous for his work of political economics, *The Wealth of Nations*.

Favoured philosopher of Margaret Thatcher and darling of Conservative economists, Smith is famous for his views on private property, the free market economy and the doctrine that 'unintended consequences of intended action' will be to the benefit of society at large. The idea behind this most fortunate if true of principles is that in intentionally serving one's own interests one unintentionally serves the interests of society as a whole.

A simple example will illustrate the essence of Smith's idea. Suppose that Jones, in seeking his own fortune, decides to set up and run his own business, manufacturing some common item of everyday need. In seeking only to provide for his own fortune, Jones' entrepreneurial enterprise has a number of unintentional benefits to others. First, he provides a livelihood for the people in his employ, thus benefiting them directly. Second, he makes more readily available some common item which previously had been more difficult or more

Intentionally serving one's own interests one unintentionally serves the interests of society as a whole

expensive to obtain for his customers, thus easing one, if only minor, aspect of their lives. The forces of market economy ensure that these unintentional benefits occur, for if Jones' workers could find more profitable employ elsewhere they would either cease to work for him or he would have to raise their salaries in order to secure a workforce. Likewise, if Jones' product was available more readily or less expensively from some other source, Jones would either go out of business or be forced to lower his prices to a competitive rate. The model assumes the absence of a monopoly, both in the labour and economic markets.

The belief that 'unintended consequences of intended action' will be of benefit to society held great imaginative power over the industrial philanthropists of the 18th and 19th centuries and provided the philosophical groundwork for the later ethical theories of **Bentham** and **Mill**.

However, criticism is not hard to come by. It is surely a blinkered view, if comforting for the entrepreneurial capitalist, to suppose that pursuing one's own self-interest constitutes a magnanimous and philanthropic act towards society at large. One has only to review the social history of industrial Britain, to witness the treacherous and exploitative working practices of the industrial age, the extreme poverty and degrading social conditions of the suffering working classes, to realize Smith's idealistic model has far more serious 'unintended' consequences. What has largely brought an end to such conditions in the industrialized West is not a triumphant adherence to Smith's principles in Western economics, but a shifting of the poverty and exploitative working practices from one part of the world to another. In other words, the living conditions of those in the West has improved to the detriment of other countries insofar as the labour required to support Smith's economic philosophy has been removed from Western societies and transferred to those of the Third World.

Regardless of one's political views on Smith, *The Wealth of Nations* is one of the most important and deservedly read works of economic and political philosophy in the history of Western thought. It needs to be read and understood by its detractors as much as it does by its supporters.

In 1759, Smith received private patronage and financial support, and was able to resign his chair at the University of Glasgow.

▌ ESSENTIAL READING ▐

The Theory of Moral Sentiments (1759)

In this work, a bestseller in its day and the book that launched Smith's career, he asks why we regard certain actions with approval and condemn others. At the time, some regarded the law as the only standard of right and wrong, while others believed that moral principles could be worked out rationally. Smith offered a different answer: he argued that people are born with a moral sense, just as they are born with notions of beauty or harmony. We have an innate conscience, bolstered by a natural fellow-feeling, which Smith terms 'sympathy'. It is by these natural senses that humans live together in orderly society.

The Wealth of Nations (1776)

Smith's great work was published at a time when the power of free trade to stimulate industry and innovation was poorly understood, and monopolies and restrictive practices were rife. Smith demonstrates his belief that free trade, choice and competition can encourage economic development and reduce poverty. His book provided people with a new understanding of the wealth-creating process and laid the philosophical foundations for the economic expansion of the 19th century.

SOCRATES

c.470–399BC

Socrates lived through times of great political upheaval in his birthplace of Athens, a city which would eventually make him a scapegoat for its troubles and ultimately demand his life. Much of what is known about Socrates comes through the works of his one time pupil **Plato**, for Socrates himself was an itinerant philosopher who taught solely by means of public discussion and oratory and never wrote any philosophical works of his own.

Unlike the Greek philosophers before him, Socrates was less concerned with abstract metaphysical ponderings than with practical questions of how we ought to live, and what the good life for man might be. Consequently, he is often hailed as the inventor of that branch of philosophy known as ethics. It is precisely his concern with ethical matters that often led him into conflict with the city elders, who accused him of corrupting the minds of the sons of the wealthy with revolutionary and unorthodox ideas.

By Plato's account, Socrates was a larger-than-life figure who valued wisdom and teaching above all material wealth.

Socrates was certainly a maverick, often claiming to the consternation of his interlocutors that the only thing he was sure of was his own ignorance. Indeed much of his teaching consisted in asking his audience to define various common ideas and notions, such as 'beauty', or 'the good', or 'piety', only to show through reasoned argument that all of the proposed definitions and common conceptions lead to paradox or absurdity. Some of his contemporaries thought this technique disingenuous, and that Socrates knew more than he let on. However, Socrates' method was meant to provide salutary lessons in the dangers of uncritical acceptance of orthodoxy. He often railed against, and made dialectic victims of, those who claimed to have certain knowledge of some particular subject. It is chiefly through the influence of Socrates that philosophy developed into the modern discipline of continuous critical reflection. The greatest danger to both society and the individual, we learn from Socrates, is the suspension of critical thought.

'The only thing I know is that I know nothing'

Loved by the city's aristocratic youth, Socrates inevitably developed many enemies throughout his lifetime. In his 70th year, or thereabouts, after Athens had gone through several changes of leadership and a period of failing fortunes, Socrates was brought to trial on charges of 'corrupting the youth' and 'not believing in the city gods'. It would seem that the charges were brought principally to persuade Socrates to renounce his provocative public speaking and convince the citizens of Athens that the new leadership had a tight rein on law and order. With a plea of guilty he might perhaps have walked away from the trial and lived out the rest of his life as a private citizen. However, in characteristic style, he robustly defended himself, haranguing his accusers and claiming that god himself had sent him on his mission to practice and teach philosophy. When asked, upon being found guilty, what penalty he thought he should receive, Socrates mocked the court by suggesting a trifling fine of only 30 minae. Outraged, a greater majority voted for Socrates to be put to death by the drinking of hemlock than had originally voted him guilty. Unperturbed, Socrates readily agreed to abide by the laws of his city and forbade his family and friends from asking for a stay of execution.

‖ ESSENTIAL READING ‖

Socrates wrote no philosophical works, and we rely on other writers, especially Plato, to provide information about his beliefs and teaching. Three key works by Plato are the *Apology*, *Crito* and *Phaedo*.

Apology

The *Apology* records Socrates' defence speech when he was put on trial for supposed impiety and allegedly corrupting the young people of Athens.

Crito

This consists of a conversation between Socrates and Crito, in which Socrates explains his ethical views.

Phaedo

This book recounts Socrates' final hours after being sentenced to death at the trial mentioned above, and includes his views on death and immortality.

Socrates' trial on charges of corrupting the youth of Athens and his subsequent death have been immortalized in Plato's accounts.

268

SPINOZA, BENEDICT DE

1632–1677

Dutch philosopher of Jewish origin, Spinoza remains one of the most compelling if difficult philosophers of the rationalist school. Greatly influenced by **Descartes** and Euclid, he takes rationalism to its logical extremes, determining to set out the principles of an ethical system in axiomatic format, much as Euclid proved his theorems of geometry. Spinoza's ambitious project is perhaps one of the greatest ever undertaken in philosophy and it is a mark of his greatness that, to a considerable extent, he was remarkably successful in this undertaking.

In the posthumously published *Ethica ordine geometrico demonstrata (Ethics demonstrated in geometrical order),* Spinoza sets out the axioms which he takes to be self-evident and then proceeds, step by step, to deduce ethical conclusions. Like Descartes, he is concerned to set knowledge on logical foundations: his ethical conclusions must therefore first be founded on a number of ontological, metaphysical and epistemic beliefs. Each of these is, in turn, demonstrated in geometric fashion. Central to Spinoza's philosophy is the idea, similar to that of **Parmenides**, that everything in the universe is One. There is only one substance and that substance we can conceive of as either Nature or God. This substance has infinitely many attributes but human beings, being finite, can only

BENOIT SPINOSA né en 1632, mort en 1677.

Spinoza's rationalist philosophy was deemed to be incompatible with Jewish orthodoxy and in 1656 he was expelled from the synagogue.

perceive two of them, extension and thought. Unlike Descartes, who thought mind and body were two separate kinds of thing, Spinoza argues that

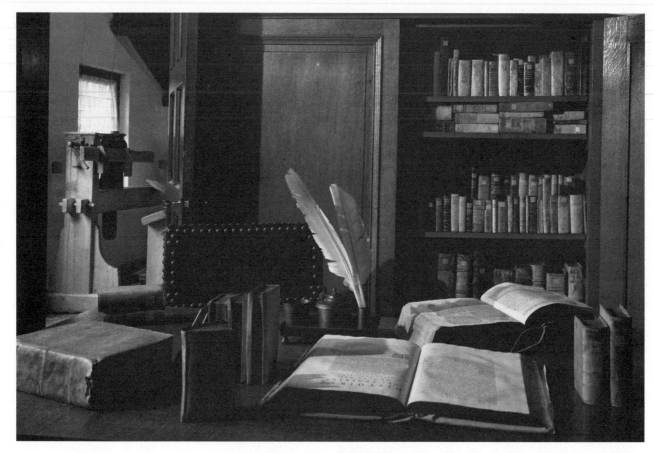

Following his expulsion from the synagogue, Spinoza earned a living from lens-grinding and teaching in Rijnsburg in the Netherlands.

mind and body are just different ways of conceiving the same reality.

This reality, Nature or God, is wholly self-contained, self-causing and self-sufficient. Everything in the universe is part of God, and everything that happens is a necessary part or expression of the divine nature. The upshot of this pantheistic view is to remove free will from the realm of human actions. After all, if human beings are part of the divine reality there is no room for independent causal actions. Spinoza is more than happy with this conclusion, he is a thorough-going determinist:

'...experience tells us clearly that men believe themselves to be free simply because they are conscious of their actions and unconscious of the causes whereby these actions are determined; further, it is plain that the dictates of the mind are simply another name for the appetites that vary according to the varying state of the body.'

Nevertheless, Spinoza does find a way of making room for a kind of freedom, though it is not of the sort that philosophers are generally used to. Each individual, says Spinoza, is a localized concentration of the attributes of reality, really a

There is only one substance and that substance we can conceive of as either Nature or God

quasi-individual, since the only true individual is the universe in totality. Insofar as the quasi-individual is ruled by his emotions, he is unfree and at the mercy of finite understanding. To become free, the individual must, by means of rational reflection, understand the extended causal chain that links everything as one. To become aware of the totality of the universe is to be freed, not from causal determinism, but from an ignorance of one's true nature.

What then, of wickedness, sin and evil?

Since everything is part of one reality, there is no such thing as evil from the viewpoint of the whole – 'sub specie aeternitis' (from the aspect of eternity).

That which appears evil does so only because we lack the understanding to see the bigger picture, the chain of causes that makes all events a necessary part of divine reality. Though many were shocked by this in Spinoza's day, it reflects the same sentiment expressed by those Christians who persevere in the face of adversity by claiming that 'God moves in mysterious ways' and 'ours is not to reason why'. Of course, for Spinoza, to reason why is exactly what we must do to attain freedom.

Interestingly, Spinoza's philosophy is both mystical, rational and theistic. Yet he was excommunicated from the Jewish community for his views, denounced as an atheist by Christians and declared so wicked that at one time his books were publicly burnt. **Leibniz**, who owes a great deal to him, rarely acknowledges the debt. Despite the rigour and integrity of his work, Spinoza remains one of the lesser studied and least regarded of all the rationalist philosophers.

‖ ESSENTIAL READING ‖

Theological-Political Treatise (1670)
Bertrand **Russell** has described this book as 'a curious combination of biblical criticism and political theory'. Published anonymously, it met with fierce criticism. Spinoza argues for freedom of thought and religion, and he advocates taking political power away from the clergy. His biblical criticism and interpretation are well ahead of their time.

The Ethics (1677)
This is Spinoza's major work, published shortly after his death. It is written in the form of definitions, axioms and propositions, which makes it quite hard to read. Although principally a work on ethics, it also sets out Spinoza's metaphysical views, among which is the idea that reality consists of one single substance which can equally well be called 'God' or 'Nature'.

TARSKI, ALFRED

1902–1983

Perhaps the greatest logician of the 20th century, Tarski's work is fundamental to much of modern philosophy of language and philosophical logic. At Warsaw University he studied mathematics, biology, philosophy and linguistics. Early in his career he made a name for himself for his work on the foundations of mathematics. But it is principally for his work in semantics and his definition of truth in formal languages that Tarski's influence has been greatest.

Philosophy has long struggled to find an adequate account of the concept of truth. Exactly what is it for a sentence to be true? The most popular answer, since **Aristotle**, has always been to think that a sentence is true when it somehow corresponds with the facts. However, trying to explicate the notion of 'correspondence' without referring to the concept of truth in the definition has proven notoriously difficult. Tarski solves that problem for formal languages. He was himself pessimistic of applying his solution to natural

Raised and educated in Warsaw, Tarksi left Poland just in time to escape the German invasion in 1939.

languages like English or French. Nonetheless, this has not stopped some philosophers from trying to complete such a project.

According to Tarski, any proposed definition of truth must entail as a consequence all equivalences of the following form:
1. Some sentence S is true in some language L, if and only if p. Where p represents a translation of S in a second-order, or 'meta' language.

This condition, which Tarski calls 'Convention T', might have as an instance, for example:
2. 'Schnee ist weiss' is true in German, if and only if snow is white.

But also equally:
3. 'Snow is white' is true in English, if and only if snow is white.

These examples highlight that what is important for any proposed definition of truth, according to Tarski, is the distinction between an 'object language' and a 'meta-language'. The complete sentences, (1), (2) and (3) are all sentences couched in a meta-language, that is, they are used to mention and assert something of another sentence. Now in the case of (3), it is clear that the meta-language and object language are both English. Natural languages, such as English or German (or other world languages), are in fact their own meta-languages, a peculiar feature which allows them to both use and mention their own sentences. Such languages Tarski calls 'semantically closed'. Formal languages, such as those found in logic, mathematics and computer programming, may be 'semantically open', just insofar as no sentence which mentions another sentence in the same language counts as a well-formed formula.

The distinction between a 'semantically open' and 'semantically closed' language is important for Tarski. First, because he maintains that only semantically open languages can have a definition of truth. Second, because when, as in natural languages, the object language and the meta-language are identical, paradoxes such as the 'liar paradox' can be generated which are un-decidable. Consider:
4. This sentence is false.

(4) is un-decidable because in referring to itself, if it is true, it is false, and if it is false, it is true. Accordingly, Tarski insists that truth can only be completely defined for 'open' languages, languages where truth is ascribed from 'outside' of the language (i.e., in a meta-language) under consideration. This makes him pessimistic for the chances of ever providing a definition of truth in natural language (a pessimism that has not always been shared by his philosophical descendants, such as **Kripke**).

Since truth is, according to Tarski, a property of sentences, not of the world or of states of affairs, then any definition of truth must ascribe that property to a sentence, just so long as that sentence says how things stand in the world. That relationship is precisely what the T-convention represents. Consequently, Tarski's view of truth is in line with the 'classical' conception of truth as a correspondence between language and world. However, though Tarski's account has stimulated much work in an attempt to solve the problem of defining truth in natural, or 'closed' languages, many philosophers remain convinced that his pessimism in this regard was well-placed.

273

Only semantically open languages can have a definition of truth

‖ ESSENTIAL READING ‖

The Concept of Truth in Formalized Languages (1933)
In this classic paper, published in Polish, Tarski set out his mathematical definition of truth for formal languages. The German translation appeared in 1936.

Logic, Semantics and Metamathematics (1956)
This landmark paper contained the first English translation of *The Concept of Truth* and made a powerful contribution to semantics and the philosophy of language.

THALES OF MILETUS

c.620–?540BC

Credited as the first philosopher of Ancient Greece, and therefore the founder of Western philosophy, Thales hailed from the Ionian seaport of Miletus, now in modern Turkey. Miletus was a major centre of development for both science and philosophy in Ancient Greece. Thales, probably born somewhere around 620BC is mainly remembered as the presocratic philosopher who claimed that the fundamental nature of the world is water. **Aristotle** mentions him, as does Herodotus, and these are really our only accounts of Thales' background.

The first natural scientist and analytical philosopher in Western intellectual history

However, his significance as a philosopher is not so much what he said, but his method. Thales was the first thinker to try to account for the nature of the world without appealing to the wills and whims of anthropomorphic, Homerian gods. Rather, he sought to explain the many diverse phenomena he observed by appealing to a common, underlying principle, an idea that is still germane to modern scientific method. He is also credited by Herodotus with correctly predicting that there would be a solar

eclipse in 585BC during a battle between the Medes and the Lydians. As such, Thales can with some justification be thought of as the first natural scientist and analytical philosopher in Western intellectual history.

Thales had other modern traits, for it also seems that he was something of an entrepreneur. According to one story, Thales made a fortune investing in oil-presses before a heavy olive crop – certainly he would have had to be wealthy in order to devote time and thought to philosophy and science in 7th century BC Ancient Greece.

According to his metaphysics, water was the first principle of life and the material world. Seeing that water could turn into both vapour by evaporation and a solid by freezing, that all life required and was supported by moisture, he postulated that it was the single causal principle behind the natural world. In a crude anticipation of modern plate tectonics, Thales professed that the flat earth floated on water. Aristotle tells us that Thales thought the earth had a buoyancy much like wood, and that the earth floated on water much like a log or a ship. Indeed, many floating islands were said to be known to the sea-farers of Miletus, which may have served as either models or evidence for Thales' theory. He even accounted for earthquakes as being due to the rocking of the earth by subterranean waves, just as a ship may be rocked at sea. From the port of Miletus he would have been familiar with the phenomenon of sedimentation, possibly believing it to be the spontaneous generation of earth from water, an idea held as recently as the 18th century.

Having sought to give a naturalistic explanation of observable phenomena, rather than appealing to the wills of gods, Thales claimed that god is in all things. According to Aetius, Thales said the mind of the world is god, that god is intermingled in all things, a view that would shortly appear contemporaneously in a number of world religions, most notably Buddhism in India. Despite his metaphysical speculations being clearly mistaken, it seems that Thales was a modern thinker in more ways than one, pre-empting many ideas in religion, philosophy and science.

According to historical accounts, Thales was a wealthy man, a polymath and probably the first philosopher of the Western tradition.

‖ ESSENTIAL READING ‖

No writings of Thales survive, and there have even been doubts as to whether he wrote anything at all. We know of the man and his philosophy through references to him in the works of other classical authors, such as Herodotus, Plutarch, Aristotle and particularly Diogenes Laertius.

TURING, ALAN

1912–1954

English mathematician, code-breaker and founder of computer science, Turing has bequeathed the possibility of artificial intelligence to science, and a criterion for intelligence to the philosophy of mind. His definition of a universal computing device, named 'the Turing machine' in his honour, set generations of eager scientists to work in the quest to develop algorithms that would describe the computational processes of human thought. His 'imitation game', sometimes simply called 'the Turing test' has taxed philosophers' understanding of concepts such as 'intelligence', 'consciousness' and 'mind'. During the Second World War, Turing was the leading cryptographer at Bletchley Park, where he made an invaluable contribution to the Allied cause

Turing's belief in the possibility of artificial intelligence has stimulated an ongoing philosophical debate about the nature and processes of the human mind.

Hut 3 in Bletchley Park, the Second World War intelligence base where Turing helped to crack the German Enigma code.

by helping to crack the notorious 'Enigma' code used by the Germans.

Turing's seminal work is contained in his famous paper *Computing Machinery and Intelligence* in which he poses the question 'Can machines think?'. The answer to such a question, of course, depends exactly on what is meant by the terms 'machine' and 'think'. But since any analysis of the terms is likely to presuppose an answer to the question rather than help us investigate it objectively, Turing proposes to replace the question with a hypothetical game.

Suppose, says Turing, that we define a game with three players. Player A is to act as an interrogator, and the object of the game for the interrogator is to guess the sex of the other two players, one of which is a man, the other a woman. All the players are in separate rooms and send and receive questions and answers via teletype terminals. For Player B the object of the game is to confuse the interrogator and hide the identity of his or her gender. For Player C, the object of the game is to help the interrogator to guess his or her gender correctly. Clearly, since the interrogator does not know which player is trying to help him and which is trying to deceive him, he must be very canny in his questioning.

Now Turing asks, what will happen if a machine takes the place of Player B in this game? Will the interrogator guess more or less correctly than he would when the players are both people? The answer to this question, Turing tells us, will settle the question of whether a machine can think. Why? Because any machine sophisticated enough to replace a person in the game without the detection of the interrogator (or at least with a detection rate no worse than a person) must possess just the same intelligence as a person. The assumption, in other words, is that anything that responds intelligently is, by that very fact, intelligent.

Turing's 'imitation game' raises a number of interesting issues for philosophers. In particular, is it true that imitation is really enough to satisfy us that a machine can think? A child can imitate the behaviour of an adult, but is not thereby an adult, and neither is player B, if he is a man and successfully fools the interrogator that he is a woman, thereby a woman. So why should we suppose that a computer that imitates the behaviour of a thinking person, is really thinking? The issue is complex, and turns in part on the assumption that the level of sophistication required to fool the interrogator might only be achieved by something that was, indeed, a thinking being. On the other hand, and this is probably closer to Turing's own view, since the only criterion we have of conscious thought is how it is manifested in behaviour (including verbal behaviour), it can make no sense to call one thing 'thinking' and another non-thinking' if their behaviour is indistinguishable to a competent judge.

Of course, the imitation game does not imply that any machine ever could pass the test, but does give us, if one agrees with Turing, a test that any candidate machine should have to take. Turing himself professed that by the end of the 20th century we would have machines capable of passing the test over 70 per cent of the time. His optimism in this regard has yet to be been borne out.

Why suppose that a computer that imitates the behaviour of a thinking person, is really thinking?

‖ ESSENTIAL READING ‖

Proposed Electronic Calculator (1946)
Turing's plan for ACE, the world's first design for a stored program computer, was presented in a paper to the National Physical Laboratory on 19 February 1946. The full-scale version of ACE was only completed in 1957.

Computing Machinery and Intelligence (1950)
In this famous paper, Turing addresses the possibility of artificial intelligence and proposes an experiment, now known as the Turing test, in an attempt to define a standard for a machine to be considered intelligent. The paper also proposed the theory now known as computationalism, which states that cognition is a form of computation.

The Chemical Basis of Morphogenesis (1952)
In this paper, Turing looks at Fibonacci phyllotaxis, the existence of Fibonacci numbers in plant structures. He devised a type of mathematical system called reaction-diffusion equations, which are now central to the field of pattern formation (a science dealing with the visible, orderly outcomes of self-organization in nature).

VOLTAIRE

1694–1778

Voltaire was born Francois-Marie Arouet, to a wealthy Parisian family. Intended for the legal profession, Voltaire rebelled against his family's wishes and pursued a literary career, much to the embarrassment, at times, of his parents. He was imprisoned in the Bastille for penning libellous poems, during which time he wrote tragedies and adopted the name of Voltaire. After a second spell in prison, he quit France for England, where he came under the lasting influence of the works of **Locke** and **Newton**.

Following Locke and Newton, Voltaire championed reason over superstition and, though he held certain deistic beliefs, denounced the power of the clergy. He later contributed to what proved to be perhaps the greatest intellectual project of the times, the

Politically and socially engaged, Voltaire was the archetypal rational humanist of the Enlightenment era.

Voltaire's *Candide*, in which he satirizes mankind's blind optimism, was in part a reaction to the devastating Lisbon earthquake of 1755.

Encyclopaedia edited by **Diderot** and Jean d'Alembert. The *Encyclopaedia* was to become the subject of further controversy for Voltaire, as it was considered to be a challenge to faith by encouraging people to look to the power of reason.

Alongside his championing of reason, Voltaire became a strong voice in calls for freedom of expression. Since he had himself been persecuted for his writings this was, perhaps, a natural consequence of his own experience. Accordingly he wrote many satires on what he saw as the abuse of power by society's elite, inevitably bringing himself into conflict with this elite once again. Typical of his view of religion is the following excerpt from his *Philosophical Dictionary*, an eminently readable work even by today's literary standards, in which he relates the qualities of a theist: 'Reconciled in this principle with the rest of the universe, he does not embrace any of the sects, all of which contradict each other; his religion is the most ancient and the most widespread; for the simple worship of a God has preceded all the systems of the world. He speaks a language that all peoples understand, while they do not understand one another. He has brothers from Peking to Cayenne, and he counts all wise men as his brethren. He believes that religion does not consist either in the opinions of an unintelligible metaphysic, or in vain display, but in worship and justice. The doing of good, there is his service; being submissive to God, there is his doctrine. The Mohamedan cries to him: "Have a care if you do not make the pilgrimage to Mecca!" " Woe unto you," says a Recollet, "if you do not make a journey to Notre-Dame de Lorette!" He laughs at Lorette and at Mecca; but he succours the needy and defends the oppressed.'

Voltaire did more to popularize and instigate 'the age of reason' than any other philosopher

It is small wonder the Church found him vexatious. But Voltaire's interests were much wider than theology. During his time in England, he had also greatly admired the English constitution. On considering democracy, he writes, 'One questions every day whether a republican government is preferable to a king's government. The dispute ends always by agreeing that to govern men is very difficult. The Jews had God Himself for master; see what has happened to them on that account: nearly always have they been beaten and slaves but do you not find today they cut a pretty figure?'

As a philosopher Voltaire is not by his own work particularly original. However, he must be included in any retrospective of Western thought for the huge influence his writings have had. Voltaire did more to popularize and instigate 'the age of reason' than any other philosopher. His style is always readable, provocative and laced with wit. Not until the plays and stories of the existentialists in the 20th century would philosophy be again so popularly read.

‖ ESSENTIAL READING ‖

Letters Concerning the English Nation *(1733)*
Written in English after a two-year exile in England, and published in French in 1734 as the *Lettres philosophiques*, this book consists of a series of essays in the form of letters, supposedly written to a friend, describing English society. It includes discussions on politics, philosophy, religion, commerce and literature.

Treatise on Metaphysics *(1734)*
A short work on metaphysics, greatly influenced by the philosophy of John Locke. Among other things, it argues in support of deism.

Candide *(1759)*
In this humorous and ironic novel, Voltaire recounts the life and adventures of a young man, Candide, who suffers mishap after mishap. The novel ridicules the doctrine of **Leibniz** that this is the best of all possible worlds.

A Treatise on Toleration *(1763)*
In this book Voltaire condemns all forms of religious intolerance and persecution. It was written after a Protestant, Jean Calas, was wrongly executed for supposedly having murdered his son to prevent him from becoming a Roman Catholic.

Philosophical Dictionary *(1764)*
This book includes articles on a wide range of topics, such as beauty, final causes, free will, reason, truth and virtue; animals, climate and corn; and perhaps more unexpectedly, adultery, kissing and nakedness.

VYGOTSKY, LEV SEMENOVICH

1896–1934

Soviet psychologist whose 1930s work on language and thought, although suppressed in his own land and not known in the West until 1958, has had a strong influence in the philosophy of mind and language, in particular because of its affinities with the later work of **Wittgenstein**.

Vygotsky studied in the fields of linguistics, psychology, philosophy and the arts before completing his most famous work *Thought and Language,* published shortly after his death. His main concern is with the relationship between thought and language which, he believed, psychology had never investigated systematically or in detail. The traditional view, articulated by **Augustine**, was that speech is the outer expression of an inner process, thought. In this view, language and thought are logically distinct but contingently related. In other words, we happen to use vocalizations as a convenient means for expressing the ideas that independently occur in our minds. The picture is intuitive and compelling, but Vygotsky, like Wittgenstein, found it conceptually flawed.

Part of Vygotsky's work on developmental psychology was to investigate the phenomenon of children's play.

Vygotsky states, 'The structure of speech is not simply the mirror image of the structure of thought. It cannot, therefore, be placed on thought like clothes off a rack. Speech does not merely serve as the expression of developed thought. Thought is restructured as it is transformed into speech. It is not expressed but completed in the word. Therefore, precisely because of the contrasting directions of the movement, the development of the internal and external aspects of speech form a true unity.'

The picture Vygotsky paints here is one of language use combining with conscious activity to form a unity. There is no causal relation to be explained between the thought had and the word formed, but rather meaningful expressions are a result of conscious processes operating upon a linguistic medium. The two are conceptually dependent, an idea that is vigorously argued for in Wittgenstein's famous 'private language argument' and given similar expression by Vygotsky's account of language-acquisition in childhood.

An infant, as a dependent individual, cannot live an isolated existence: 'He lives a common life as one term in a personal relationship'. Accordingly, he learns first by exposure to social stimuli, which he later internalizes. Vygotsky says, 'Every function in the child's cultural development appears twice: first, on the social level, and later on the individual level; first, between people (interpsychological), and then inside the child (intrapsychological).

Vygotsky's work connects with a famous philosophical hypothesis known as the 'Sapir-Whorf' hypothesis, or 'linguistic determination'. Put simply, it is the argument that the conceptual scheme one possesses directly affects the way one thinks about and perceives the world. Different cultures, with different languages, literally perceive the world in different ways. Whereas in English there is only one word for snow, for example, the Inuit language has many words for it. Whorf argues accordingly that since Inuit make many finer discriminations about snow than English speakers, they literally 'see' snow differently. They see subtle differences in snow that others do not.

'The structure of speech is not simply the mirror image of the structure of thought'

Vygotsky is thus forced to conclude that in growing up within a particular linguistically structured relationship, 'the child begins to perceive the world not only through its eyes but also through its speech. And later it is not just seeing but acting that becomes informed by words'.

The Inuit people have many words for snow, while the English language has only one – an example of 'linguistic determination.'

▌ ESSENTIAL READING ▌

Thought and Language (1934)

Vygotsky's principal work is a highly original exploration of the interrelationship of thought and language. Vygotsky argues that thought is originally non-verbal and language is non-intellectual. The separate curves of thought and language development only meet at the age of around two, at which point thought becomes verbal and speech becomes rational. Vygotsky goes on to argue that cognitive skills and patterns of thinking are the products of the particular culture within which an individual grows up. In this process, language plays a crucial role in determining how a child will think because modes of thought are transmitted to the child by means of words.

283

WHITEHEAD, ALFRED NORTH

1861–1947

284

English philosopher and co-author, with **Russell**, of the *Principia Mathematica,* Whitehead is best known for his 'philosophy of organism'. He rejects materialism in favour of a philosophy centred around 'the concepts of life, organism, function, instantaneous reality, interaction, order of nature'. Whitehead tries to repair the gap made by materialism which split the notions of purpose, value and meaning from scientific explanation.

Whitehead's project is to integrate science as part of the social sciences

To understand Whitehead's 'philosophy of organism' one must start with his critique of materialism, 'a scheme of scientific thought framed by mathematicians, for mathematicians'. This scheme, originally intended to serve a set of social and epistemological purposes which have now been served, not only remains intact, but, Whitehead believed, has now got out of control.

The principal problem with the scheme is the way it has left no room for notions of value, meaning and purpose within scientific explanation. Such notions are criticized by materialists as subjective, immaterial and non-factual. They proclaim to uphold a science unencumbered by value judgements, a science that is valueless and objective, and thereby, universally true. Whitehead finds such a view hypocritical and inconsistent. For in rejecting values in this way, the materialist is upholding a particular value system. Moreover, the history of science cannot be separated from the cultural, social and political environment in which it is pursued. History shows that generalizations from scientific research to political and social conclusions are widespread. The values of society and the outcome of scientific research are not so clearly delineated as the materialist believes.

In place of materialism, Whitehead suggests we operate with the concept of 'organism' rather than 'substance', and 'event' in place of the parameters of space and time. Whitehead's project is to integrate science as part of the social sciences, reversing the modern trend to think of the social sciences as 'folk theories', naïve scientific theories awaiting development.

Central to this project is a reinterpretation of what we understand by 'nature'. Materialism has always conceived nature as that which lies behind sense

Whitehead taught Bertrand Russell at Cambridge before collaborating with his former pupil on the *Principia Mathematica.*

WHITEHEAD, ALFRED NORTH

WHITEHEAD, ALFRED NORTH

experience, as that which is causally responsible for sense-perception. The view engenders the split between primary and secondary qualities first made explicit by **Locke**, where secondary qualities are thought to be merely ephemeral effects caused in the mind by the primary qualities of objects. Whitehead thinks such a split unwarranted and undesirable, for if true, he says, 'The poets are entirely mistaken'. Rather than praising the rose for its scent, or the nightingale for its song, 'they should address their lyrics to themselves, and should turn them into odes of self-congratulation on the excellency of the human mind'. For Whitehead, nature is not the underlying causal substrate of our perceptual experience, but rather nothing more than that which is observed by perception. Science should address itself to the relations between perceptual events and do away with the outmoded claim to be investigating an underlying, abstract 'matter'.

Whitehead may have been a philosopher before his time. His 'philosophy of organism', while not widely accepted, does form one of the first, and most systematic, attempts of 20th century philosophy to break away from the traditional problems of contemporary philosophy. It is important as a source of stimulating and useful ideas to the growing number of philosophers, who, like Whitehead, see materialism as fundamentally wrong-headed.

‖ ESSENTIAL READING ‖

Principia Mathematica (3 volumes: 1910, 1912, 1913)
This was written jointly with Bertrand Russell. See page 232.

Process and Reality (1929)
In this, perhaps one of the greatest books in metaphysics, Whitehead sets out his 'philosophy of organism', and suggests that it is process rather than substance that should be taken as the fundamental metaphysical constituent of the world.

Adventures of Ideas (1933)
This is a less technical work than most of Whitehead's later writings, and a good point of entry into his thought. It considers the parts played by 'brute forces' on the one hand and aspirations and beliefs on the other in the development of Western civilization. There is also a discussion of beauty, truth, art, peace and adventure.

Modes of Thought (1938)
Intended as 'a free examination of some ultimate notions, as they occur naturally in daily life'. Two important concepts are 'assemblage', which is the creating of 'notions of large, adequate generality', and 'importance' to which he accords a central role in development of civilization.

WILLIAM OF OCCAM

?–1347

Occam was a political and religious maverick, in trouble with the Church for much of his life on account of his teachings. He is well-remembered in philosophical schools today for the adage known as 'Occam's razor' (see below). A Bachelor of Oxford, he fled to Munich after being called to defend his views in front of a Papal commission at Avignon in 1324. He died in 1347, probably from the Black Death which was raging in Munich at around that time, still hoping for reconciliation with the Church. His name is sometimes given the variant spelling 'Ockham' on account of speculation that he was born either at Ockham in Surrey or Ockham in Yorkshire. Neither can definitively lay claim to be the place of his birth.

'It is vain to do with more what can be done with fewer'

This principle now famously known as 'Occam's Razor' is a methodological principle concerning ontology. *'Entia non sunt multiplicanda praeter necessitatem'* translates from the Latin as 'Entities are not to be multiplied beyond necessity'. The principle reflects the idea that given two theories that equally explain the data, one should choose that theory which posits the minimum number of entities. Why one should opt for the simplest theory is not a judgement that can easily be philosophically defended, but nevertheless maintains a strong intuitive appeal. 'Occam's Razor' (so-called because the principle encourages one to cut out unnecessary complications from theory) is ultimately aesthetic: why postulate two things when one will do? Or as Occam is said to have put it, 'It is vain to do with more what can be done with fewer'. In other words, simplicity is always preferable where possible. It is a principle strongly adhered to today in both scientific and philosophical theory building, despite being difficult to justify rationally.

The principle underlies both Occam's epistemology (theory of knowledge) and his metaphysics. Occam held that universals only exist as part of human understanding. In reality everything is singular. In other words, concepts like 'species', 'redness', or even 'man', which name a range of objects that are united by some common form or feature, are purely inventions of the human understanding: ways of collecting together many individual objects for psychological simplicity. In reality there are only individuals. Universals do not exist. In modern terminology, this makes Occam a 'nominalist', and opposed to **Plato**'s idea of abstract, universal forms that are the archetypes of individual, material objects.

Universals only exist as part of human understanding – in reality everything is singular

Along with nominalism, the principle of 'Occam's Razor' can also be seen as a reflection of an atomistic world-view. In some sense a precursor of the logical atomism of Bertrand **Russell** and the early thought of **Wittgenstein**, Occam held that reality is ultimately composed of simple, singular objects that exist independently and absolutely. No single thing depends on any other for its existence and change is merely the re-ordering and rearranging of singulars. These singulars, according to Occam, gained their existence by being posited by God but remain independent of any divine machinations in their causal and operative powers. In this way, Occam upholds both the possibility of free will and moral responsibility in human affairs.

Ockham taught in Oxford before being accused of heresy and fleeing to plague-ridden Continental Europe.

∥ ESSENTIAL READING ∥

Sum of Logic (before 1327)

In this work, his most important work of philosophy, Occam sets out the basis of his logical approach to questions of metaphysics. The approach he uses is syllogistic logic, in which a proposition is inferred from the combination of two existing statements.

WITTGENSTEIN, LUDWIG

1889–1951

Raised in a prominent Viennese family, Ludwig Wittgenstein studied engineering in Germany and England, but became interested in the foundations of mathematics and pursued philosophical studies with **Russell** and **Frege** before entering the Austrian army during the First World War. The notebooks he kept as a soldier became the basis for his *Tractatus Logico-Philosophicus* (1922), which later earned him a doctorate from Cambridge and exerted a lasting influence on the philosophers of the Vienna Circle. Despite being only 32 when it was published, he declared that in it he had solved all the problems of philosophy and promptly retired from academic life.

The central concern of the *Tractatus* is the relationship between language, thought and reality. Language, Wittgenstein insists, is the perceptible form of thought and bound to reality by a common logical form or structure. Following Frege, Wittgenstein insisted that the meaning of linguistic expressions must be determined by the nature of the world, since otherwise the meaning or sense of an expression would be infected with vagueness and uncertainty. From Russell, he borrowed the idea that both language and the world must be understood in terms of their constituent or atomic parts. However, Wittgenstein broke away from his teachers by arguing that the underlying logical structure of sentences must exactly mirror or picture the essential structure of the world. This became known as his 'picture theory' of meaning: sentences are representations – literally pictures – of possible states of affairs. Since logical order is necessary for sense, Wittgenstein claimed, ordinary language could not be logically imperfect as both Russell and Frege had thought. On the contrary, claimed Wittgenstein, language is ordered as it is, anything that can be said at all can be said clearly and what cannot be said clearly must be passed over in silence.

It is a mistake to conceive of meaning as essentially tied to the nature of reality

After publication of the *Tractatus*, Wittgenstein went into self-imposed exile, giving away his inherited fortune and living and working in Austria, first as a schoolteacher and later as a gardener. By 1929, however, he had become unhappy with elements of his early work and returned to Cambridge. Meanwhile, in his absence the *Tractatus* had won critical acclaim and was beginning to exert major influence in European schools of thought.

Wittgenstein now found himself in the unusual position of being the most vehement critic of his own early work. He spent the following 20 years, until the end of his life, trying to clarify and dispel the philosophical confusions that had informed his early thinking. The corpus of his later writings were published posthumously as *Philosophical Investigations* (1952).

In the *Investigations*, Wittgenstein remains concerned with the nature of language, thought and reality. Now, however, he repudiates both the claim that meaning is dependent on reality and that language is essentially concerned with representation. Objects are not literally the meanings of names, rather they serve as elucidations of meaning – pointing to a table helps explain what the word 'table' means. Likewise, Wittgenstein realized, language has many functions. Words are like instruments or tools that we employ for many different purposes in different contexts. Language is not just used to represent or describe, but also to ask questions, play games, give orders, throw insults and so on. What a word means depends both on what it is being used to do and the context in which it is employed. This gives rise to Wittgenstein's famous

Wittgenstein gave up academic work in 1922 and worked as a teacher and a gardener, returning only in 1929 when he felt his work needed revision.

notion of 'a language-game': roughly, that it is the context which explains the meaning of an expression used in particular circumstances. The essence of Wittgenstein's later work is that it is a mistake to conceive of meaning as essentially tied to the nature of reality. Meaning cannot be divorced from the activities and behaviour of language users, which both reflect and explain the meaning of our words.

It is hard to overestimate Wittgenstein's influence on modern philosophy. His later work had a direct influence on J.L. **Austin** and the Oxford 'ordinary language' school of philosophy as well as the modern speech-act theorists. The assumptions present in and worked out through his early work, on the other hand, are still enshrined in the modern philosophical programs offered by **Quine**, Donald Davidson and Michael Dummett, to name just a few.

The 'Wittgenstein house', designed by the philosopher for his sister, 1926–8.

‖ ESSENTIAL READING ‖

Tractatus Logico-Philosophicus *(1921)*

The only book of Wittgenstein's published during his lifetime, the *Tractatus* is written in the form of numbered paragraphs, often containing only one short sentence. The book is mainly concerned with the nature of language and its relationship to the world, and outlines Wittgenstein's 'picture theory' of meaning.

Philosophical Investigations *(1953)*

Like the *Tractatus*, this book is largely concerned with the nature of language. Wittgenstein introduces the notion of 'language-games': words can only be understood in the context of human activities in which they are used, and a word and its context of use together constitute a 'language-game'.

The Blue Book and the Brown Book *(1958)*

These books originate from notes dictated to students between 1933 and 1935. They are the easiest to read and understand of all Wittgenstein's writings. They include discussions on thought and meaning, on sensation and imagination, on language-games, and on realism and idealism.

On Certainty *(1969)*

In this book, Wittgenstein discusses knowledge, doubt and certainty, and distinguishes between mistakes and madness.

WOLLSTONECRAFT, MARY

1759–1797

The original feminist, Wollstonecraft, who died in childbirth at the early age of thirty-eight, was a radical thinker who campaigned both for the rights of women but also for the rights of man, in similar style to Thomas **Paine**. Wollstonecraft's most important work, *Vindication of the Rights of Women* was preceded by a pamphlet, *Vindication of the Rights of Man,* in which she argued that the British people had the right to remove a bad king and that slavery and the treatment of the poor at that time were immoral. Indeed, unlike some strands of the modern feminist movement, Wollstonecraft saw the rights of both men and women as mutual and inextricably linked.

For Wollstonecraft, the evil of her days and the means by which to put them right, lay in education. In the introduction to the *Rights of Women,* she observes, 'I have turned over various books written on the subject of education, and patiently observed the conduct of parents and the management of schools; but what has been the result? A profound conviction that the neglected education of my fellow-creatures is the grand source of the misery I deplore'.

In particular, she was concerned with the way women's natural abilities were being suppressed through an education that emphasized the qualities required to flatter and serve men rather than enhance their natural abilities as people. She writes, 'One cause of this barren blooming I attribute to a false system of education, gathered from the books written on this subject by men who, considering females rather as women than human creatures, have been more anxious to make them alluring mistresses than wives; and the understanding of the sex has been so bubbled by this specious homage, that the civilized women of the present century, with a few exceptions, are only anxious to inspire love, when they ought to cherish a nobler ambition, and by their abilities and virtues exact respect'.

Although Wollstonecraft is clear that it is male-dominated society that has encouraged women to be 'docile and attentive to their looks to the exclusion of all else' and that marriage is merely 'legal prostitution', she is adamant that this is as much to the detriment of men as it is to women. 'Let woman share the rights and she will emulate the virtues of man', proclaims Wollstonecraft. Since the good of society proceeds from the increase of reason, knowledge and virtue, it can only be to the benefit of both sexes to maximize these qualities. To treat women as mere trifles encourages them to be cunning and sly, debases their natural talents and fosters discord in the home that can only be reflected upon and perpetuated in the children.

In the cause of female suffrage Wollstonecraft argues that whilst men reject the rights of women they can make no appeal to women's duties, as either wife or mother. Can women not vote because they are not rational? If, so, quips Wollstonecraft, sardonically, 'it will be expedient to open a fresh trade with Russia for whips; a present which a father should always make to his son-in-law on his wedding day, that a husband may keep his whole family in order by the same means; and without any violation of justice reign, wielding this sceptre, sole master of his house, because he is the only being in it who has reason: the divine, indefeasible earthly sovereignty breathed into man by the Master of the universe. Allowing this position, women have not any inherent rights to claim, and by the same rule, their duties vanish, for rights and duties are inseparable'.

Wollstonecraft's book was truly revolutionary, shocking many of her contemporaries. She was once patronisingly described as 'a hyena in petticoats', not just for her views on women's rights but also for calling for the abolition of the monarchy and the dissolution of the power of the Church, both of which she saw as oppressive regimes. Had she not

The first feminist philosopher, Wollstonecraft grew up in a troubled household and was largely self-taught.

suffered an early death the cause of women's rights might have advanced much quicker than it did. As it is, philosophy would have to await the arrival of Simone de **Beauvoir**, nearly 200 years later, before finding another female thinker of such influence.

'Let woman share the rights and she will emulate the virtues of man'

‖ ESSENTIAL READING ‖

A Vindication of the Rights of Women (1792)

Wollstonecraft wrote her classic of feminist philosophy at the time of the French Revolution, when there was much talk among intellectuals about the rights of man. She believed that the realities of life a woman had been mostly overlooked during this debate. In the book she argues forcefully that women deserve an education that will enable them to carry out their responsibilities, including the education of children and to be proper companions to their husbands. Although Wollstonecraft argues for equality between the sexes in certain areas of life, she does not explicitly state that men and women are equal. Nevertheless, her work paved the way for modern feminism.

XENOPHANES OF COLOPHON
c.570–?475BC

Like many of the presocratic philosophers whom we know of mainly through mention by later authors, exact dates for Xenophanes are uncertain. What is known is that **Heraclitus** mentions him as a contemporary and critic of **Pythagoras**, and we can thus date him as living roughly at around the same time.

Exiled by the Persian wars in Ionia to southern Italy, Xenophanes wandered the polities of Ancient Greece as a poet and freethinker. Following **Thales**, he criticized the Homerian concept of anthropomorphic gods. Homer's gods, Xenophanes complained, had all the immoral and disgraceful traits of flawed human beings and should hardly be the object of veneration.

In one of the earliest known expressions of cultural relativism, Xenophanes remarked that Homer's gods were simply a reflection of Homerian culture. As he proclaimed, 'the Ethiopians make their Gods black and snub-nosed; the Thracians say theirs have blue eyes and red hair'. If oxen and horses had hands and could paint, Xenophanes said, oxen would no doubt paint the forms of gods like oxen and horses would paint them like horses. Likewise, he criticized Pythagoras' doctrine of the transmigration of souls, making fun of the idea that a human soul could inhabit another animal.

Xenophanes' criticism of anthropomorphic Gods was that they were culturally relative and could not therefore be universal.

Xenophanes held some vague concept of a single deity that was 'in no way like men in shape or in thought' but rather 'causing all things by the thought of his mind'.

From his observations of fossil remains, Xenophanes speculated that the underlying principle of the natural world was mud

Like Thales before him, Xenophanes speculated about the underlying principles of natural phenomena. Whereas Thales had conceived the first principle to be water, Xenophanes proposed the rather less glamorous possibility of mud. The speculation was not entirely unreasonable at the time, having the virtue of at least being based on observation. For Xenophanes had noticed the fossil remains of sea-creatures embedded in the earth, and guessed that perhaps the world periodically dried up, returning to its original muddy state, trapping and preserving the earth's creatures as it did so before reversal of the process.

Xenophanes was also the first known thinker to anticipate **Socrates**' caution regarding claims of certain knowledge. Philosophical certainties could not be had, according to Xenophanes, for even if we chance to hit upon the truth, there is no way of knowing for certain that things are as we think they are. Nevertheless, this does not make philosophical inquiry useless, for exposing errors in our thinking can at least tell us what is certainly not the case, even if it cannot tell us what certainly is the case. This idea has a modern counterpart in the falsificationist methodology of Karl **Popper**.

There is little coherent or underlying structure to Xenophanes' thought, or at least not that we can tell from the fragments that have come down through history. This is perhaps unsurprising for someone who was essentially a refugee of the political turbulence in Asia Minor and who propagated his thoughts and speculations mostly in the form of oral poems and stories. Nonetheless, Xenophanes clearly had enough influence to be remembered and mentioned by those that followed him. Quite probably it is his criticism of the Homeric gods, still revered throughout the Hellenistic world during and long after Xenophanes' time, that attracted a great deal of attention to him.

‖ ESSENTIAL READING ‖

Xenophanes of Colophon: Fragments: A Text and Translation with Commentary (1992)

This contains the Greek texts of the existing fragments of Xenophanes' philosophy, together with an English translation, commentary and notes.

Further information on Xenophanes can be found in books on the Presocratic philosophers, such as *The Presocratic Philosophers* (1979; 2nd edition 1982) or *Philosophy before Socrates* (1994).

ZENO OF ELEA

490BC–?

There are two Zenos known to philosophy: Zeno of Elea, and the later Zeno of Citium (c. 320BC), who is now only remembered as the founder of Stoicism (see **Seneca** and Marcus **Aurelius**). Zeno of Elea, a student of **Parmenides**, is best known for his defence of Parmenides against the followers of **Pythagoras** in a series of graphic paradoxes. Zeno's paradoxes are the first recorded example of argument by the logical technique of 'reductio ad absurdum' (literally, reduction to absurdity) in which an opponent's view is shown to be false because it leads to contradiction.

Defending Parmenides' view that the common-sense notions of change and plurality are illusory, Zeno developed a series of paradoxes to show that they lead to very uncommon, nonsensical conclusions, thereby proving that they cannot represent the true nature of the world.

Zeno offers two series of arguments levelled against the idea of the plurality of things and against the idea of motion. First, Zeno wants to show that there cannot be many different things in the world, despite the seemingly obvious evidence of our senses. Any three dimensional object is divisible into many parts. It can be repeatedly divided until one gets down to the very basis of matter, or substance. But then even atoms can be split, as can - modern science tells us - the constituents of atoms, neutrons and protons. Indeed it seems that logically anything that has a physical magnitude can be divided into half that magnitude. Therefore one cannot say that matter is composed of a collection of spatially extended units or points, since one can continue dividing anything that is extended, ad infinitum. Therefore matter must be continuous, not discrete.

Achilles can never catch the tortoise no matter how fast he runs

Zeno's arguments against the idea of motion take essentially the same form. Suppose Achilles decides to see how fast he can run the track in a stadium. Before he can reach the end he must first get to the halfway point, but before he does so he must get to the halfway point of that, and the halfway point of that, and so on indefinitely. If space is made up of an infinite series of points one can never move any distance at all; to complete a journey one would have to pass every point, and one cannot pass an infinite series of points in a finite amount of time. Similarly, in the famous Achilles and the Tortoise paradox, Zeno asks us to imagine Achilles giving the tortoise a head start. But before he can get to where the tortoise is, it will have moved a little farther on, and before he can get to that spot it will have moved a little farther on again, and so on indefinitely. Achilles can never catch the tortoise no matter how fast he runs, for every time he moves the tortoise moves too. Therefore motion through time (i.e. change) is impossible.

Zeno's argument seems to show that space cannot consist of an infinite series of points. We cannot make the obvious move of claiming that space is infinitely divisible, for the same argument given earlier against the idea of plurality. Any line or distance can be divided into a smaller line, and that into a smaller line still, and so on indefinitely. If one can talk about a physical magnitude one can also talk of half that magnitude. In this way, Zeno tried to defend Parmenides' view that the true nature of reality is an unchanging, indivisible whole. **Kant**, **Hume** and **Hegel** all offered solutions to Zeno's paradoxes, none of which were entirely successful. Only by using modern set-theoretic mathematics, which abandons the Euclidean definition of a line as a series of points, has a reasonably satisfactory answer to Zeno been found.

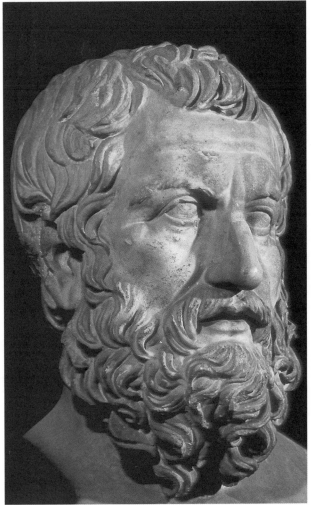

Zeno's paradoxes sparked a debate about the nature of reality that remains active today.

‖ ESSENTIAL READING ‖

Only a few fragments of Zeno's work still survive, and most of what we know of Zeno and his philosophy comes **Plato**, Proclus and **Aristotle**. Plato, in *Parmenides* 127, has Zeno say that Zeno's work, written in his youth to protect the arguments of Parminides, was stolen and published without his consent. Proclus, in his *Commentary on Plato's Parminedes,* claims that Zeno produced 'not less than forty arguments revealing contradictions'.

GLOSSARY

(**Bold type** within the text indicates a cross-reference)

the Absolute

The opposite of relative, conditioned or dependent. The idea of the Absolute dates back to pre-Socratic times. For Plato, the Ideal Forms were the Absolute. For other philosophers the idea has been associated with that of the Godhead. Certain rationalist thinkers, such as Spinoza, held the absolute to be an all encompassing principle and the true source of all reality, as did the idealist philosophers (see **idealism**), most notably Hegel.

aesthetics

The branch of philosophy that deals with the nature and expression of beauty, or in Kantian philosophy the branch of metaphysics concerned with the laws of perception.

agent

The self that acts, chooses and decides, as opposed to the self that knows.

agnostic

One who believes that God's existence cannot be proven, but doesn't deny the possibility that God might exist.

agnosticism

belief that no proof can be given for the existence ... the concept of God, like those of soul, ... first cause, lies beyond the reach of the ... only know the world of natural

analytic philosophy

Originally a branch of philosophy concerned with the analysis of language and the concepts it expresses, typically formulating its precise and rigorous analyses in the symbolism of formal logic, as in the work of Russell and Wittgenstein. Still dominant in the English-speaking philosophical world, its subject matter now ranges well beyond linguistic analysis, but it can still be characterized by its emphasis on rigour, precision and clarity of argument, an objectivity similar to that of mathematics and science, and a concern for setting out clear evidence for the views proposed. In addition to Russell and Wittgenstein, proponents of analytic philosophy include Carnap, Quine, Kripke, Rawls and Nozick. Analytic philosophy is generally contrasted with **continental philosophy.**

a priori

Something known to be true or false prior to experience. Its opposite would be a posteriori, which is knowledge derived from experience.

atheism

The absolute disbelief in and denial of the existence of a God or gods.

atomism

The theory of Democritus and Epicurus, among others, which claims that the entire universe is composed of minute, indivisible and indestructible particles.

behaviourism

The branch of psychology, most radically developed and advocated by B.F. Skinner, that focuses exclusively on observable behaviour, excluding all subjective phenomenon, such as emotions, memories and motives.

Cartesian

Relating to René Descartes or his philosophy.

category

In philosophy, categories are the most basic group into which things can be classified. A category, then, would be an irreducible and fundamental concept that can be applied to other concepts and objects. Aristotle and Kant each attempted a definitive list of categories, which included substance, relation, place, time, passion, and action, among others.

causality or causation

The connection between cause and effect, or the relationship between two things when the first is perceived as the cause of the second. Ordinarily, the relationship between cause and effect seems inevitable. Nevertheless, philosophers have asked why we think in terms of causation, where the idea comes from, and when it is correct to apply it. David Hume is one philosopher who challenged the concept of causation.

cognition

The forms of knowing and perceiving, such as attention, memory, reasoning, and perception (visual, aural, tactile), through which we synthesize information.

concept

In philosophy, concept can stand for an idea, a thought, the form of a thought or even the meaning of a term, though concept is largely used in its most general application. For example, to have a concept of table means that one might 1) distinguish table from every other thing and 2) reason about tables in some way.

continental philosophy

European in origin though by no means limited to mainland European philosophers, continental philosophy is generally contrasted with **analytic philosophy**, from which it differs in being more metaphysical and speculative in approach and less concerned with rigorous, formal proofs. Closely related to the humanities, it is concerned with the human condition in all its complexities, and is sometimes expounded in the form of works of literature, such as Sartre's novel *Nausea* and Nietzsche's *Thus Spake Zarathustra*. Other philosophers associated with this tradition are Kierkegaard, Heidegger, Merleau-Ponty, Foucault and Derrida.

cosmogony

The study of the origin and development of the universe.

cosmology

The study of the whole universe as a totality of phenomena in time and space.

Cynic

A member of a school of Ancient Greek philosophy, namely **Cynicism,** wherein virtue was seen as the only good and self-control as the only means of attaining virtue. Cynics not only showed a complete disregard for pleasure, but also expressed contempt for human affection, preferring to find fault with most individuals for their lack of virtue. Diogenes was perhaps the most renowned Cynic.

deduction

A form of argument in which the conclusion logically and necessarily follows from the premises, with the general leading to the particular. An example would be, 'If all human beings are born, then Plato as a human being, must have been born.' It is an agreed upon fact that deduction is valid. Its opposite would be **induction**.

determinism

The view that whatever happens has to happen, for every event is the inevitable, hence necessary, outcome of its specific, preceding causes, which themselves were the necessary result of yet previous causes. The chain of cause and effect might be seen as determined by God or the laws of nature. In science, an entirely mechanistic view is deterministic. In the Ancient World and in the Christian idea of predestination, the idea of fate is thoroughly deterministic. See **causality**.

dialectic

A Greek term originally used to describe the Socratic method, according to which argument and reasoning took the form of dialogue. For Hegel and Marx, dialectic is an interpretive method whereby the contradiction between a thesis and its antithesis is resolved into a synthesis that includes elements from each of the opposing positions.

dualism

The view that reality is made up of two fundamental and fundamentally different elements, as opposed to monism, which perceives reality to be made up of only one substance. The dualism of Descartes, perhaps the most famous, advances the view that material substance and the mind's activity (thinking, reflecting, etc.) bear upon each other but are separate, unlike and essentially distinct.

empiricism

The view that sense experience is the only basis for true knowledge. An empiricist would doubt any statement claiming truth regardless of experience. Among the empiricist philosophers are Locke and Hume.

Epicureanism

Named after the Greek philosopher Epicurus, this strain of moral philosophy advances the claim that pleasure, mainly understood as the avoidance of pain by opting for intellectual pleasure, needs to be understood as the basis for leading an ethical life.

epistemology

The branch of philosophy concerned with the nature of knowledge – with what and how we know and the limits of human understanding.

essence

The fundamental qualities that make something what it is and not something else are what constitute its essence. In other words, the essence of a dog is what makes it a dog and not a cat or a horse. See also **universal**.

ethics or moral philosophy

The branch of philosophy that examines human values, beginning with questions about how we should live and act. Hence its focus on questions of conduct, duty, responsibility, good and bad, right and wrong.

existentialism

The modern philosophical view which takes the individual human being, possessing free will and standing in an absurd and meaningless world, as its starting point. Existentialists argue for human responsibility and judgement in ethical matters, seeing the individual as the sole judge of his/her own actions, with human freedom understood precisely as the freedom to choose. Among the best-known existentialist philosophers are Kierkegaard, Heidegger, Sartre and Camus.

free will

The doctrine that human beings are free to control their own actions, which are not determined by cause and effect, God or fate. Its opposite is **determinism**.

hedonism

The philosophical doctrine that pleasure is the sole good or at least the chief good.

hypothesis

A theory that is held to be true and seems like it might be true until confirmed or proven wrong by empirical testing or experience. An element belonging to the scientific method.

idealism

The philosophical view that the empirical world does not exist independently of the human mind and hence can only be known according to our conceptions of it. Its opposite is **materialism**. Among idealist philosophers are Berkeley, Kant and Hegel.

induction

The opposite of deduction, induction moves from individual instances to general principle. Unlike **deduction**, induction does not lead to necessarily true results.

instrumentalism

A pragmatic theory in which ideas, such as scientific theories, are instruments that function as guides to action, and serve to deal with problems in the real world. As such, ideas do not give a true account of reality. Rather, their validity and value are determined by their success in enabling us to act, problem-solve, and predict outcomes.

intentionality

The attachment of meaning to an object, such as a belief about it, a desire for it, a dislike of it, the assigning to it of a function, etc. Intentionality is what, according to some philosophers, such as John Searle, distinguishes human consciousness from artificial intelligence.

intuition

A form of direct, conceptual knowing that does not rely on reason or derive directly from the senses. For example, as human beings, we might be said to have an intuitive or innate idea of God, the beautiful, or justice.

intuitionism

A philosophical doctrine according to which basic truths and moral values can be known by **intuition**.

liar paradox

The paradox that if a sentence such as 'I am lying' or 'This sentence is not true' is true, then it is not true; on the other hand, if it is not true, then it is true.

libertarianism

The political philosophy that advocate the greatest possible freedom of the individual and the least possible interference by the state in the lives of its citizens.

logic

The branch of philosophy that examines the nature of rational argument, focusing on the principles of reasoning, the structure of propositions, and the methods and validity of deductive reasoning.

logical atomism

The theory, associated mainly with Russell and Wittgenstein, that all language can be analysed into 'atomic propositions' – simple, independent, irreducible elements of meaning (the 'atoms' of language) which correspond to 'atomic facts', the simplest facts about the world.

logical positivism

The view that philosophy should be based on observation and testing and that propositions are only meaningful to the extent that they can be verified empirically. It is opposed to any type of metaphysical speculation. Among the most prominent logical positivists are Schlick, Carnap and Ayer.

materialism

The view that only matter or material things actually exist. In other words, there is nothing in existence other than matter, one of the consequences of which is the nullification of the possible existence of a God or gods. Materialism is opposed to **idealism**, which holds the mind to be generative of objective reality. Marx, Engels and Lenin are among the best-known materialists.

metaphysics

The branch of philosophy concerned with first principles, particularly being (**ontology**) and knowing (**epistemology**), as well as with the ultimate nature of what exists. Central to metaphysical speculation are all the traditional questions of philosophy, such as: the origin of life, the nature of mind and of reality, and the meaning of concepts such as time, space, causation and free will, among others.

methodology

The system of principles, practices and procedures that are employed within a specific branch of knowledge. For instance, while historical, philosophical and scientific methodologies might converge, they largely differ from one another.

modal logic

In a narrow sense, the logic of constructions involving the concepts of possibility and necessity, but in a wider sense also including the concepts of obligation, permission, time, etc.

monism

The view that reality is a unified whole and that all existing things follow from or can be described by a single concept or system. Its opposite is **dualism**. As regards human beings and the relationship between mind and body, in this view both would be seen as like entities, formed from the same substance. Hegel's philosophy, for example, is monistic.

mysticism

A belief in the existence of realities beyond intellectual or perceptual apprehension that are germane to 'being' and directly accessibly through subjective experience. The 'One' of Plotinus would be an example of such a reality.

natural law

Laws considered 'natural' in the sense of being derived from nature and therefore seen as providing universal moral standards that are binding. Natural law is often associated with divine law, with reason as arbiter. It's opposite is positive law, namely, the laws established by particular societies. A good example of the concept of natural law is given by the opening of 'The Declaration of Independence' of the United States of America:

'When in the Course of human events, it becomes necessary for one people to dissolve the political bands which have connected them with another, and to assume among the powers of the earth, the separate and equal station to which the Laws of Nature and of Nature's God entitle them, a decent respect to the opinions of mankind requires that they should declare the causes which impel them to the separation.

We hold these truths to be self-evident, that all men are created equal, that they are endowed by their Creator with certain unalienable Rights, that among these are Life, Liberty and the pursuit of Happiness.'

naturalism

The view that reality can be understood without resorting to anything outside of or beyond nature to serve as an explanatory principle.

nominalism

The theory that universals are not real and existing in the world, but rather are words and names for phenomena.

ontology

The branch of philosophy that deals with the nature of being.

open society

This term was first proposed by French philosopher Henri Bergson and further developed by the Austrian philosopher Karl Popper. Philosophically speaking, the concept of an open society is based on the recognition that people act on imperfect knowledge and that no one possesses the ultimate truth. Consequently, the best form of social organization and government, as advanced by Popper, is a pluralistic democracy characterized by the rule of law, a diversity of opinion, a division of power and a market economy.

pantheism

The doctrine that identifies God or gods with the forces and workings of nature.

phenomena

For Plato, things as perceived by the senses (versus noumena, which are things as reflected upon by thought). For Kant, the distinction between phenomena and noumena was that between things as objects of experience and things as they are in themselves, a state of being not accessible to human reason.

phenomenology

The philosophical view introduced by Edmund Husserl according to which objects are objects of experience rather than independently existing entities. This approach aims to explore the ways in which people conceive of and interpret the world as they experience it. In this view, reality is relative and subjective.

philosophy

Literally, 'the love of wisdom.' Traditionally, philosophy was comprised of Metaphysics, Epistemology, and Logic. Modern philosophy also encompasses political theory, ethics, aesthetics, and the philosophies of religion, science and law. Most generally, philosophy might be described as the rigorous, systematic analysis and critical examination of such topics as reality, nature, time, causation, free will, human beingness, reason, moral judgements, and perception, among others.

positivism

The theory introduced by Auguste Comte that limits knowledge to what can be derived from observation and comprehended within the bounds of science.

pragmatism

A strain of **empiricism**, this view, founded by C.S. Pierce, interprets truth in terms of its practical effects, and as such might be seen as a theory of truth. When applied to science, this view holds that the 'truth' of a theory depends on whether or not it works. William James took this approach to ethical judgements and religious beliefs, measuring 'truth' in terms of the usefulness or benefit of a belief or judgement to a person's life.

Presocratic

Of the time before Socrates.

rationalism

The theory that reason is the fundamental source of knowledge and spiritual truth and that the exercise of reason, rather than empiricism (sense-perception), authority or revelation, provides the only valid basis for action and belief. Rationalists include Descartes, Spinoza and Leibniz.

realism

Philosophically, the theory that **universals** exist independently of the human mind and that the essences of things are objectively given in nature.

relativism

The theory that there are no objective standards with regard to knowledge, truth and moral principles, which are influenced by cultural or historical context.

scepticism

The view that it is impossible to know anything with certainty. Hence, absolute knowledge is unattainable and doubt is central to human knowledge and experience.

scholasticism

The theological and philosophical methods and systems of Medieval Europe (12–14th centuries), which aimed to reconcile Christian thought with Aristotelianism.

scientism

The theory that the investigative methods used in the natural sciences should be applied in all fields of inquiry.

semiotics

The study of signs and symbols.

solipsism

The view that only the self can be known to exist.

Stoicism

The Greek school of philosophy founded by Zeno of Citium around 308BC. The Stoics believed that happiness lay in accepting the law of the universe and advised equanimity in the face of good and bad fortune alike. They held that human beings would be happiest if they freed themselves from passion and calmly accepted all occurrences as the result of divine will.

structuralism

The 20th-century philosophical movement that has had a great influence on anthropology, linguistics and literary criticism. Following Ferdinand de Saussure's work in linguistics, structuralists hold the view that objects should not be investigated as independent entities, but rather as entities formed by or within systems of relations.

syllogism

A form of reasoning in which a conclusion is drawn from two premises.

tautology

A necessarily true statement, such as 'red is red.'

teleology

The study of final ends, from the perspective that there is a purpose to life and the universe, and hence also some sort of blueprint or overall design that makes all development purposive and meaningful.

theism

Most specifically the belief that a single personal God is present in the world as well as transcendent.

theology

The study of God and the nature of religious truth. Though philosophy does not posit the existence of God, its arguments and methods have nevertheless had a significant influence on both natural and revealed theologies over the centuries.

transcendental

Something outside the world of sense experience. Neither empiricists, nor pragmatists, nor existentialists believe in anything transcendental, such as God or a separate sphere of moral ideas.

universal

A property belonging to each individual of a specific class or a general concept that can be applied to all the members of a group: for example, since all cold things instantiate 'coldness,' 'coldness' would be the universal property of all cold things. In the Middle Ages, philosophers who believed that 'coldness' existed in and of itself were called 'realists' (see **realism**). Those who argued that such a property did not actually exists were called 'nominalists' (see **nominalism**).

utilitarianism

The ethical theory sketched out by Bentham and elaborated by J.S. Mill, which argues for a morality based on actions that lead to happiness. In this framework, an action that leads to unhappiness would be morally wrong. What follows from this is the view that society should aim for the happiness of the greatest number. A modern development of utilitarianism is the 'preference utilitarianism' of which Peter Singer is a leading advocate. Preference utilitarianism defines the moral rightness of an action by the extent to which it satisfies desires or preferences rather than creates happiness.

validity

A property of arguments. An argument is valid if its conclusion is the necessary outcome of its premises, even if the conclusion is false on account of a false premise. In other words, an argument may be logically valid even if its conclusion is wrong.

verifiability

The property of a statement or proposition that allows us to test, using empirical evidence, whether it is true or false. In the 20th century, many **logical positivists** and **empiricists** made verification a requirement of knowledge. However, since few statements or even scientific laws are verifiable, there were others who argued against verifiability as a theory of proof and meaning.